EXETER BRANCH LIBRARY
Date Due

FEB - 3 1992			
FEB 1 8 1992			
DEC 2 8 1992			
Jan-11			
FEB 2 0 '95			
APR 11 '98			

97
Gr

BRODART, INC.   Cat. No. 23 233   Printed in U.S.A.

GRANATSTEIN, J.

WAR AND PEACEKEEPING.

+1CDN

WAR AND PEACEKEEPING

WAR AND PEACEKEEPING

From South Africa to the Gulf —
Canada's Limited Wars

J.L. Granatstein and David J. Bercuson

KEY PORTER BOOKS

Canadian Cataloguing in Publication Data
Granatstein, J. L., 1939–
        War and peacekeeping

Includes index.
ISBN 1-55013-355-1

1. Canada - History, Military. I. Bercuson, David Jay, 1945–
II. Title.

FC226.G73 1991   971
C91-094512-8
F1028.G73 1991

Key Porter Books Limited
70 The Esplanade
Toronto, Ontario
Canada M5E 1R2

Cartography: James Loates
Picture research: Gena K. Gorrell
Typesetting: Maher Design

Printed and bound in Canada by John Deyell Company

Printed on acid-free paper

91 92 93 94 95 6 5 4 3 2 1

Photo page i: A sentry on duty at Oka, summer 1989.

Photo page ii: An exhausted private of the RCR loads Bren-gun magazines the morning after a Chinese attack on Hill 187—the assaults had started before 9:00 P.M. and had gone on for over six hours.

Photo page iii: Imperial forces spent almost five weeks outside Bloemfontein, recuperating and waiting for provisions, but Boer raids kept food in short supply. One private complained of an hour's pack drill for eating emergency rations on the march: "Of course it is a disobeyed order but I think they might have let us off this time...."

CONTENTS

ACKNOWLEDGEMENTS

Our thanks to Julie Green and Bob Perrins for doing a super research job; also to the staff at the Directorate of History, Department of National Defence, especially Dr. W.A.B. Douglas, Norman Hillmer, Bill McAndrew, and Steve Harris, Sergeant Bob Zubkowski of the PPCLI Archives in Calgary, and John Saywell for assistance with photographs. Thanks also to Ted Zuber, Canada's war artist in the Gulf, for his co-operation. Gena Gorrell did a splendid job as our editor and photo researcher. We are most grateful.

J.L.G. & D.J.B.

INTRODUCTION

Most Canadians know something of the Great War: the trench warfare in France and Flanders that cost the lives of sixty thousand Canadians, the triumph at Vimy Ridge at Easter 1917, the Hundred Days that saw the Canadian Corps score some of its greatest victories in the last three months of war. They know somewhat more about the Second World War, with its disasters at Hong Kong and Dieppe, where the lives of Canadian men were thrown away because of misguided imperial patriotism and optimistic, incompetent planning. But few know much about the earlier and later battles in which their country has been involved: the Fenian raids on the eve of Confederation; the first Riel rebellion—almost an archetypal frontier war—and the second one fifteen years later, handled almost wholly by the fledgeling Canadian militia. The Boer War at the turn of the century marked the first time that Canada sent troops abroad—though this step onto the international stage was more an emotional response to the British imperial spirit than a measured act of national maturity. Even so, Canadians from every part of the dominion made a name for themselves and their country at Paardeberg.

The Riel rebellions and the Boer War set the pattern for the Canadian military in the first four decades of this century. There was a strong sense that civilians enlisted off the street, or militiamen, who were almost always without real military training, could hold their own against the professional soldiers of any country. Canadian pluck would carry the day, or so such politicians as Colonel Sam Hughes, Militia minister at the time of the Great War, fervently believed. The evidence did not sustain that belief, to be sure, but the idea persisted nonetheless, and even the horrendous casualties of the Great War did not eliminate it entirely. There was also more than a lot of muddle in the way these early campaigns were conducted. As the technology of the new century began to replace the traditional bayonets and rifles, Canada's weaponry was in short

1

supply, and usually obsolete. Military leadership was often wanting as well, in part because the dead hand of political patronage still controlled the granting of officers' commissions and promotions.

The Second World War seemed to knock some of those faults on the head. The experience of hastily raising an army, navy, and air force, the shock of defeat and débâcle, and the increasing complexity of war led the military and, more surprisingly, the government to conclude by 1945 that amateurism was finished. Canada needed a professional military, and though the post-war armed forces were small, they were much larger and better trained than the nine or ten thousand regular soldiers, sailors, and airmen with which the country had gone to war in 1939.

Even so, when the Korean War erupted in 1950 the government decided to limit its involvement by enlisting a brigade off the street rather than using the regular army. The result was that for Canada the Korean campaign began in a fashion not unlike the Boer War half a century before: many of the wrong people rushed to the colours and, for a while at least, improvisation was the order of the day.

Although the Korean War was officially a United Nations operation, it marked the first great confrontation between the two ideological poles of the twentieth century, capitalism and Communism. As Britain's power waned in the long ordeal of the Second World War, Canada had finally been forced to cut its colonial apronstrings and turn instead to the United States. Throughout the fifties, as China loomed in the Orient and post-war Europe lay in a precarious balance between the vast and increasingly sophisticated armies of the North Atlantic Treaty Organization and the Warsaw Pact, Canada's military forces grew to maturity. The army, navy, and air force became substantial forces of some 120,000 professional officers and enlisted personnel at their peak, and the defence budget rose to astronomical heights: in 1947, defence spending amounted to only 1.7 per cent of the Gross National Product; in 1953, however, with the GNP substantially larger after years of boom, defence accounted for 7.6 per cent. The Canadian forces' equipment, much of it produced in Canada, was first class, and morale was sky-high.

In this atmosphere of confidence and competence, Canada was able to begin responding to calls for United Nations peacekeepers around the world, from Kashmir to Cairo to Cambodia. In 1954, when an International Control Commission was formed to help end France's colonial involvement in Indo-China, Canada agreed to play a key role even though the U.N. was not involved in any way. And two years later, when External Affairs minister Lester Pearson helped create the United Nations Emergency Force to cool the Suez crisis, Canada participated in a major way. Pearson's Nobel Peace Prize told Canadians that their country had arrived on the world stage. Peacekeeping suddenly was something that Canadians did and did well, so much so that the U.N. came to depend on Canada's good will and military competence. The Canadian media and public—if not necessarily the soldiers and flyers who found themselves stuck at a scruffy airfield in remote New Guinea or encamped at an observation post on the Golan Heights—were clearly in love with the idea of their country helping to keep the world's peace. Few thought of the dangers or the casualties that servicemen and servicewomen had to suffer in the Congo or Cyprus or along the border between Iran and Iraq. Eventually, even the staff officers at National Defence Headquarters came to see that peacekeeping was their best guarantee that Canada's military would not go the way of the dodo. In peacekeeping, Canada has apparently found its métier.

This book, a companion volume to *Marching to Armageddon: Canadians and the Great War 1914–1919* and *A Nation Forged in Fire: Canadians and the Second World War 1939–1945*, is the first to examine Canada's "other wars" from Confederation to the present in text and illustrations. Together the three books cover the whole of the Canadian military experience, but each can be read on its own.

Following page: This *Illustrated London News* celebration of the Boer war scrupulously represents the forces of the Empire. Its caption, from Kipling's "Song of the English," notes that "...I do not press my will, / Because ye are Sons of The Blood and call me Mother still."

PART ONE
THE AGE OF INNOCENCE

I
THE CANADIAN MILITARY, 1866–1900

In the early hours of February 27, 1900, the 2nd Battalion of the Royal Canadian Regiment (RCR) attacked Boer General Piet Cronje's perimeter in the valley of the Modder River at Paardeberg Drift. It was Majuba Day, the anniversary of a British defeat by the Boers at the Battle of Majuba Hill nineteen years before. The date was symbolic for both sides and the expectation of an attack had hung heavily in the air when the fighting men bedded down the night before. For men about to enter combat, sleep comes hard. But even those who did sleep were soon awake; the new day was less than two hours old when the officers and NCOs of the RCR prodded their men awake, moved them into attack formation, and sent them into position through the pre-dawn dark.

One of those officers was Lieutenant-Colonel William Dillon Otter. Otter's military career up to that point paralleled the military development of the young Dominion of Canada; he had played a role in virtually every important event in the country's military history. He had joined the militia before Confederation and had fought the Fenian raiders on the Niagara frontier in 1866. By the early 1880s he had risen to command the Queen's Own Rifles of Canada, a Toronto militia regiment, and when the government established a tiny permanent force in 1883—the Infantry School Corps, which later became the Royal Canadian Regiment—Otter had been chosen to command it; in that capacity he had led one of three columns of Canadian troops against the Métis in the North-West Rebellion of 1885. It was only natural that he would volunteer to serve in South Africa when the Boer War broke out in 1899 and local imperialists clamoured for Canadian participation. He was, after all, a soldier, and war was his profession.

Although virtually every member of the Canadian contingent at Paardeberg was new to combat, and most were new to military life itself, the regiment they were part of had developed as the result of almost fifty years of experience. In times of peace Canadians like to think of themselves as an unmilitary people, but military events have moulded the very shape of Canada and Canadians have a military tradition that goes back to the beginnings of European settlement. Wars between French and Indians, between English and French, and between Britain and the United States determined not only the map of Canada but also its political institutions, its trade patterns, its rate and direction of expansion, and even, to a surprising degree, its cultural and social institutions.

THE BRITISH MILITARY PRESENCE

In the first half of the nineteenth century, the British colonies in North America were defended primarily by the British, supported by a rudimentary militia. As far as the British were concerned, British North America was just one more outpost in a vast empire which underlay British power and prestige and guaranteed a steady flow of raw materials for British factories. British naval bases at Esquimault on the west coast and Halifax on the Atlantic helped guard the sea routes of empire; their army garrisons at Quebec City and Kingston were intended to protect British American colonists from any northward expansion by the United States.

While it was in Canada, the British military had a dramatic impact on Canadian society. Great public works such as the Rideau Canal were built and maintained for defence against the Americans. British officers often invested in Canadian enterprises—the Dunsmuir coal empire on Vancouver Island was partly financed by officers stationed at Esquimault. British military purchases formed a large part of the economy of Halifax. British officers and their wives and families were at the core of the colonial elite, and many stayed in Canada at the end of their military service to become important landowners and social leaders.

By the mid to late 1850s British North America consisted of a number of widely scattered colonies: there were Newfoundland, Nova Scotia, New Brunswick, and Prince Edward Island, there was the United Province of Canada, which consisted of French-speaking Canada East and English-speaking Canada West, and far to the west lay the Pacific Coast colonies of Vancouver Island and British Columbia, which were joined in 1858. Between the Rocky Mountains and Canada was Rupert's Land, a virtual fiefdom of the Hudson's Bay Company. With the exception of Rupert's Land, each colony had its own government, which was responsible for local and internal matters, including local defence. Overall foreign and defence policy was set in London.

Around this time British imperial thinking began to undergo a major shift. For years the flow of trade had been channelled by a tariff system favouring colonial goods. But Britain now led the world in manufacturing, and its merchants and industrialists, not to mention their liberal (and Liberal) political supporters such as William Ewart Gladstone, were less and less interested in paying for the upkeep of a colonial empire. What need had Britain of colonies when it could abolish all tariffs and take on any commercial competition from Europe or the United States and win? At the same time the British were increasingly eager to cut unnecessary government spending, and nothing seemed more unnecessary than maintaining armed forces along Canada's southern border—especially when Britain's own military experts were convinced that it was impossible to defend Canada against the United States in any case.

But much as the British wanted to cut spending in North America, they were reluctant to do so until the colonists began to take their own defence needs seriously. For a time that seemed wishful thinking. Although the colonies boasted a militia strength of several hundred thousand by 1850, the militia was almost non-existent in most localities. Its volunteers, who were supposed to train and, if necessary, fight to defend their farms, towns, and cities, were part-time soldiers, usually led by a local notable. In times of great crisis the local militias were expected to join with other militia units and with British regulars to form an effective fighting force. In fact, the members were underpaid, poorly armed, badly trained, and virtually without leadership. Shortly after the outbreak of the Crimean War in 1853 the government of the United Province of Canada passed a Militia Act which was supposed to provide financial support for an "active militia" of five thousand men. Thousands of young men rushed to the colours with the hope of defending Canada against Russia, and within a short time a number of units had been established. With the end of the war and the onset of economic recession, however, government support collapsed, and so did much of the militia.

The colonial governments were so apathetic about defence matters that they did little to bolster their own defences even during the American Civil War. For most of the war, Britain's sympathy lay with the south—the source of much of Britain's raw cotton. Relations with the north were further soured when the Yankees seized two Confederate agents from the British mail packet *Trent* in 1861. They grew worse yet after a Confederate raid on St. Albans, Vermont, was launched from Canada in 1864, and after a series of attacks on Yankee shipping by the *Alabama*, a Confederate commerce raider built in a British shipyard.

At the end of the Civil War, prominent U.S. politicians seemed intent on annexing the British North American colonies as partial compensation for shipping destroyed by the *Alabama*. There was little the colonies could do to defend themselves; British troops were still stationed in their midst—eleven thousand additional men had been sent to Canada during the Civil War—but there were not nearly enough to defend all of British North America against hundreds of thousands of hardened veterans of Civil War battlefields.

The danger of American invasion was one of the factors that spurred the colonies towards Confederation. The movement had begun in 1864, when Canadian and Atlantic political leaders had met at Charlottetown to discuss the formation of a political union to expand their markets, improve the credit of their governments, strengthen their defences, and solve a political deadlock. There was vigorous opposition in some parts of Atlantic Canada, but union prevailed nonetheless. Nova Scotia, New Brunswick, and Canada joined together, with Britain's active encouragement, on July 1, 1867, and John A. Macdonald, one of the leaders of the Confederation movement, was Canada's first elected prime minister later in the year.

THE FENIANS

If the American threat was one factor in speeding Confederation, another was the attacks of the Fenians. In 1866 this handful of Irish republicans began to mount raids on British American soil. The Fenians, who were mostly Irish Americans, hoped to create enough trouble along the Canadian border that Britain would be forced to divert troops to Canada—thus giving republican rebels in Ireland a chance to throw the British out—or even to capture Canada outright. The first major attack took place in the Niagara Peninsula when young "General" John O'Neill, a Civil War cavalry officer, led between eight hundred and a thousand men across the Niagara River north of Fort Erie after nightfall on May 31, 1866. Two days later they ran into a mixed force of British regulars and Canadian militia near the little town of Ridgeway. The militia, under Lieutenant-Colonel Alfred Booker, were eager but, as usual, badly trained and poorly equipped. They had come to Ridgeway by rail, and Booker's first need after disembarking was food for his men and wagons to carry the equipment. That arranged, the company marched north under the hot morning sun. O'Neill and his men were waiting.

After a march of three kilometres, Booker's scouts spotted the Fenian

skirmish line across the Canadians' line of march. He called a halt and
ordered his column extended into battle line across the road. The Canadians then advanced in good order towards the Fenians, with the Queen's
Own Rifles in the van. Fenian sharpshooters fired their muzzle-loaders,
bullets cracked through the hot air, and men fell, but the Canadian line
advanced at a brisk pace.

The Fenians were mostly Civil War veterans; the Queen's Own Rifles
were largely students from the University of Toronto. Even so, the Queen's
Own held their own at first; they moved relentlessly towards the Fenian
lines as other militia units began to clear the woods on their flanks. But
just as the Canadians seemed on the verge of winning the battle, Booker
received an erroneous report that Fenian cavalry had been spotted (in fact,
they had none) and ordered his men to form a square in the narrow defile
through which the road ran. The square was the traditional tactic for
defence against cavalry. The result, as Captain John A. Macdonald (no
relation to the prime minister) later described it, was a disaster:

> The Fenians, who were about ready to quit the fight and flee from the
> field when this unfortunate circumstance occurred, now saw their
> opportunity and were quick to avail themselves of it. Their rifle fire now
> became hotter and more incessant than ever, and as the Canadian
> troops were all huddled up in a narrow road, their [the Fenians'] mur-
> derous volleys were very destructive.

The volunteers broke under the hail of bullets. Officers—including
Otter, a young adjutant—tried to stem the tide of retreating men, but fear
of imminent death dissolved what little discipline there had been. It was
fortunate indeed that the Fenians were only slightly better prepared for
combat and had little stomach to take full advantage of their triumph.
Their pursuit was half-hearted but the Canadians suffered ten deaths, with
thirty-eight of their number wounded. The dead and wounded were carried back to the Ontario capital on the steamer *City of Toronto*. A newspaper described the scene:

> At 9 o'clock in the evening the bells of the city began to toll mournfully
> as the lights of the "City of Toronto," freighted with dead and wounded
> from the battlefield, were seen entering the harbour, and every street
> and avenue began to pour their throngs of sympathizing citizens to
> Yonge Street wharf, where strong pickets of volunteers were drawn up
> to keep the dense crowd already assembled from pressing over the
> dock.

O'Neill had won the day but his victory had been exceedingly lucky; thinking better of their adventure, he and his men soon withdrew across the Niagara River. There he was interned by U.S. authorities for the attack.

Ridgeway was not the last Fenian thrust into Canada—another assault was mounted in Quebec and a second series of attacks would be launched under O'Neill in 1870. Without the active support of the United States, however, several hundred ragged Fenians could not hope to conquer Canada or even to defeat the Canadian troops, however poorly disciplined or badly led they were. Nonetheless, the British felt it necessary to send further troops to Canada following Ridgeway—achieving at least one of O'Neill's aims, the diversion of troops from the United Kingdom, and reminding all sides that the colonies were hopelessly unprepared to defend themselves.

In an effort to augment the country's defence, the new federal government passed Canada's first Militia Act in 1868, establishing a Department of Militia and Defence which was supposed to provide an organizational and bureaucratic structure for an active militia of forty thousand men. In fact, the only action of any consequence that Macdonald's government took was to establish two permanent batteries of artillery at Kingston and Quebec in 1871, to double as artillery training schools for the militia. Those who manned these artillery schools were Canada's first full-time "professional" soldiers, and for a long time the schools provided the only suitably trained militiamen in the country.

The 1868 election of the Liberals in Britain under Prime Minister Gladstone led to sweeping army reforms. Gladstone's government announced that British forces would be withdrawn from those overseas posts that were not considered vital for imperial defence. That meant that the British garrison and naval presence in Halifax and Esquimault would be retained, but that troops in Kingston and Quebec would be pulled out. It was Britain's hope that Canada would at last assume responsibility for its own defence, and indeed that was the case—at least in theory.

EXPEDITION TO RED RIVER

The one concession that Britain did make prior to its troop withdrawal proved to be politically important. In 1869, Canada had negotiated to buy Rupert's Land from Britain for $1.5 million. This vast area was defined as all the land comprehended by rivers draining into Hudson Bay, and extended from present-day Ontario to what is now Alberta and the Northwest Territories. But buying land was one thing, buying people was something else—and there were people in the north-west: Indians and Métis. The Métis—of mixed European and Indian blood—lived mainly by buffalo hunting, farming, and carrying freight to and from Hudson's Bay Company posts. They were proud of their two heritages and angered at being sold and bought without regard for their rights or the impact joining Canada would have on their lives. In the fall of 1869 the Métis of the Red River area (in present-day Manitoba) united behind Louis Riel, a Métis who had been educated in Canada East, to stop the transfer of Rupert's Land. Riel and his men seized Lower Fort Garry and imprisoned a number of local white leaders there, and proclaimed a provisional government. Macdonald's response was to insist that Britain send an expedition to Red River to put the rebellion down. Britain agreed, but only on condition that Canada open negotiations with the Métis. Macdonald had little choice but to comply, and sent Donald Smith of the Hudson's Bay Company (the future Lord Strathcona) to Fort Garry to meet with Riel. An agreement was reached that formed the basis of the Manitoba Act, passed in May 1870, which admitted Manitoba into Confederation and gave the Métis guarantees of land ownership and a modicum of self-government.

While those negotiations were going on, Colonel Garnet Wolseley and four hundred British regulars, together with approximately seven hundred Canadian militia volunteers, were still preparing to depart from Toronto for Red River, to put down the revolt. They were forced to wait until May, since there was no overland route to the remote colony and they would have to follow the old canoe route for much of the journey. The troops travelled by steamer to Port Arthur and then followed the water trail via Rainy Lake, Rainy River, and Lake of the Woods. Aided by French-Canadian boatmen, the force hauled all their equipment, and the heavy boats that carried the expedition, over an endless chain of heavily forested portages connecting the lakes and rivers of north-western Ontario. The heat, the mosquitoes and black flies, the mud and muskeg, and the rain made the journey a supreme trial of physical strength and mental endurance, and Wolseley did not enter Fort Garry until August 24. Since the Manitoba Act was already law—and Riel and other leaders of the rebellion had taken flight—there was little for the force to do except occupy the settlement and attempt to keep the peace.

The militia stayed at Fort Garry over the winter of 1870–71 but Wolseley and the British regulars withdrew almost immediately, as British garrisons were being withdrawn from Canada as rapidly as possible. Henceforth Canada would be on its own.

Manitoba's entry into Confederation was followed by that of British

Columbia a year later and, in 1873, that of Prince Edward Island. No other provinces would be created until Saskatchewan and Alberta were formed out of the Northwest Territories in 1905.

In 1873 Macdonald was forced to resign as the country was rocked by a scandal over the financing of the Pacific railway. His successor, Alexander Mackenzie, was himself a former militiaman who had served against the Fenians, and he was not unfriendly to the notion that Canada had to take more effective steps to defend itself. He set up the Royal Military College (RMC) at Kingston in 1876, patterned partly after the United States Military Academy at West Point (both schools had a four-year engineering-oriented course) and the British military academy at Sandhurst. Arrangements were soon made to have four graduates of the RMC receive commissions in the British army each year.

Mackenzie's approach to defence was more aggressive than Macdonald's but he held office at a time of deep economic recession. Canada faced no obvious enemies from abroad, and the sabre-rattling that had followed the American Civil War had long since ended. The only useful role the militia seemed to play was in the maintenance of public order. In October 1875, for example, the Toronto-based Queen's Own (now under the command of Lieutenant-Colonel Otter) was called upon by the mayor to maintain order during a Catholic procession through the city, as there was a well-established tradition of Irish Catholic–Irish Protestant violence in Canada in that era. As it happened, violence did break out but the militia was not involved, and the men went home none the worse for wear. In December 1876 the Queen's Own was again called out when striking locomotive engineers tried to tie up the Grand Trunk Railway, the most important railway link in Canada. When the Grand Trunk hired strikebreakers who attempted to restore normal service, strikers attacked trains all along the route between Montreal and Toronto. The worst incident took place at a key section point in Belleville on New Year's Eve, when a large crowd of strikers tried to halt all movement. The local militia was considered unreliable—it contained too many strikers and sympathizers—and the Queen's Own was called in. For several hours on that bitterly cold night, militiamen battled a crowd who assaulted them with stones, iron bolts, chunks of ice, and anything else that was lying around. By 3:00 A.M. the battle was over and the strikers had dispersed, leaving the militia in control of the station and roundhouse. Despite this "victory", the Grand Trunk capitulated the next day, much to Mackenzie's disgust.

Mackenzie's Liberal government was unable to solve the country's economic woes, and in 1878 Macdonald and the Conservatives regained

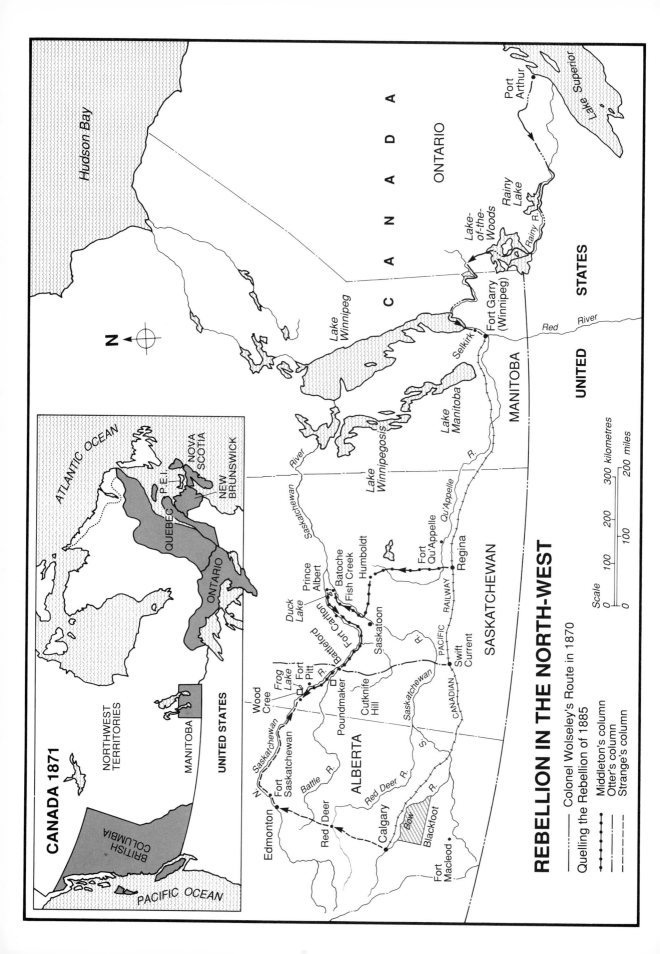

REBELLION IN THE NORTH-WEST

——— Colonel Wolseley's Route in 1870

Quelling the Rebellion of 1885

●—●—● Middleton's column

●——● Otter's column

- - - - - Strange's column

CANADA 1871

ATLANTIC OCEAN

NOVA SCOTIA

P.E.I.

NEW BRUNSWICK

QUEBEC

ONTARIO

NORTHWEST TERRITORIES

MANITOBA

UNITED STATES

BRITISH COLUMBIA

PACIFIC OCEAN

Hudson Bay

C A N A D A

ONTARIO

Lake Superior

Port Arthur

Rainy Lake

Rainy R.

Lake-of-the-Woods

Lake Winnipeg

Fort Garry (Winnipeg)

Selkirk

Red River

MANITOBA

UNITED STATES

Lake Manitoba

Lake Winnipegosis

Saskatchewan River

Qu'Appelle

R.

Fort Qu'Appelle

Regina

SASKATCHEWAN

CANADIAN PACIFIC RAILWAY

Swift Current

Saskatchewan River

Humboldt

Saskatoon

Batoche

Fish Creek

Prince Albert

Duck Lake

Fort Carlton

Battleford

Fort Pitt

Frog Lake

Wood Cree

Poundmaker

Cutknife Hill

R.

S. Saskatchewan R.

N. Saskatchewan River

Fort Saskatchewan

Edmonton

Battle R.

Red Deer R.

Red Deer

Bow R.

Blackfoot

Calgary

Fort Macleod

ALBERTA

N

Scale

0   100   200   300 kilometres

0   100   200 miles

power. By this time the state of Canada's defences had sunk so low that it was patently obvious that unless some action was taken the militia would deteriorate into a bad joke. The artillery schools in Kingston and Quebec City began to train infantry and cavalry officers as well, while the RMC course was upgraded to more professional standards. Permanent schools for militia officers were established in Toronto, Montreal, and Fredericton, and all prospective officers were required to attend. A government-owned arsenal was established at Quebec City to produce ammunition for the Snider-Enfield Long Rifle. A third battery of militia artillery was established at Victoria. Finally, in 1883, a small permanent force based on Quebec City's Cavalry School Corps and Toronto's Infantry School Corps was initiated. The latter was commanded by Otter, who now became a full-time soldier.

THE CANADIAN MILITIA

Despite the improvements, Canada was still virtually defenceless. Theoretically a large force of militia units existed, backed by reserves, but in reality there was no military to speak of. Most weapons were hopelessly obsolete: the standard gun was the Snider-Enfield, a former muzzle-loader of .577 calibre which had been converted into a single-shot breech-loader, so it could be reloaded from a prone position. The first shipment of thirty thousand had been "lent" by Britain in 1867 to help the Canadians against the Fenians. Despite the shortage of other basic equipment, the government had refused to buy surplus British stores left over when the British withdrew. With the exception of a handful of militia officers who had seen service with the British army, almost no one knew anything about the profession of arms. This was a major hazard: without the right training, men under fire quickly become an unruly mob and surrender to the urge for self-preservation.

The only rudimentary training a militiaman was likely to receive came at the annual militia camps, when twenty thousand or so men would gather near some village or town to don uniforms (often dirty or ill-fitting), drill, and engage in a mock battle or two. When the weather was good it could be great fun: they escaped their mostly menial jobs, and their wives and families, to hang around with other men, play cards, smoke, swear, and pay frequent visits to the local watering hole (liquor was never permitted in the camps). They were paid a mere pittance but it was more vacation than the average Canadian received in those days. When the weather was rotten, of course, the camps became a sodden, miserable mess. The camps were highly prized by the towns as a boost to the local economy; it is doubtful if they served any other purpose.

Officers reaped somewhat greater rewards. They were expected to share in expenses for much of the equipment, including the regimental uniforms. Many of these uniforms were quite elaborate: that of the 10th Royal Grenadiers, for example, included a Havelock cap (not unlike that used by the French Foreign Legion), a full red tunic (the Queen's Own used green), heavy corduroy trousers, and a wide leather Sam Browne belt. In return for their contribution, the officers received both social and political benefits. A militia officer was thought of as a notable in his community, someone to be respected, a member of the local elite. But even an ordinary militiaman could derive some status from membership in a famous regiment. A drygoods clerk at Eaton's might also be a corporal in the Queen's Own Rifles, something that would impress the girls at the Saturday night dance!

If the militia was an important social and political instrument, why was it so neglected? In part it was because Canadian governments throughout the 1870s and 1880s were convinced that the militia was militarily useless. John A. Macdonald himself believed that if the United States was truly determined to conquer Canada it could do so with little trouble, and that Canada's only real defence lay in trying to get along with the Americans. Since Britain controlled Canadian foreign policy, he thought it was Britain's responsibility to ensure that the Americans were not provoked into an invasion—and if they were, it followed that it was Britain's responsibility to defend Canada.

The militia was also neglected because of the peculiar idea of the *levée en masse*. This was the notion that at a time of crisis all males in the country would present themselves at their local militia headquarters, rifles in hand, ready to fight for queen and country—indeed, they were compelled by law to do so. In some mysterious fashion this large and undisciplined mass of untrained men was expected to fight like demons for home and hearth and repel any invader taking the field against them. Had this not happened when the Yankees had invaded during the war of 1812? In fact, it had not. The Canadian militia of the time would have been useless without the considerable stiffening that the handful of British regulars—Sir Isaac Brock foremost among them—provided. But the popular myth of the Loyalists repelling the Americans—the myth of the militia—was at its height in the 1880s as the fever of imperialism swept across English-speaking Canada. The idea that determined young farmers and mechanics clutching the Union Jack in one hand and a flintlock in the other had saved Canada for the Empire was all-pervasive.

The militia myth made life exceedingly difficult for the men periodically sent from Britain to try to mould the Canadian militia into some semblance of a real fighting force—the General Officers Commanding (GOC) Canadian Militia. These men were supposed to fill several roles at the same time. They were to give advice to the Canadian government on a broad range of defence matters—advice that was often ignored. They were to prepare the militia to serve alongside British regulars in time of war—an impossible job as long as the Canadian government was unwilling to buy modern military equipment or to support an effective training program. They were also to keep the British government informed about the state of Canada's defences—but no one in Whitehall could possibly grasp how apathetic Canadians were on defence issues. And these British officers, with little or no political experience, were supposed to do all this while paying close attention to the sensibilities of Canadian politicians, who reacted with horror to even the semblance of British military interference in internal Canadian affairs—especially when it was suggested that patronage be eliminated from the appointment of militia officers.

Patronage—the granting of favours to one's political friends—was a fact of life in nineteenth-century Canada. Virtually every government job, from local postmaster to deputy minister, was a patronage appointment, to be granted, not for ability, but for the right politics. Militia officers were, almost without exception, patronage appointments. There was no pay in the position, but there was prestige, and for those who could not get postmasterships (which did pay) it was better than nothing.

BOATMEN ON THE NILE

The 1880s were the springtime of the second British Empire. The first Empire had all but melted away after Britain adopted free trade—all but India, which Britain called the "jewel in the crown" and refused to relinquish. But other European countries soon began to match Britain's industrial power, and in the last two decades of the nineteenth century a race began for new colonies, territories, and possessions around the globe. With its powerful navy, Britain took first place, but its pre-eminence did not come without a struggle. One major battle was fought in far-off Sudan in 1884.

The Sudan was vital to the defence of Britain's position in Egypt and, so the British thought, to control of the Suez Canal, the lifeline of Britain's link to India. Led by the Mahdi, a holy man who proclaimed himself to have been sent by Muhammad to establish God's kingdom on earth, many Sudanese wanted to expel the British and take control of the Nile. Major-General Charles George "Chinese" Gordon, a tempestuous, self-righteous, and highly religious man, had come to Khartoum, capital of the Sudan, to pacify the country. But by the summer of 1884 the Mahdi's forces, vastly outnumbering Gordon's small contingent, had laid siege to Khartoum. The British were determined to rescue Gordon and decided to dispatch an expedition up the Nile. The problem was that the river tumbled over six cataracts, which made it virtually impassable.

In the War Office the adjutant-general, Major-General Garnet Wolseley—the man picked to lead the rescue—cast his mind back to the Red River expedition of 1870. He had been impressed with the efforts of the Canadian boatmen who had transported his troops west over the long and arduous river route, and he prevailed upon the Colonial Office to ask Macdonald to send three hundred *voyageurs*, commanded by three militia officers, to help out. Macdonald refused to give any official assistance "to get Gladstone and Co. out of the hole"—for the sake of his position in Quebec he did not want to be seen as supporting a strictly imperial adventure. He did, however, agree to let the British recruit directly in Canada, as they had done during the Crimean War. Close to four hundred boatmen (none of them true *voyageurs*—they had all died years before), accompanied by three militia officers and an engineer, eventually went to the Sudan on civilian contracts.

The work of moving the large troop-carrying boats through the Nile rapids was difficult and time-consuming, for the convoy had to be physically hauled through each rocky cataract. One of the Canadian officers, Lieutenant-Colonel Frederick Charles Denison, described this scene after his return from Egypt:

> When they came to a bad rapid...3, 4 or 5 crews...would be put on [the boat ropes].... It was generally necessary also to unload the arms, and perhaps part of the load. In these cases a voyageur was put in the bow, another in the stern.... If there was too much slack rope, the current would catch the boat, running her out into the stream broadside on, and sometimes filling the boat. She would turn over, throwing the voyageurs into the water....

Despite these valiant efforts, the troops arrived at Khartoum too late to save Gordon, who was captured and beheaded when the city fell to the Mahdi's forces on January 25, 1885.

The Battle of Ridgeway. In 1866, Fenian raiders crossed the Niagara River and routed a mixed force of British soldiers and militia (including students) before withdrawing across the U.S. border. The Fenians' main goal was to speed Ireland's liberation by forcing Britain to divert troops to Canada. (NAC C-18731)

Colonel Wolseley's Camp, Prince Arthur Landing, July 1870, William Armstrong. When the Métis first rebelled in 1870, British soldiers and Canadian militia had to spend months on the canoe route from Toronto to Fort Garry, camping every night and portaging heavy boats. By the time they arrived, the rebellion was over. (NAC TC-472)

The Fight at Duck Lake In the second rebellion, Louis Riel proclaimed Métis government on March 19, 1885. Major Crozier of the NWMP was first on the scene and rashly attempted to seize the supply and munitions depot at Duck Lake, in the heart of the Métis territory; the Métis drove his men off but let most of them escape. (NAC)

The Battle of Fish Creek With the new Canadian Pacific rail line covering most of the route, troops reached the west by April 6, 1885. On April 24 General Middleton's men fell into an ambush at Fish Creek and suffered heavy losses; Métis tactics had again carried the day. (NAC TC-406)

The Battle of Cut Knife. On May 2, 1885, Col. Otter's column was surrounded by Cree at Cut Knife Hill. Otter might have gone down in history as Canada's Custer if the Cree chief, Poundmaker, had pressed home his advantage. (NAC TC-407)

The Capture of Batoche, 1885, Sgt. Grundy. In May the armies met at Batoche, and although Middleton's grand stratagem of a gunboat failed, his troops won the decisive battle. Six months later Louis Riel was hanged for treason. (NAC C-55581)

The Surrender of Poundmaker to Major General Middleton at Battleford, Sask. on May 26th, 1885, R. W. Tutherford. Fears of a great Indian war came to nothing; the few Cree who had supported the Métis surrendered and the revolt was over. (NAC C-2769)

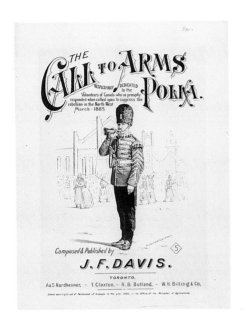

In the 19th century every campaign found its way to the parlour piano; these pieces commemorate the North-West Rebellion and the Boer War. The lyrics of the latter extol the Union Jack "baptized in blood and tears" over "more modern flags with stars and bars," and celebrate the Empire from "torrid strand to far-thest North ice pack." (NAC)

The Dawn of Majuba Day, R. Caton Woodville. In 1899 Britain asked the dominions to help in the war brewing in South Africa; to many Canadians it seemed a glorious adventure. The battle of Paardeberg (Feb. 27, 1900), in which the Royal Canadian Regiment played the major role, avenged the Boer victory at Majuba 19 years before. (Courtesy RCMI and the RCR Museum)

REBELLION IN THE NORTH-WEST

Meanwhile, trouble was brewing much closer to home, and it was almost solely the fault of John A. Macdonald. Acting as his own Minister of the Interior, he had been ignoring growing signs of unrest among Métis, Indians, and even whites in the north-west. The whites opposed his policy of high tariffs and were bitter about the monopoly of the Canadian Pacific Railway, as well as the federal government's indifference to their claims to public lands and natural resources. The Indians were dismayed by the way the whites were swallowing up the land—a concept utterly foreign to Indian life—and with the disappearance of the buffalo they were facing starvation. The Métis were angry because they had been cheated out of lands promised at the time of the Red River Rebellion in 1869, and their repeated pleas for action had been ignored by Ottawa. In 1884 they invited Louis Riel to come back to the north-west.

In the years since the first rebellion, Riel had suffered prolonged periods of mental instability during which he had been confined to an asylum in Montreal. Although he had eventually received a pardon from Macdonald, he was still hated in Ontario. Embittered and frustrated, he moved to Montana, where he waited for an opportunity to return to Canada and resume leadership of the Métis. Although there is still controversy about his sanity at the time, there is no doubt that he suffered religious delusions: he had started to call himself Louis "David" Riel, and he proclaimed that he was founding a new religion combining aspects of Catholicism with prophetic Judaism as he understood it—a proclamation deeply offensive to the Catholic Church and its clergy.

Now, it seemed, Riel's second chance had come. He eagerly returned, determined to repeat the role he had played fifteen years before. When he too was ignored, he moved to rebellion. On March 19, 1885, he proclaimed a Métis provisional government with its capital at Batoche.

Riel badly miscalculated. Too much had changed since the days when the proclamation of a provisional government at Red River had led to negotiations and the passing of the Manitoba Act. In 1869 Canada had had no military to speak of; Macdonald had needed to beg help from Britain, and the only way west had been the arduous river route. By 1885 the country had a nearly completed railway—the CPR—and both the nucleus of a standing army and a militia, however badly organized or equipped.

As it happened, the first response was from the North-West Mounted Police, who had been established as a temporary force in 1873 to maintain order during the years of settlement. Major L.N.F. Crozier led a small party of fifty-six police and forty-three militiamen from the Prince Albert

Volunteers through the snow from Fort Carlton to Duck Lake, in the Northwest Territories. Riel's proclamation had been like a red flag to Crozier, and he was determined to defy the Métis leader by taking control of supplies and munitions stored at Duck Lake, in the heart of the provisional government's territory. His force was small and ill-prepared for combat and he should have waited for reinforcements on their way from Regina under the command of NWMP Colonel A.G. Irvine. But Crozier was hot-tempered and was determined to teach the Métis a lesson they would not soon forget.

As Crozier's troops approached Duck Lake, they encountered a loose Métis skirmish line set up across the road. There was a brief attempt to parley but neither side would give way. Suddenly shots rang out. Within moments the smoke and sound of gunfire drifted over the little battlefield. Riel stood to the rear of his line, encouraging his troops, while Gabriel Dumont, his adjutant general, directed the Métis riflemen from the firing-line. For a few brief moments Crozier and his largely mounted force returned the fire, but suddenly they were caught by enfilading fire from a group of riflemen hidden in a farmhouse up a hill to their right. Within minutes ten men were dead, thirteen wounded. Crozier was only able to extricate his group because Riel stopped Dumont from pursuing them.

Crozier retreated to the small settlement at Fort Carlton. Colonel Irvine and his troop of almost a hundred had arrived about a half hour before. Irvine quickly concluded that discretion was the better part of valour, and that his best course was to consolidate the small detachment of NWMP available to him in defensible positions until help arrived from the east. As their first duty was to defend the scattered white settlements, he gave the order to abandon Fort Carlton and concentrate in Prince Albert, the principal white settlement in the area. Even there, he had only a handful of police and poorly trained and equipped volunteers at his disposal. With Métis and Indian bands throughout the Saskatchewan country apparently ready to join the uprising at a moment's notice, it looked as if Canada's hold on the north-west was in jeopardy—especially when news arrived shortly after that two Catholic missionaries had been killed by the Cree at Frog Lake.

By this time the militia was on the move. The GOC Canadian Militia, Major-General Frederick Middleton, had left for the west within days of the clash at Duck Lake, while militia volunteers rushed to join up from the Maritimes to the west. For many of the volunteers, the rebellion was a chance at high adventure. Quebeckers were insulted at Riel's attempts to undermine the Catholic Church in the north-west and angered by the killing of the missionaries at Frog Lake. Ontarians wanted vengeance for Thomas Scott, an Orangeman from Ontario who had been imprisoned and executed by some of Riel's men in 1870. Within a short time a combined force of close to eight thousand men had been raised, half from the east and half from the west. Two of the militia regiments were francophone. The "regulars"—the Infantry and Cavalry School corps and the batteries at Kingston and Quebec City—formed the core of this force.

The soldiers did not have a quick and easy journey to the west. There were two gaps in the CPR line through northern Ontario, and both men and supplies had to be ferried over the gaps by sleigh. On another part of the trip no enclosed railway cars were available and the troopers were forced to endure long hours on freezing, snowswept flatcars, with no protection from the elements except low wooden sides that had been staked on.

By April 6 enough men and supplies had arrived in the north-west to allow Middleton to begin his push northward. His strategy was simple: three columns would march north from supply bases on or near the CPR main line to relieve the white settlers who were under siege or otherwise threatened in the area south and west of Prince Albert. The ultimate objective was the capture of the Métis "capital" at Batoche, which Middleton reasoned would bring the rebellion to an end. He took command of the most easterly column, which moved north from Fort Qu'Appelle; Colonel Otter commanded the central column, which moved north from Swift Current to relieve Battleford; and Major-General T.B. Strange, retired commander of the Artillery School, led the third column north and east from Calgary and Edmonton towards Frog Lake.

Measured by numbers, the two sides were vastly uneven. Riel's main force numbered about a thousand riflemen under the command of Gabriel Dumont, a crack marksman who had polished his tactical skills as leader of the Métis buffalo hunt. In addition Riel was counting on the help of several hundred Indians, mostly Cree, from Big Bear's and Poundmaker's bands; it was Big Bear's men who had killed the two Catholic missionaries. These were the only two groups of Indians in the north-west to throw their lot in with Riel. The Indians never actually joined up with the Métis, however, and the Métis never fought as one single group. They were poorly armed, they had little ammunition, and although they were used to the quasi-military organization of the buffalo hunt and had once inflicted a major defeat on the Sioux, they were not inclined to go on the offensive. They had little or no understanding of the principles of war. Throughout the brief rebellion, their greatest handicap was Riel's refusal to allow Dumont to "hunt the soldiers down like buffalo". Although Dumont knew

nothing of formal military doctrine, he was a natural tactician who understood instinctively how to use the terrain and how to deploy his forces for
ambush and defence.

The militia enjoyed tremendous advantages over the Métis. They had
better rifles, a small number of old cannon, and even a Gatling gun—a
crank-operated, multi-barrel weapon that was forerunner to the modern
machine-gun. Moreover, they were led by trained soldiers. But many of the
militiamen, especially those from the east, had never fired a shot, while
the officers, including Otter, had no concept of the tactics that Métis and
Indians were likely to employ. Middleton spent several extra days at Fort
Qu'Appelle to ensure that his troops received at least rudimentary training.
He was often accused by his officers and men of being overly cautious,
even ponderous, in his march to Batoche. In light of his uncertainty about
the terrain and the true strength of the enemy, and his ignorance of the
Métis and Indians, his caution was understandable.

On April 24—the same day that Otter's column arrived in Battleford—
Middleton ran into a Métis ambush at Fish Creek. He had previously divided his force, sending one half up the west side of the South Saskatchewan
River, the other up the east side. Concentration of force is usually the best
way to organize an attack; Middleton paid the price for not adhering to
this principle. Dumont's men were hidden in riflepits dug into the brush
and coulees on the east side of the river, and although they were discovered by Middleton's scouts, Middleton did not have enough troops to outflank them. Firing upwards from the dry creek beds, the Métis easily shot
down the militia silhouetted on the skyline. Middleton was unable to dis-
lodge the Métis and was forced to withdraw with fifty-five dead and
wounded. The newspapers claimed victory, but with many more such "victories" the war would be lost.

In any case, the real danger to the government's hold on the north-west
was not Riel's motley band of riflemen—not even when he was backed by a
few bands of Cree. The real danger was that the Blackfoot of southern
Alberta and the bulk of the Plains and Woods Cree of south and central
Saskatchewan would join in a general Indian uprising of the type which
had broken out in the northern United States in 1876, and which had led
to General Custer's "last stand". Custer was never far from Middleton's
mind. In fact, although the Blackfoot and the other Cree had much reason
to be angry with Ottawa and to sympathize with the Métis and the two
rebellious Cree bands, they held back from joining the fight. For one thing,
Blackfoot Chief Crowfoot had developed a healthy respect for white power
during a trip to Winnipeg in the summer of 1884. There he had seen brick

buildings (Lieutenant-Governor Dewdney made certain he saw Stony Mountain Penitentiary), gas lamps on the streets, the CPR railway yard, and more whites than he had ever set eyes on. At the time Crowfoot had been impressed. But if those whites could not easily defeat Riel, he might yet allow himself to be drawn into the fight.

On May 2, the Canadians suffered another dubious victory. This time it was Otter's turn. Against Middleton's advice, he moved out of Battleford to punish Poundmaker's Cree somewhere to the west. He found the Cree at the foot of Cut Knife Hill and they quickly found him; within minutes they had surrounded his force of 350 men. His few cannon proved useless; his Gatling gun was little better, although it made a great show:

> A few seconds sufficed to get the Gatling at work. Its "growl" as the bullets streamed out reminded one more of the explosion of a huge bunch of fire-crackers than anything else. The bushes were fairly mowed down, and how anything...could have lived through that leaden hail is a mystery.

But live they did; Gatlings were notoriously difficult to aim and, although it shredded the foliage, the gun had no apparent effect on Poundmaker's warriors. Otter was forced to withdraw. He missed the chance to go down in history as Canada's Custer when Poundmaker forbade his men to follow.

The Canadians actually lost every "battle" in the campaign except the last one—Batoche—but that one victory was enough to effectively end the uprising. The battle began after Middleton left the vicinity of Fish Creek with 850 men on May 7 and advanced to the Métis capital. Most of the men marched the short distance but some travelled aboard the *Northcote*, a paddle-wheel steamer used for transporting supplies on the North Saskatchewan. Middleton's idea was to turn it into something of a gunboat, and to make a two-pronged attack: one by land, the other from aboard the *Northcote*.

The "naval" assault turned into a disaster. Around 8:00 A.M. on May 9, as the steamer moved into midstream just upriver from Batoche, it came under fire. One correspondent aboard the paddle-wheel "dreadnought" later described the events:

> We were raked fore and aft by a fierce storm of bullets coming from both banks. From almost every bush rose puffs of smoke, and from every house and tree on the top of the banks came bullets buzzing. The fire was steadily returned by the troops on board.... Volley after volley

was fired, and several of the lurking enemy were seen to drop headlong down the sloping banks.

As the steamer moved into the thick of the action, two Métis lowered a cable, normally used to haul a small wooden ferry across the river, across the path of the paddle-wheeler. The *Northcote's* twin smokestacks struck the cable and toppled onto the deck. Middleton's "gunboat" was out of the fight.

Over the next two days Middleton's troops bombarded the town and launched several unsuccessful attacks to improve their positions, all turned back by Métis riflemen dug in around a defensive perimeter. The Métis were vastly outnumbered and were running out of ammunition, but struck back with short, sharp raids on the militia positions. This undoubtedly increased Middleton's caution—he did not want any more Fish Creeks or Cut Knife Hills. Finally, on May 11, an unauthorized attack led by two militia officers exasperated by their commanding officer's caution broke the Métis lines. A Toronto cavalry officer later recalled the climax of the battle:

> The infantry were steadily advancing through the bush, supporting one another by hearty cheers. The guns took an advanced position and opened fire.... I gave the word to mount and advance, and within minutes...we had galloped up to the skirmishing line and dismounted.... The whole line stretching upwards of a mile from the river bank, now advanced steadily but rapidly through the bush...we came to a gully, at the bottom of which lay a number of the enemy.... Poor Ted Brown...was instantly killed.... This exasperated our men, who, with the 90th on the left, rushed furiously down the gully and drove the enemy before them.

The battle lost, Dumont escaped to the United States; Riel was captured, tried for treason, and sentenced to be hanged.

The trial and sentencing sparked months of political controversy. Although the jury found Riel guilty of treason, they recommended mercy, a recommendation the judge ignored in sentencing him. There was also some question of Riel's sanity, though he himself refused to plead for mercy on those grounds. Although the vast majority in English-speaking Canada probably welcomed the death sentence, some thought he should not be executed because Macdonald's bungling of Métis grievances had set the stage for the rebellion. Opposition to the death sentence was especially strong in Quebec, where many sympathized with the Métis; they were, after all, another threatened minority. For months Macdonald wavered, fearing he would alienate large numbers of voters whatever he decided. In the end he declared that Riel would "hang though every dog in Quebec bark in his favour". On the morning of November 16, 1885, Louis Riel died on the scaffold in the courtyard of the Regina jail.

Although the expeditionary force which had defeated Riel was welcomed home as conquering heroes, it was clear to anyone who seriously examined the events that it had been a close thing. The lack of Métis aggressiveness and Poundmaker's refusal to allow Otter's troops to be slaughtered were the chief reasons for the government's victory. The militia had suffered from poor training, lack of effective equipment, and, more important, uneven leadership—if Middleton had been too cautious, Otter had been too impetuous. There were still a lot of lessons to be learned.

STANDING ON GUARD

In 1887, Canadian representatives attended the first Colonial Conference, in London. One of the chief items on the agenda was the colonial role in imperial defence. Britain's point of view was simple, and had changed little over the previous hundred years: since the self-governing colonies were benefiting from the protection of the imperial defence system, especially the Royal Navy, they ought to contribute to its upkeep. Macdonald had rejected that proposition when asked to contribute troops to the Nile expedition and he rejected it now. The Australians and New Zealanders agreed to contribute to the maintenance of a Royal Navy squadron in the southwestern Pacific, but Canada refused to make any commitments. It was a pattern the Canadians would follow for years to come. The political balance between English- and French-speaking Canadians was delicate, and must not be upset by anything not directly and demonstrably linked to the national interest.

On the other hand, real efforts were made to improve the state of Canada's own defences following Macdonald's death in 1891. The man most responsible for the changes was General Ivor J.C. Herbert, who came from England to assume the position of GOC Canadian Militia that same year. Herbert, a vigorous young officer who was both Catholic and bilingual, was determined to stiffen the Canadian military, primarily by shoring up the tiny forces. He transformed the Infantry School Corps and the Cavalry School Corps into miniature regiments—the former became the Royal Canadian Regiment of Infantry(RCR), commanded by Otter, and the latter the Royal Canadian Dragoons. The artillery was reorganized and enlarged as the Royal Canadian Artillery. Herbert dispatched a handful of officers and NCOs to England to receive special training, and organized a training camp at Lévis, Quebec, in the summer of 1894 at which the four companies of the RCR trained together for the first time with officers and men of the militia.

Herbert's emphasis on the permanent force proved to be his undoing. Not only did he concentrate his efforts on improving the training and efficiency of the regulars, he also cancelled the militia summer camps to free up funds for the purchase of new rifles. This was too much for the militia, which was increasingly jealous of the attention being showered on its full-time rivals. When Herbert foolishly persuaded the Militia minister to offer the RCRs to help garrison Hong Kong in 1895, his career in Canada came to an end. Following his departure, the rifle purchases were cancelled and the militia camps were reinstated.

The sorry state of Canadian defences was again evident in 1895, when a British–American dispute over the boundary between Venezuela and British Guiana came close to precipitating a war. Herbert's successor, General W.J. Gascoigne, discovered to his horror that there were no contingency plans for countering an American invasion. There weren't even enough rifles or light arms of any kind to equip an adequate defensive force. Orders were hurriedly sent to England for more than 40,000 rifles and carbines, 12 artillery pieces, and ammunition, while the government tried to keep the request secret lest the U.S. discover just how unprepared Canada was. The crisis soon evaporated; so too did the government's resolve to shore up the military.

In 1896 the Conservatives were tossed out of power and replaced by the Liberals under Wilfrid Laurier. At the 1897 Imperial Conference, called to mark the sixtieth anniversary of Queen Victoria's accession to the throne, Laurier found himself fêted as an imperial hero. Here was a French-Canadian Catholic, once considered a Quebec nationalist, who was prime minister of Britain's oldest and largest self-governing colony, and sworn to preserve British institutions in far-off Canada. Laurier was flattered at the attention he received, but not enough to move away from the position Macdonald had adopted more than a decade before. When it was proposed that the self-governing colonies contribute to imperial defence, Laurier demurred. Canada would still make no commitments.

Once again, however, Canada would make an effort to improve its own position, and this time the man responsible would be the Minister of Militia and Defence himself. Frederick Borden set out on the difficult task of trying to improve the permanent force while placating the militia. Despite complaints that he was overspending, Borden was able to bring in a number of improvements in key ancillary services such as supply and transport. This, together with a new plan for the mobilization of the militia, put the defence of Canada on a firmer footing than it had been on for years.

At first Borden got on well with his new GOC, General E.T.H. Hutton, who was determined to build up Canada's defences. Up to this point the GOCs had usually concentrated on enlarging the pool of manpower that might be available to Britain in time of war. But Hutton repeatedly called for the creation of a "national army". This would entail the reorganization of Canada's mixed force of militia and regulars—whose primary role was to train the militia—into one integrated structure, with the necessary support and ancillary troops, that could be rapidly mobilized in times of national emergency.

There was nothing wrong with this idea; there was much wrong with the way Hutton tried to achieve it. He believed that if reform was to come about, patronage had to be expunged from the system. He thus aimed to diminish the authority of the Militia and Defence minister and increase the responsibility of the GOC. There were two problems with that: the GOC was a British officer, perceived by many to be serving British and imperial interests first; and the GOC was a military man and, as such, had to be responsible to the Canadian government. There were therefore two principles at stake—autonomy and civilian control of the military—and Frederick Borden was not about to let either be undermined. A major rift developed that would eventually lead to Hutton's dismissal.

THE YUKON FIELD FORCE

In August 1896, George Washington Carmack, Skookum Jim, and Tagish Charlie had struck gold on Bonanza Creek, a tributary of the Klondike River in the Yukon Territory. By the following summer thousands of gold-seekers had swarmed into the region from all over the world, and the Klondike Gold Rush was on, as the population of the Territory swelled with goldminers and those—storekeepers, saloon operators, prostitutes, etc.—who sought their gold from the miners. There was a small detachment of Mounties in the Territory, and as soon as word reached Ottawa that a major gold rush was in the offing, reinforcements were sent north, until there were more than 230 police there under the command of Superintendent Sam Steele—a militia man during the Fenian raids and the Red River Expedition, a Mountie since 1873, and a cavalry commander during the North-West Rebellion. Steele was a man of powerful personality and exceptional strength. But would he and his men be enough? Aside from the possibility that the Mounties might not be able to maintain law and order, there was the chance that Canada's very hold over the region might be in jeopardy. On several occasions in the nineteenth century, U.S. settlers—farmers, prospectors, and so on—had moved into non-U.S. territory, put down roots, and claimed the protection of the U.S. government. The last time that had happened, in the late 1840s, Britain had lost a large chunk of territory in the Oregon country. Now, as a result of the gold rush, Canada and the United States were locked in another boundary dispute over the exact location of the Alaska–British Columbia border along the Alaska Panhandle. Prudence seemed to dictate a more tangible Canadian presence—and soldiers cost half as much as Mounties. In the early spring of 1898 the federal government announced the creation of the Yukon Field Force, made up of 203 regulars (all volunteers), most from the RCR, with a number of Royal Canadian Dragoons thrown in for good measure. In May 1898 they set out for the Yukon, taking two seven-pounders, two Maxim machine-guns, and $30,000 worth of tinned beef, hardtack biscuits, and flour. They travelled by steamer from Vancouver up the Stikine River to Telegraph Creek. Then they hiked overland to Fort Selkirk, about 320 kilometres upriver from Dawson City. They were forced to contend with almost constant rain, clouds of mosquitoes, and packs weighing as much as 80 kilos. Trooper Edward Lester kept a diary:

> We struck camp this morning at 9 o'clock.... We did about 18 or 19 miles, only halting once for about 15 minutes. The trail was if anything in a worse condition than yesterday and we had a lot of difficulties to overcome...the way lay along the margin of a chain of lakes, sometimes along the very margin and sometimes hundreds of feet up, now running through the depths of a forest, now running through a gloomy gorge with beetling crags overhead, now crossing a mountain torrent, now winding over a shaking bog, over a corduroy road a slip from which meant a plunge to the knees in black peaty slime.

The Yukon Field Force reached Fort Selkirk on September 11. A detachment of fifty was sent on to Dawson City while the main body of the force spent the winter at Fort Selkirk standing watch, cutting wood, enduring the cold, and fighting boredom. The following fall half the garrison was withdrawn, while the remainder were concentrated in Dawson City until they left in June 1900.

There was good reason for the early withdrawal of half the garrison. In mid-October 1899, a long-simmering dispute between Britain and the British colonies in South Africa on the one hand, and the Afrikaans-speaking republics of the Transvaal and the Orange Free State on the other, exploded into war. Within months a large force of Canadians would be serving on a distant battlefield for the first time in Canadian history. After years of vacillation and half-hearted preparation, Canada was sending its soldiers onto the world stage—and this time they would not be fighting skirmishes or small rebellions, but a full-scale, deadly war.

The Cannington militia—part of the 34th Battalion of the Ontario County Volunteers—around the 1860s. Note frock coats and Kilmarnock caps, and the colour sergeant, who carries the flag into battle, in the middle. Although the militia was supposedly a bulwark of home defence, inadequate training and inept leadership made the militia woefully inadequate. Canada's only real protection remained the British army.

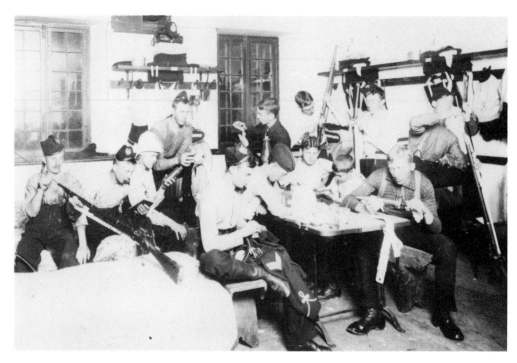

The 57th Peterborough Rangers, a militia unit, spiffing up their uniforms in the late 19th century. Note the young boy at the table, perhaps helping his father. Spit and polish are the inevitable lot of the soldier. So is PT, or physical training. Below, the gymnasium of the new Fort Stanley barracks in 1887, with the men frozen in "lightning moves" for the camera's interminably long exposure time.

Expedition to the Red River in 1870 under Sir Garnet Wolseley. Advanced Guard Crossing a Portage. Frances Hopkins' painting suggests the labour and organization demanded by this extraordinary voyage against the first Métis rebellion: trees are felled, stripped of branches, and aligned in a "staircase" for the men carrying the heavy boats.

Louis Riel poses in a buffalo coat. The Métis leader's early success in the Red River Rebellion led him to expect a similar triumph in the North-West Rebellion 15 years later. But Canada had changed— and Riel's vision of himself as "Prophet of the New World" had cost him many supporters.

A party of Métis traders. The wagons are the famous Red River carts—the versatile two-wheeled carts of wood and leather, which could pass through mud and marsh and float across streams.

In May 1885 the *Illustrated War News* published this portrait of General Middleton, who was charged with defeating Riel's new revolt. Middleton was able but cautious, and many of his officers were exasperated by his lack of daring.

Even with the new rail line running much of the way, moving an army across the country to defeat the rebellion remained a daunting task. Here the Halifax Garrison Artillery fords a stream, at Swift Current, towing a gun.

Many of Middleton's supplies were transported via the North Saskatchewan River, on freight scows like this one, towed by river steamers. When these arrangements broke down, Middleton had to rely on horse-drawn wagon trains as long as five kilometres. Local farmers did their part by selling hay to the government for $20 a ton—10 to 20 times the going rate.

Washing up near Qu'Appelle, Saskatchewan. Note the logs laid down to form a boat landing, and the shirts spread out to dry on the tall, stiff grass.

This unusual piece is a collage of photographs glued to a hand-drawn background. In the centre is Lt.-Col. Otter, commander of one of Middleton's columns; left of him is Superintendent Herchmer of the NWMP, who would be made commissioner of the Mounties the next year. The uniforms are a jumble of dress and undress, showing a fine disregard for regulations.

A contemporary lithograph captures the action of the fight between Col. Otter and Chief Poundmaker at Cut Knife Hill. While the Gatling guns chopped up the surrounding trees, they had little effect on the Indians, and Otter was lucky not to be pursued when he ordered a withdrawal.

W.D. Blatchly's portrayal of the bayonet charge that finally broke the Métis lines at Batoche is more heroic than accurate, with its ordered ranks of steadfast militiamen rushing resolutely forward against disorganized savages. In fact the Métis had constructed well-engineered rifle pits, but were driven out by Middleton's men—who outnumbered the defenders three to one.

The whaleboats were towed up the Nile by steamers as far as the cataracts, and then hauled through on a complex system of ropes. With such arduous means of travel, it was hardly surprising that relief arrived too late to save General Gordon.

When the Gold Rush brought Americans flooding over the border from Alaska, there were serious concerns for Canadian sovereignty. This customs house at the summit of Chilkoot Pass was more a token than a barrier.

Between the expertise of the NWMP and the extra manpower of the hastily mustered Yukon Field Force, a slightly more credible Canadian presence was mounted; as it turned out, the force had little to do but keep warm. Here the men of the YFF capture Christmas 1898 for posterity, in Dawson.

II
THE BOER WAR

For years the Uitlander has suffered under the oppression of a horde of ignorant Dutch farmers." That blunt opinion, expressed by the editors of the Vancouver *Province*, was widely held in English Canada in the summer of 1899. Britain and The Netherlands had been squabbling over South Africa, and especially the Cape of Good Hope, for generations. In 1814 the Congress of Vienna had awarded the area to Britain, which proceeded gradually to take over more and more of southern Africa—to the bitter resentment of the Dutch farmers (Boers) already settled there. When the Boers succeeded in creating their own republics in the Transvaal and the Orange Free State, they retaliated by imposing severe restrictions on what they called Uitlanders—largely British "foreigners" working the gold and diamond fields of the Transvaal. The Uitlanders were undoubtedly discriminated against by the Boer majority and its tough, grey-bearded leader, President Paul Kruger. That was bad enough. What made it worse was that it was the Uitlander who had made the Transvaal, or so the *Province* argued in full-throated rhetoric. "He defrays three-fourths of the cost of the state. He pays the piper and he is not allowed to join in the chorus, much less set the tune." Worse still, "The Uitlanders' children are compelled to learn a hideous Boer dialect...or grow up uneducated. The English language is forbidden in the Transvaal to school children who have passed the third standard. No indignity is too great to put upon the Uitlander," complained the newspaper. "Only quite recently a law was actually passed requiring Englishmen in the Transvaal to carry passes like the Kaffirs [blacks]. The Boers think more of their dogs, and feed their dogs better, than their Kaffir servants....".

The message of the *Province* was crude but very plain: no one with English blood in his veins could long put up with such injustice. Britain had the right and, indeed, the duty to go to war to protect the Uitlanders—

and every Britisher in the world had a duty to help squash the Boers' hateful tyranny.

What British partisans conveniently overlooked was that the Boers were desperately trying to maintain their hard-won independence from Britain. Many had moved inland from the Cape in an epic long march to get free of British control; they had fought wars against the Zulus and brutally subjugated them as they carved out the countries of the Transvaal and the Orange Free State, and they had fought battles with British troops, some successful, some not, to keep their independence.

Then the discovery of the immense Transvaal gold fields of the Rand in 1886 posed a new threat to the Boers, all at once making their dusty pasture lands and arid hills (or kopjes) "the richest spot on earth". Exactly as had happened in California, exactly as would happen in the Yukon a few years later, speculators and sharpsters from all over the world flooded into Johannesburg to dig for treasure. Most failed to find it, and the few who did almost always lost it to the tougher and more ruthless among them. But all, the successes and the failures, were soon demanding their God-given civic rights. At the beginning of 1896, a large raiding party of horsemen secretly sponsored by the millionaire Cecil Rhodes, premier of Cape Colony, tried to topple the Transvaal government. Rhodes looked to the day when Africa, from the Cape to Cairo, would be painted British red on the world's maps, and had been trying to foment rebellion for several years. But the raiders were crushed and any trust remaining between Boer and Briton was irrevocably shattered. War began to seem inevitable.

For Wilfrid Laurier, the situation in South Africa was a major political problem. He personally had little sympathy with the Boers' treatment of the Uitlanders, and in the summer of 1899 he had Parliament pass a resolution to condemn the Transvaal's persecution of them. On the other hand, he had no more sympathy with the jingo patriotism being whipped up by the press in Britain and Canada, which he thought destructive.

To be a jingo, in Canadian terms, was to believe that British was best and to be ready to back up that conviction anywhere in the world, with a punch or a pistol. Britain ruled the waves; and according to Canada's 1898 Christmas postage stamp, showing a world map with the vast extent of the Empire boldly coloured in red, "We hold a vaster empire than has been." That "we" was significant. It was Canada's Empire too, and some Canadians, looking at their country's potential, dreamed of a day when they might pick up the sceptre from Britain and rule the Empire themselves— or, at the very least, share in its management.

Too many Canadians carried their jingo attitudes into their dealings with their fellow countrymen. They decried Catholics as servants of the Church of Rome (the less polite railed at the "Whore of Rome"), people who owed allegiance to a foreign throne. Religion, as a result, was a major political issue in federal, provincial, and municipal politics. The toughs of the Loyal Orange Lodges were always ready to crack papist heads—and often did—and some Protestants felt threatened enough that organizations like the Protestant Protective Association sprang up to ensure that the pope did not take over Canada. The Catholic French Canadians were defined by the jingos as second-class citizens and disloyal to boot: they wanted schooling in their own language, they wanted to be taught by nuns, and they just wouldn't step up to their patriotic duty to the queen. Didn't they realize that they had been conquered by General Wolfe way back in 1759?

Adding to the racial tensions were the foreigners or "aliens" who had been pouring into Canada from Eastern Europe in the tens of thousands since 1896. These Ukrainians (or Galicians, as they were usually called), these Jews, these Romanians, were here on sufferance, barely tolerated as long as they knew their place and kept it. Tolerance had never been a Canadian virtue, and certainly it was not one in the 1890s.

Laurier, a Roman Catholic and a French Canadian, was the first of his race and religion to be prime minister. His outrage over Riel's hanging in 1885 and his support of free trade with the United States in the 1891 election had already raised doubts in some minds about his loyalty to the queen and the Empire. All it would take to get English-Canadian dander up would be any hint that Laurier was prepared to sell Britain short.

Through September 1899, the newspapers filled their front pages with increasingly alarming dispatches from London about the worsening situation in South Africa. Inside the papers, column after column rehashed the history of the Boers, their "trumped-up" grievances against Britain, and the story of the Uitlanders' maltreatment. "The spectacle of thousands of British subjects kept permanently in the position of helots," the Toronto *Globe* quoted from one dispatch from South Africa, "steadily undermines the influence and reputation of Great Britain...." What would Canada do if war came?

On September 29, the *Montreal Star* reported on what it called "Canada's proposal to offer a regiment for service in South Africa", adding that this had "awakened the keenest interest" in London, where the able, aggressive, and imperialistic colonial secretary, Joseph Chamberlain, was determined that, if war came, it should be turned into a glorious opportunity for the whole Empire to display its unity. But what proposal was the

Star referring to? Individuals, most notably the firebrand Conservative member of Parliament Lieutenant-Colonel Sam Hughes, had offered to raise regiments, but so far the government had done nothing. Or had it? No one was more mystified than the prime minister.

The story was complex. On July 3, 1899, Chamberlain had telegraphed Lord Minto, the governor-general of Canada, to ask if Canada would be willing to send troops to South Africa as part of an imperial force. Here, the colonial secretary said, "is an opportunity of showing the solidarity of the Empire, and if a really spontaneous request were made from any Canadian force to serve with H.M. troops...it would be welcomed...." Minto was a British appointee, the only channel of communication between the governments in London and Ottawa. He knew Canada, he knew Laurier would not be enthusiastic about a military commitment in South Africa, and he knew well the constitutional niceties. That made his response to Chamberlain's message all the more astonishing.

The governor-general immediately summoned General Hutton, the GOC. Hutton had already quarrelled with the Militia minister, Frederick Borden, and was fed up with the political interference to which "his" militia was subjected. Without consulting the prime minister or the Minister of Militia, Minto told his general to prepare a plan for a contingent "consistent with the dignity of the Dominion"—something that his own actions that day were violating. By late that afternoon, Hutton (who was nothing if not efficient and eager) had produced a scheme for a 1,200-man force of infantry, cavalry, and artillery, a list of officers to command it, and a draft cable that Minto could send to the War Office in London. Hutton had not consulted Borden, nor would he so much as mention the plan to him until early September.

Instead Hutton talked to his friends in imperialist circles in Montreal and Toronto, and most especially to Hugh Graham, the owner of the Montreal *Star* and a practitioner of the new "yellow" journalism that William Randolph Hearst had used shamelessly, but effectively, to whip up public passions in the United States and provoke "a splendid little war" with Spain in 1898. These fire-eaters desperately wanted Canada to participate in its own glorious little war, and if the government was reluctant, then the government would have to be forced to do its duty. The *Star*'s dispatch on September 29 was part of the process; so too were sensational fabrications of Boer "outrages" against women and children fleeing the onrushing war. The appeals for calm by some rural newspapers and the outright opposition to the war from a few Irish and German-language journals in Canada made little or no headway.

More pressure was to come. On October 3, Chamberlain sent yet another telegram to Ottawa, effusively thanking the dominion for its offer of troops—and promptly handed copies to the press. There was certainly an element of calculation here, but the telegram was a circular to all those dominions that had officially offered men, a list that included Canada—so the War Office and Colonial Office claimed—and it had been released only because of some junior clerk's mistake. The government in Ottawa scrambled to explain, but on the same day the *Canadian Military Gazette*, a Toronto publication "in close touch with the headquarters staff at Ottawa", as the *Globe* described it, hit the newsstands with the full details of the contingent that Hutton had prepared in July. The Cabinet was now playing catch-up, and the Minister of the Interior, Clifford Sifton, wired the editor of the *Globe* that "The whole story about the Canadian contingent to the Transvaal is foundationless...not warranted by any existing emergency." To no avail. A supporter of Laurier though it may have been, the *Globe* was already beating its own nationalist tomtoms, demanding a contingent that would be "Canadian from colonel to drummer-boy.... Canada's offering to the empire should set forth the good service which her sons can render in every rank."

Laurier tried to squelch the agitation in an exclusive interview with the Toronto paper. The Militia Act simply did not permit troops to be sent overseas, he argued. "They are Canadian troops to be used to fight for Canada's defence." Of course, he conceded, there were times when attack was the best method of defence, but this was not one of them. "There is no menace to Canada, and, although we may be willing to contribute troops, I do not see how we can do so...without Parliament's granting us the money." Parliament was not in session, a convenient additional roadblock. But while Laurier's interpretation of the situation was correct in law, it ignored the growing zeal for war in English Canada.

In Montreal, the *Star* denounced the government. "It is not constitutional authority that the Government lacks...it is moral courage to do its duty at the risk of offending a disloyal element which objects to any[thing] that tends to strengthen the bonds which unite England and Canada." Humbug, said *Le Temps* of Ottawa: "Let those who are burning with the desire to shoulder a rifle against the Boers enlist in a British regiment." And *La Patrie* put it simply: "What interest have we in the Transvaal?... Why should we take the money and blood of our people to spend them in such far-away regions?" That infuriated the Toronto *News*: "Canadians with whom loyalty is not merely an empty word are held in check by an element that to all intents and purposes are foreigners.... [The] Loyalists did not come to Canada to live in bondage to the habitant, and their sons will not submit to such a condition."

Incredibly, while the press fought its race war, the fighting in South Africa had not yet begun. That condition effectively ended on October 9 when President Kruger issued an ultimatum to England demanding an arbitration of the points at issue, the withdrawal of British troops from the Transvaal's borders, and the return home of all troops who had arrived in South Africa since June 1 as well as the turning back of troops still on the high seas. The ultimatum was to expire on October 11. The demands were not unreasonable, but they seemed so to fevered opinion in Britain and in Canada, and the ultimatum was rejected by Whitehall. The war was on.

And war was on in Ottawa, too. While the whole Cabinet was "extremely annoyed", as Minto was informed, over his offer of a contingent, there was no unanimity on whether the country should now raise men for South Africa or, if so, how this should be done. Certainly Laurier was unpersuaded that anything more than a nominal contribution was necessary; so too believed Israël Tarte, his powerful Minister of Public Works and the editor of *La Patrie*. On the other side, favouring a contingent equipped, paid for, and commanded by Canadians, were Borden and a few others. Many ministers stayed on the fence throughout the stormy discussion.

Almost immediately apparent to everyone but Tarte was that some contribution had to be made—public opinion in English Canada demanded this. But what kind of contribution? Chamberlain had asked for four company-sized units of 125 volunteers who would serve in the British army and be paid by it at the standard pay of one shilling a day. To Laurier this suggestion, though it smacked of imperialism, constituted a gesture of support that would cost little and would not create a precedent committing Canada to future British wars. His opponents around the Cabinet table wanted the scheme worked out by General Hutton: a substantial and truly national force of 1,200 infantry, cavalry, and artillery commanded by Canadians, with all costs to be borne by Ottawa. Anything else, said the proponents of action, would be unspeakably colonial, unworthy of a full partner in the Empire.

Initially the government decided to double Chamberlain's request and send eight 125-man units for incorporation into imperial regiments—"a much larger number than that supplied by any other colony of the empire", the *Manitoba Free Press* bragged. But four days later, another scheme became public. After representations to London by Minto and Hutton, the War Office had recognized Canada's *amour-propre*. Now an infantry regiment of 1,000 officers and men, equipped and commanded by

Canadians but paid for by Britain once the troops reached South Africa, would be the dominion's contribution. Moreover, as Minto cabled his imperial masters, "My Ministers hope that Canadian contingent will be kept together as much as possible...."

For his part, Laurier was unnerved enough by the controversy that he decided against calling a fall election. He also conveniently forgot his statement that Parliament had to be consulted before Canada could participate in the war. The cost of equipping the contingent and getting it to South Africa was estimated at $600,000, and while that was a lot of money in 1899, it was not so large that parliamentary propriety would be raped if approval took place after the fact. To keep French Canadians happy and Tarte in the Cabinet (and *La Patrie* supporting Laurier), the government explicitly stated that its dispatch of troops could not be construed "as a precedent for future action". That statement provoked Henri Bourassa, a young Liberal MP from Quebec who promptly resigned his seat in protest, to state—quite correctly—that "The precedent, Sir, is the accomplished fact."

The government's policy was nonetheless clever. Laurier could tell Ontario, truthfully enough, that he had done more than Britain wanted; he could say to Quebec with equal conviction that participation was voluntary, costs were low, and no precedent had been set. He could also argue that the British cause was "the cause of justice, the cause of humanity, of civil rights and religious liberty.... The object is not to crush out the Dutch population but to establish in that land...British sovereign law, to assure to all men of that country an equal share of liberty." Most Canadians bought his argument, but some remained bitter. In Quebec, *nationalistes* like Bourassa felt Laurier had sold out to the demands of Ontario instead of refusing to take part in subjugating the Boers—a people, after all, much like the Canadiens. For the first time, Laurier had been tried and found wanting by important segments of Quebec public opinion. In English Canada, on the other hand, a few nationalists argued that the government's temporizing policy had cost Canada the opportunity to be Britain's equal.

For most English Canadians, the fine points simply didn't matter. The Boers were wrong, Britain was right, and Canada should help. The Reverend Duncan Anderson expressed the people's mood in his poem "Transvaal Ho":

Sons of a clime where freedom reigns
And brethren breathe alike God's air;

Go! Break forever serfdom's chains,
And hunt each hell hound from his lair.

CREATING THE CONTINGENT

While the political warriors declared a truce, the Canadian military machine went into action. There was much to do if the contingent was to leave at the end of October 1899, the announced goal. First, the men had to be found. The Militia department authorized recruiting for one year's service of men between twenty-two and forty years and at least five feet six inches tall, for companies in London, Toronto, Kingston, Ottawa, Montreal, Quebec, Saint John, and Halifax, with the last coming from Western Canada. Everywhere except London and Montreal, there were more volunteers than places for them. All the volunteers underwent "as stiff a medical examination as can be devised", the *Globe* reported, with special attention being paid to "all cases of short-sightedness, varicose veins, malformations of the foot, ankle and instep that might interfere with marching and tendencies to lung and heart trouble." Even "ill-shaped and overlapping toes" were stated to be a barrier to enlistment. Skilled marksmen were especially wanted, although one "noted rifle shot", Captain Tom Mitchell of the 12th York Rangers, assured the press that the Boers were overrated in this area: "Man for man, I believe the Canadian contingent will prove better marksmen than the Boers." So eager were some militia officers to serve that more than a score abandoned their commissions to join as privates; others launched telegram campaigns to get officers' billets with the contingent, calling on family political connections and demanding that their region of the country get its fair share of the glory.

The regimental commander had already been named as Lieutenant-Colonel William Otter. With his years of experience in the militia and the army, Otter, though fifty-six years old, was the best soldier Canada had to offer. He was hard and dour, efficient but colourless, a man who could take and give orders. He was a political realist, something that was immediately apparent when he suggested Oscar Pelletier, a francophone lieutenant-colonel and the son of a Liberal senator, for one of the senior positions with the contingent. And he was practical; he agreed to take forty-one officers instead of the usual battalion strength of thirty-one. The addition of eight lieutenants and two captains relieved the Militia minister of some of the political pressure for appointments, and also permitted the contingent—to be known officially as the 2nd (Special Service) Battalion of the Royal Canadian Regiment of Infantry, but popularly as the Royal

Canadian Regiment—to be divided into two smaller battalions if circumstances at the front demanded. Still other officers were to be taken along as instructors, one as commander of a machine-gun section, two as additional medical doctors, and one as "historical recorder". There were also four nursing sisters, three chaplains to care for the Anglican, Presbyterian, and Roman Catholic soldiers, and four press correspondents, two from Liberal newspapers and two from Conservative.

Equipping the regiment was the task of the Militia stores branch in Ottawa, hitherto not the most efficient of the department's branches. There were no suitable uniforms on hand, and not until October 11—the expiry date of Kruger's ultimatum—did the department ask the W.E. Sanford Co. of Hamilton to prepare some. The uniform was to be that of a rifle regiment, and each man was to receive "two rifle serges, two pairs of rifle trousers, and a tunic and pair of trousers of kharkee." The serge was to be "light in texture, suitable for wear in the hot climate of South Africa…and the kharkee," the *Globe* reported, "is the same waterproof linen material that has for years been used for the service uniforms of British troops in tropical or sub-tropical conditions." The troops would come to despise the poor-quality khaki uniforms, stiff and uncomfortable at first, then prone to rot after prolonged wettings. Included in the soldier's kit would be a white helmet (destined to be stained brown), a field service cap, two pairs of boots, blue serge puttees and leather leggings, and what was mysteriously described as an abdominal bandage.

The uniforms would not be ready for issue until the regiment concentrated in Quebec City prior to embarkation, so when the various companies set out on October 25 they were still dressed in motley mixtures of militia uniforms (the men came from eighty-two different units) and civilian clothes. In Toronto more than a hundred thousand cheered the boys through the streets, men "prepared to fight in defence of the rights of Great Britain", as the *Globe* put it. In Ottawa, Private G.R.D. Lyon wrote in his diary that the company "Left Ottawa at 6:30 and were given a great sendoff. Never saw such a crowd." In Quebec the Ottawa troops were billeted at the Citadel while others camped out in immigration sheds. Lyon's diary records the events of the first two days:

October 25: had dinner Beef & Potatoes, Bread (no tea) got beding [*sic*] in afternoon also Oliver Equipment [belts, packs, and ammunition pouches] & Rifle….went to YMCA and had a bath then had a shave.

October 26: [breakfast] of Bread Butter Preserves & Tea…got serge and trousers fitted...too late to get any meat for dinner and had some bread...some milk....were instructed by Street of the GGFG [Governor General's Foot Guards] til 4 pm who knew nothing.

By October 30, despite the usual confusion and rampant theft, the troops' equipment had all been issued, and after a final march through the streets, where tens of thousands of cheering Québécois shouted their heads off, the contingent began to board the aged Allan Line steamer *Sardinian*, hastily refitted at vast expense ($160,543) as a troopship. At 4:10 P.M., the ship cast off. "From the Citadel above the minute guns thundered their farewell," wrote Norman Patterson in *The Canadian Magazine*. "A thousand brave Canadian lads cheered and wept on the decks and in the rigging; fifty thousand Canadian men and women on the shore, waved and hurrahed—and prayed....the bands played 'Auld Lang Syne', 'the Maple Leaf', and 'God Save the Queen', and I saw no more because I rejoiced with those who rejoiced, and my joy blinded my eyes and scorched my throat." Going off to war was still a great adventure in those innocent days, and the emotions generated by imperialism let almost everyone forget that the costs of battle could be terrible indeed.

THE RCR

Who were the soldiers of the RCR? Just over seven in ten had been born in Canada, with one-quarter coming from Britain. Overwhelmingly, the regiment's officers and men were English-speaking. Most were city-dwellers, only 5 per cent coming from rural areas; and roughly equal numbers, just over 35 per cent in both cases, came from white-collar and blue-collar employment. Only one in twelve listed his occupation as soldier.

This state of affairs alarmed Colonel Otter, as well it might. He was quick to discover that even those volunteers who claimed to have militia experience were, as his biographer, Desmond Morton, noted, "almost as ignorant of drill, discipline and military routine as the rawest recruit." The officers often were no better trained, and "even those from the permanent corps knew nothing much beyond their drill manuals and the monotonous round of Canadian barrack life". The month-long voyage to South Africa should have provided an opportunity to begin the process of turning the recruits into a military unit.

It didn't. The *Sardinian* was a small, cramped scow, a former cattle boat. Charles Frederick Hamilton, the war correspondent of the *Globe*, wrote privately to Toronto that "This is in many respects an ill-found transport", and grossly over-crowded. "The fellows (& everyone) are terribly close packed & in some respects very uncomfortable, but in wonderfully good spirits." Though tonnes of food and comforts (six barrels of oranges and forty-five of apples, two cases of cocoa, twenty-two of canned corn and twenty-two of canned tomatoes, three cases of sardines, and ten cases of biscuits, etc., etc.) pressed on the contingent by individuals across the country had been loaded aboard, the daily ration of food was dreadful; Private Albert Perkins of Fredericton wrote home that coffee and tea were boiled, and "The soup is very bad always. The drinking water is lukewarm, if not warmer, though there are thousands of tons of ice on board"—but, he cautioned, "Don't think I complain." All this was bad enough, but a few days out of Quebec the ship ran into heavy storms. Private Lyon wrote wretchedly in his diary that the sea was "pretty rough was on deck for a while but could only bring up blood which came up for over half an hour." Soon after, the weather turned warm, and Perkins wrote his father that "Every third morning...we have a bath, using the ship's hose." Later there was a dysentery epidemic. The ship, to put it kindly, reeked. Still, as Private Tom Wallace—the son of prominent Tory politician N. Clarke Wallace—cheerfully wrote, "we have not much room to drill on board but we are kept busy doing something all the time.... We had target practice on board...and I happened to make enough to be classed as a 1st class marksman." For all the discomfort, Otter saw no reason to revise his initial conclusion that "I have a splendid regiment as far as the men, and fair officers."

On November 30, 1899 the *Sardinian* finally pulled into Cape Town harbour. Cut off from news during the long voyage, many of the contingent had feared that the war would be over before they had a chance to show their stuff. Now they learned that they need not have feared. The Boer armies had moved quickly into the field, and though most of their ranks were full of simple farmers, their professional artillery had already demonstrated its skill. Their mounted infantry were hard-hitting and fast, their riflemen every bit as good as rumoured, and their generalship seemed impressive—much more so than the lacklustre showing thus far provided by General Sir Redvers Buller and General Lord Methuen, the senior imperial commanders. In fact, when the RCR arrived the Boers had a large force of British troops besieged in Ladysmith, while a smaller imperial army was struggling to defend Kimberley. Relief expeditions under Buller and Methuen were making slow, hesitant progress. The RCRs also learned that Ottawa had offered a second contingent on November 2, but that this had been refused; not until December 18, after further reverses to British arms, would the Canadian Cabinet announce the acceptance of its offer. The war clearly was going to be no cakewalk, and the RCR would get its share.

On December 1, after a march through the streets of Cape Town, the troops boarded trains for the interior and the real beginning of their service, leaving much of their kit behind in storage. The first camp was at De Aar, the base camp for the advance on Kimberley. "This place is one of the most important that the British have to hold," Tom Wallace wrote home. "We are part of the brigade that is to relieve Kimberley....we expect to leave to-morrow." Otter was no better informed; when his battalion moved forward on December 7, now equipped with transport in the form of 130 mules and wagons and carts, he, like his men, apparently believed it was towards action.

Happily for the raw Canadians, it was not to be. A Scottish battalion that had arrived in South Africa at about the same time as the RCRs got the call instead, while the Canadians took on the inglorious task of constructing a railway siding. Just as well, for the Scots were slaughtered, and their survivors put to panicked flight, by well-concealed Boers firing from rifle pits at Magersfontein on December 11—the first of a series of defeats in what the London press called "Black Week". On December 9 General William Gatacre had been roundly trounced at Storm Berg, and on the 15th Buller, still attempting the relief of Ladysmith, lost a thousand men and twenty artillery pieces. The war seemed in danger of being lost, and the War Office was quick to name Field Marshal Lord Roberts, the aged, diminutive, one-eyed, and much-loved "Bobs", to the supreme command. Sir Herbert Kitchener, appointed as Roberts' chief of staff, had defeated the "fuzzy-wuzzies" (as Kipling called them) at Omdurman in 1898, in one of the epic colonial battles of the Empire, and had been part of the unsuccessful attempt to save Gordon at Khartoum. London also scrambled to find vast new armies—almost two hundred thousand troops would arrive in the first months of 1900.

For the RCR, spared the Scots' fate at Magersfontein, there was only another move up the line to Belmont, the site of an earlier clash with the enemy. "There are dead Boers & horses lying all around us," Private Frederick Lee of the Montreal company wrote to his parents, "so you can imagine the smell," while Tom Wallace complained, "We are now down to hard tack and tea three times a day no milk or sugar." For his part, the *Globe* correspondent, Hamilton, reported privately to his editor that "the reg't is stuck here at garrison work and the indications are that it will remain for a while." That was correct.

Whether Hamilton's other comments were equally true is less clear.

"Our battalion is as curious an affair as ever.... Otter has been a great disappointment to me—he has fairly been at sea and has made himself very unpopular by what I can only describe as peevishness & irritability." Nor was the reporter happy with the battalion's training: "we have not fired a shot since [aiming practice on ship]—they are reluctant to do any firing so near the enemy.... When we once get under fire things will improve if we have good luck.... I wish we could get a little fighting, for it would do us a world of good." Just why Hamilton believed that the RCR, spirited though it undoubtedly was, would benefit from exposure to an enemy who had destroyed well-trained, if ill-led, British regiments, is as hard to fathom as his strictures on Otter.

For Otter, acting as camp commander at Belmont as well as regimental commander, was desperately trying to get his command into shape. The RCR practised parade-square drill, learned discipline, and mastered the military art of outpost duty. As Hamilton reported to the *Globe* on December 21—in a letter that would be published in February, after the six weeks' sea voyage—heavy enemy fire had forced changes in tactics, and these the RCR was practising:

> A succession of thinly extended lines advance upon the enemy, one line behind another, each so extended as to present the minimum target. As the objective point is reached the rear "waves" come up and join the "wave" in front, thus feeding the firing line and developing its fire with gradually increasing intensity.

Hamilton added that this formation had forced the elimination of volley firing and that, because the Boers unsportingly aimed their fire at officers and NCOs, swords were being left behind, rank badges were being removed, and gold buttons were being painted over.

At the very least, this training helped the grumbling men of the RCR get their ship-softened muscles back into shape. Part of the problem with Otter—and there was a problem—was that his humourless and unrelenting personality did not endear him to his troops. He expected discipline, discipline, and discipline, and he disdained the little comforts that canteens could provide. Volunteer soldiers felt entitled to tobacco and small sweets as well as regular meals—though even the latter were a problem, because the British army provided its men with "tea" at 4:00 P.M. and nothing more until breakfast. There was real bitterness in a letter from Albert Perkins, published in the Fredericton *Gleaner*, lamenting that "Col. Otter refused to let a fellow sell some stuff here—it consisted of two loads of

jam, biscuit, etc. and so we could not buy any which we would have liked
to. The boys like Col. Buchan very much." The affable Lawrence Buchan
was the battalion's second-in-command, in the rank of major, and relations
between the RCR's two senior officers were never good.

Finally one company of the RCR had the opportunity to "smell powder".
On December 31 the new station commander, a British lieutenant-colonel
named Pilcher, took a small mixed unit of RCRs, Queenslanders, and
British troops out of Belmont in search of a party of four hundred Boers
to the west. Tom Wallace of C Company wrote that his company "was chosen to go and I was lucky enough to get a place and so we were the first
Canadians to be under fire." After some twenty miles' march, the RCRs
being carried most of the way in "springless buck-waggons" or "scotch-
carts", and after a night sleeping "on the ground without any tents with
our rifles in our arms to the ready", Pilcher's force woke to the new year.

Soon scouts located the Boers at Sunnyside Kopje. After the artillery
had pounded the Boers' laager (encampment), C Company of the RCR went
forward to take up a position from which it could pin down the enemy,
and so the men came under enemy fire for the first time. As T.G. Marquis
later declaimed in his book *Canada's Sons on Kopje and Veldt*, "The fates
were with them, and although thousands of bullets splashed the brown
dust of the veldt in front, in rear, and sang overhead, no chance bullet
found a victim."

After several hours of sniping, the Canadians and Australians charged the
Boer position and took it, but not before most of the enemy escaped. The
Boers suffered eighteen casualties and lost thirty-five prisoners; Pilcher's
force had two killed and three wounded, but C Company escaped without a
scratch. It was a baptism of fire, and, as Tom Wallace noted, "The English
Colonel gave us great praise for the part we took in the engagement." Unfortunately, as he reported after his return to Belmont, "All the other companies
are jealous of us now and they try to belittle what we did." The rivalries that
had troubled the RCRs from their formation still persisted.

So did the grumbling. Albert Perkins complained that "now the Colonel
has taken it into his head to give us a march every day at 4 o'clock. If he
would only start in easy it would not be so bad, but last night we had a forced
march of thirteen miles, and I am as sore as the dickens." Those marches
continued, toughening up the troops. Frederick Lee wrote that he was going
on guard "for 24 hours which is a pretty tiresome job in this country on
account of the heat." There were also sandstorms that made life miserable.

Gruelling as the days may have been, Otter's insistence on drill and dis-

cipline was gradually getting the men into shape—and none too soon.
Field Marshal Lord Roberts' grand strategy was now taking form. After
arriving at Cape Town on January 10, Bobs had decided to mass his
armies on the Orange River, leave his base behind, and set out on a great
turning movement against the communications of General Cronje. Troops
and supplies were gathered, brigades and divisions formed. And for the
Canadians, now spoiling for a fight, there was at last the prospect of
action. Otter was summoned to meet Roberts and Kitchener and learned
to his relief that the RCR would participate in the great campaign. A few
days later Colonel Horace Smith-Dorrien passed through Belmont and
advised Otter that the regiment was to form part of his brigade. On February 12 the great advance began. That day, Tom Wallace wrote to his "dear
Papa" that "We have good officers from Col. Otter down and we go forward with confidence." That was almost the first word of praise Otter had
received, and it was a good omen.

INTO BATTLE

The Canadian contingent had yet to see any sustained action, but the contingent had already begun to dwindle as heat and sickness took their toll.
One soldier had died on shipboard; another succumbed to fever in South
Africa; many more fell victim to typhoid, which was raging through the
British armies, or to sunstroke. The result was that the RCR, which had
consisted of 41 officers and 962 men at its formation, now set off with only
31 officers and 865 men.

The regiment broke camp at Belmont, leaving much of its equipment
and tents behind before setting out by rail for Graspan, some ten kilometres up the line. The battalion's mule-drawn wagons and carts, heavily
laden despite the effort to trim away non-essentials, came along. Hamilton
of the *Globe* described the RCR as it set out:

> Right in the eye of the rising sun we marched, the regiment at loosest
> formation, quarter column shaken out to fifteen paces, ranks at five
> paces distance. Close behind the eight companies came the five or six
> Scotch carts with the ammunition and medical supplies, the stretcher-
> bearers, the Maxim gun attachment, and the water cart.

The precise formation did not last too long, or so Albert Perkins wrote in
his diary:

At three we were up and marched ten miles in the [Orange Free State]. You see we are in the enemy's country for [a] scrap. We had a horrible march. The sun was awful. We could not touch the brass on our straps or on our rifle barrels. The men from India, soldiers of years' service, said they never saw the like. Men fell overcome by the heat and some received severe sun stroke.... Our company had done 14 miles the day before and lost two nights sleep.... Then we marched into camp where there are thousands of men watching us and sang "How Dry I Am".

Perkins added that the wax candles he carried in his pack had melted, and that fifty men had dropped out, worn out and dehydrated.

The object of their exertions was Magersfontein, where General Cronje's forces were besieging Kimberley, a diamond-mining town on the border between Cape Colony and the Orange Free State. Cecil Rhodes—founder of the De Beers diamond-mining company, and a former prime minister of the colony—had been holed up in Kimberley almost since the outbreak of war, and relieving the town was one aim of the British advance; more important was to eliminate Cronje's army of five thousand men.

The old general had unaccountably failed to realize the scale of the approaching menace until February 15. Then Cronje and his forces tried to escape into the Orange Free State, the besiegers suddenly transformed into the hunted. Accompanied by three hundred wagons and in many cases by their wives, who had been brought along to keep the Boer farmers comfortable, the army moved almost fifty kilometres in a single night. British troops harried Cronje's rearguard, while cavalry led by Sir John French sped around the Boer columns to seize the high ground between Cronje and safety. His troops—and their draft animals—near exhaustion, the Boer commander formed a laager on the north bank of the Modder River at a place called Paardeberg Drift. There he would stand and fight.

Meanwhile Boer commandos—a word just coming into use to describe the superb mounted infantry that moved behind the British lines—roamed almost at will. One column threatened De Aar, the main British base on the Cape Town–Kimberley rail line. Another captured a 180-wagon supply column at a ford called Waterval Drift which the RCR had passed through just two days before. If Cronje's army was exhausted by its exertions, so too were the imperial forces—and now they would have to operate on short rations as well.

The RCR marched throughout the night of February 16, struggling through the clouds of dust raised by the British columns. The next night, now knowing that they could expect to go into action in the morning, the

RCR was the rearguard for the advance, a position that made the dust worse still. "[We] were choked with dust and parched for water," Colonel Otter wrote, "and it seemed as if daylight or the end of our march would never come." But just after 5:00 A.M. on February 18 the regiment came over the crest of a small rise and saw Paardeberg Drift before them. Knowing his men were at the end of their endurance, Otter halted the battalion so that tea, biscuits, and a half-tot of rum could be distributed. Then the orders came through: Smith-Dorrien's brigade, including the RCR, was to cross the swollen Modder and attack the Boer positions from the north and west.

That proved to be no easy task. Private Perkins noted that "Horses were put off their feet and ammunition lost. A rope was strung across and the men caught hold of it and came across in that manner." Other companies, incredibly, linked arms and marched across the river in fours, the taller helping to keep their short comrades' heads above the fast-moving water. "I put my book and my papers in my hat," Perkins said, "and in that way have kept them dry." Once across the Modder, though the men were "laughing, joking, happy" at the prospect of action, the RCR still did not know where it was going or what its task was. Otter could only urge his men forward, and hope more instructions would reach him.

The enemy fire was increasing, however, and for most of the RCRs this was the first experience of being shot at. The regiment advanced towards the east, upright at first, then in short rushes as the Boers' well-aimed firing intensified. At last the men could advance no farther, and sought shelter wherever they could find it. Casualties began to mount. The officer commanding A Company was severely wounded, and three stretcher-bearers who tried to carry him off the field were cut down as well. After that, other wounded were left where they fell; if they were lucky one of the battalion surgeons, Captain Eugène Fiset, or the Catholic padre, Father O'Leary, got to them with a bandage, a sip of brackish water from a canteen, or the last rites. And while the rifle bullets spat in the dirt around them, all the RCRs began to suffer the effects of the 40° C heat and thirst. To make matters worse, as Albert Perkins wrote, "a heavy rain drenched us and then we steamed again."

The breakdown in command that had left Otter's battalion at loose ends and under fire was unfortunately symptomatic of the whole engagement. The aged Roberts had collapsed from the heat and strain before the battle had begun, and although Kitchener was giving orders, he was both over-optimistic and interfering, and completely failed to co-ordinate the British attacks. And there was now a relieving force of Boers, under the able leader Christian De Wet, atop the battlefield's highest vantage point, so-called Kitchener's Hill.

Kitchener wanted De Wet's men dislodged, and told the Duke of Cornwall's Light Infantry to do the job. By 4:00 P.M. the British regiment had crossed the river and reached Otter's position, where the two battalion commanders had a short, sharp exchange. The British officer, Otter wrote his wife, "was offensive and insinuated that we were too slow &c." He told Otter, "I have been sent to finish this business, and am going to do it at the point of the bayonet."

The Cornwalls' commander was as good as his word, and at 5:15 P.M. he sent his battalion forward across the open terrain in a charge. Unfortunately the RCRs, intermingled with the Cornwalls, assumed the order was meant for them as well. In a few moments the whole hopeless, gallant affair was over, the survivors desperately seeking cover from a storm of rifle fire when they were still three hundred metres from the Boer trenches. The Cornwalls' colonel was killed, along with scores of his men. Frederick Lee, sending his parents "a few lines just to let you know I came through our first encounter safely", wrote that "you cannot imagine what war is until you are in it you think of nothing but killing your enemy." About sixty RCRs had fallen in the two minutes of carnage, making the dreadful total for the day eighteen killed and sixty-three wounded, and at nightfall Otter withdrew his regiment, except for those who stayed behind to collect the casualties, to a bivouac at the Modder crossing-point.

So Cronje's laager remained unbreached, though his forces had lost some three hundred. British losses were more than four times that figure, but Roberts had taken command again, and his first action was to refuse Cronje's request for a truce to allow both sides to bury their dead. The siege now got under way in earnest, the British advancing their trenches forward each day while their artillery pounded Cronje's laager.

For the next several days the slow pace of action continued, though there were rumours of relieving columns of Boers and of counter-attacks heralding a breakout. The days were hot or wet, the nights cold. Perkins noted that "There was a cold wind blowing and we nearly froze," a misery made worse by the shoddy quality of the blankets issued to the regiment in Canada. On the 24th he added that he had been on duty the night before: "It was awful. The rain fell in torrents, and I was soon soaked through. We were wet, cold and hungry." The hunger was perhaps the worst, with the continuing half-rations taking their toll. Perkins had written on February 21 that "we got a drink of weak tea and a piece of biscuit.... It seems to be very poor management." On the 26th he reported, "We are still weaker and there is nothing to eat." Water was also scarce, and most of it came from the Modder River, a source seriously polluted by the numbers of Boer and British dead floating in it. This water was not boiled before drinking—Lord Roberts had neglected to order that it should be—and typhoid fever in epidemic proportions would be the result later in the campaign.

But now the climax of the battle was at hand. On Monday February 26, the RCRs relieved the Cornwalls in the trenches facing Cronje's main positions. The British commanders believed enemy morale was weak—the Canadians kept hearing from prisoners that their comrades wanted to surrender. The Boers were certainly short of food, and were even more disturbed by the smell of dead bodies and animals than the imperials. It was time for another advance, to move the British trench line forward, and as the RCRs were in the trenches it fell to them to lead the attack.

By evening Colonel Otter had made his plans. Six companies would launch the assault at 2:00 A.M. the next morning, with Otter himself leading the troops in the centre. His two majors, Buchan and Pelletier, would command on the left and right. The battalion would advance in two lines, the first with rifles and bayonets, the second fifteen metres behind with shovels to help build a new trench as far forward as possible in case the assault was checked.

Fifteen minutes late, the RCRs set off, clambering over the parapet of their trenches in an eerie preview of the Great War. "It was very dark," Private Perkins wrote, "so dark that we were told to advance holding hands as we were apt to stray from one another if we did not." Both lines moved with painstaking care to preserve silence, trying to avoid the clank of metal on metal, and the advance, which covered some six hundred metres, proceeded at little more than fifteen metres a minute. For about a half hour they were undetected; then two shots rang out from the Boer trenches, most of the Canadians hit the dirt, and a fusillade of fire from the Boers' Mauser and Martini rifles roared out. "We dared not return the fire," Perkins said, "as it would give us away. To lift one's head would mean sure death. Had the Boers not been afraid to rise up and fire low not one of us would have escaped." The few men who rushed at Cronje's trenches sixty metres in front were all hit, falling dead or wounded. On the right flank, however, the fire left Pelletier's H Company unscathed, and the men poured covering fire on the enemy. F and G companies, just to the left, lost twenty-seven men. "Our company had nearly all the casualties," said Perkins, who was in G company. "The fire was horrible." Buchan's companies, on the left of the assault, had taken casualties but were digging in, though with difficulty.

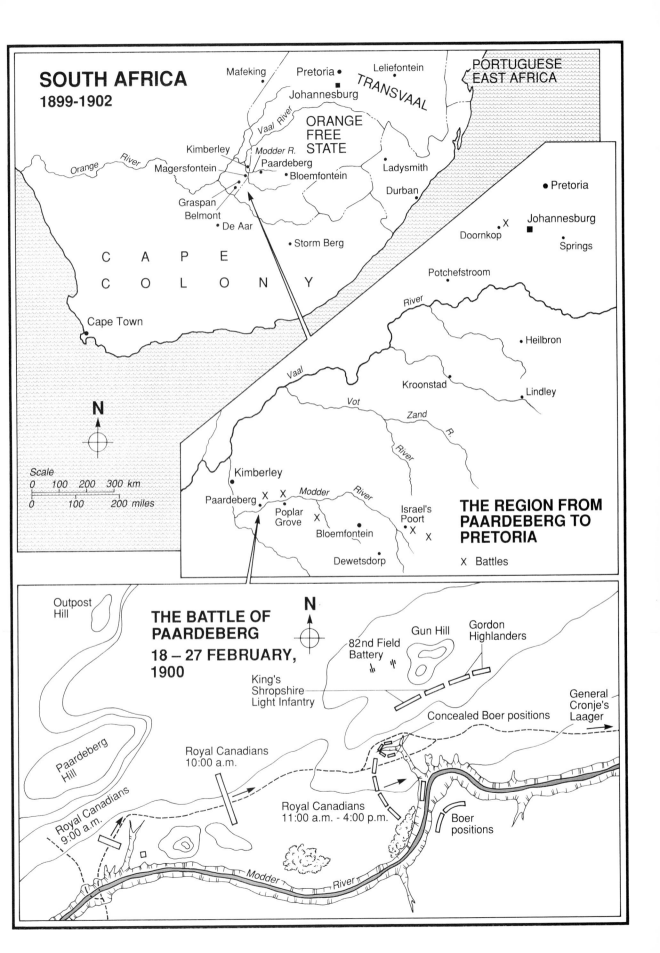

SOUTH AFRICA
1899-1902

Mafeking

Pretoria •   Leliefontein

TRANSVAAL

Johannesburg

Vaal River

ORANGE FREE STATE

Kimberley

Modder R.

Magersfontein

Paardeberg

• Bloemfontein

• Ladysmith

Durban

Graspan

Belmont

• De Aar

C A P E

C O L O N Y

• Storm Berg

Cape Town

PORTUGUESE EAST AFRICA

• Pretoria

Doornkop X

Johannesburg

Springs

Potchefstroom

River

• Heilbron

Kroonstad

Lindley

Vot

Zand

R.

River

Vaal

Scale

0   100   200   300 km

0   100   200 miles

N

Kimberley

Paardeberg   X   X   Modder   River

Poplar Grove

X

Bloemfontein

Israel's Poort

X

X

Dewetsdorp

THE REGION FROM PAARDEBERG TO PRETORIA

X   Battles

Outpost Hill

N

THE BATTLE OF PAARDEBERG
18 – 27 FEBRUARY, 1900

82nd Field Battery

Gun Hill

Gordon Highlanders

King's Shropshire Light Infantry

Concealed Boer positions

General Cronje's Laager

Paardeberg Hill

Royal Canadians 10:00 a.m.

Royal Canadians

Royal Canadians 11:00 a.m. - 4:00 p.m.

Boer positions

Royal Canadians 9:00 a.m.

Modder   River

In the confusion, someone—a Boer?—called out for the regiment to retire. With the exception of the men on the right, most did—often with humiliating speed. As Hamilton of the *Globe* put it, "three quarters of the Canadian regiment were in the depths, convinced that they had been disastrously repulsed." G and H companies—"the brave Easterners", the *Globe* called them, acknowledging that the companies had been raised in the Maritimes—had failed to hear the command and largely stayed put, improving their hasty scrapes into a serviceable trench sixty metres from Cronje's lines. Most of the Canadian wounded lay where they had fallen, with their comrades not daring to help them. There was one notable exception: Private Richard Thompson, a stretcher-bearer who had already shown great courage in the February 18 assault, "jumped to his feet, put his pipe in his mouth, leaped over the top of the trench, and cool as a cucumber, walked out to where the poor fellow lay." Unfortunately Thompson got to the man too late, but Otter recommended him for a Victoria Cross. Instead the Ottawa soldier received the "Queen's Scarf of Honour", one of only five scarves knitted by Queen Victoria and apparently intended to be of higher honour than the VC.

By daylight the Canadians discovered, to their astonishment, that they held a superb vantage point over the Boer positions. The RCRs opened fire, and quickly white flags began to flutter and Boers began to show themselves. Soon the fighters on both sides were fraternizing, the hungry RCRs seizing Boer rations and preparing breakfast. The Canadians were amazed at the quality of the Boer trenches, so much better designed and constructed than their own; the Boers' Mauser rifles were also better than anything the Canadian or British troops had. As for the 4,200 Boers themselves—a good proportion of the 35,000 men the Boers had under arms—many were grey-bearded men in their fifties and sixties; a few were boys of fifteen.

The battle of Paardeberg was over, and the RCRs, despite the confusion and panic inevitable in any night attack, had won the laurels. It was a major victory of the war, the first real success for British arms since October 1899, and the first important Canadian battle overseas. Eight RCRs had been killed and thirty-seven wounded, including Major Pelletier. Five of the wounded would soon die, and "Canada's Sad Honour Roll" would be on the front page of every newspaper in the land. Otter, humiliated by his men's unplanned and precipitous withdrawal, was more than a little surprised to find them hailed as heroes in South Africa, in Canada, and around the Empire, especially when the victory, as he admitted to his wife, "was not quite as satisfactory and complete as we had hoped for." He himself received notice in the *Times* of London for his coolness under fire. Lord Roberts rode over to deliver his congratulations to the Canadians personally, after taking breakfast with General Cronje (who was soon shipped off with his wife to a prisoner-of-war camp on the island of St. Helena, where Napoleon had ended his days). Bobs told the regiment that he had had no doubt as to the success of their attack, adding that he had been confident that the colony of Canada would prove equal to every demand made upon it. And, apparently, so it had. Paardeberg was a great Canadian triumph, Canada's first overseas victory.

Queen Victoria's Diamond Jubilee in 1897 marked 60 years of imperial glory, and evoked patriotic ardour around the Empire as bigwigs and troops massed for the celebrations. Here the revered old queen rides with the Princess of Wales while Prince Edward follows, as ever, in his mother's wake. Another carriage bore Laurier and his wife.

"One Flag, One Country, One Army," boasted the Toronto *Globe* in November 1900, in a recruiting ad that summed up the feeling of the times.

The spirit of Empire reached as far as Dawson, in the Yukon, where a concert to raise money for widows and orphans of the war in the Transvaal featured a tableau of Britain and its colonies. Note the accoutrements flanking the stage, and the military band.

It was no wonder the Canadians responded in droves. Here, the Royal Canadian Regiment turns out for morning roll-call shortly after arriving in Cape Town.

A band of Boer scouts pose with their Mauser rifles. Dressed like the farmers they were, they carried out fearless ambushes and lightning raids that left imperial infantry demoralized and—all too often—hungry.

The RCR fords the Modder River at Paardeberg Drift. According to the *Quebec Tele-graph*, "Little Bugler Williams of 'C' Company was almost swept away in the crossing, but Big Jim Kennedy reached out a strong helping hand" and carried him safely to shore.

Above: The Boer encampment at Paardeberg is ransacked after the battle. Author T.G. Marquis described the Boers as "a strange rabble...clad like the peasants of any rural district with short coats, loud-patterned trousers, narrow-brimmed light-brown soft felt hats." They carried their belongings in bundles, some dangling pots and pans from their belts, and their numbers inevitably included some "homely hard-faced women" and their children. Below: Boer prisoners—General Cronje's men—rest on the road from Paardeberg to the Modder River.

Among the nursing sisters with the first Canadian Contingent was Minnie Affleck.
The nurses' fortitude must have been formidable: another, Georgina Pope, cheerfully reported severe rains, terrible sandstorms, and a nurse afflicted with jaundice—but "the air was very fine and bracing."

III
MARCHING TO PRETORIA

The victory of Paardeberg was hailed in Canada as proof of the country's rising star, a sign of its new maturity in the Empire and the world. And now that the Boers had at last been bested in battle, no one doubted that the war would soon end. The relief of Ladysmith on February 28, 1900 and the capture of Storm Berg on March 5 added to that belief.

By this time, however, the second Canadian contingent—the one Britain had initially declined, and had finally accepted on December 18—was already on its way to South Africa. It had been decided that, instead of an infantry battalion—of which the British appeared to have more than enough—the new contribution would consist of mounted men and artillery. The South African fighting had demonstrated the superiority of the Boer commandos' tactics, with their hit-and-run attacks, and the endurance of their veldt ponies. Moreover, the Boers' artillery was better than the British army's. If the war was to be won, the Boers had to be fought by rugged outdoorsmen who could ride, shoot, and find cover in rough country.

The need was obvious (and about time, said critics of the British army's training and tactics) and Canada responded. The second contingent would have three squadrons of mounted rifles, soon increased to four, and three batteries of artillery. And if the prairies had been under-represented in the RCR, that would not be the case in the Canadian Mounted Rifles (CMR). A Squadron was to be enlisted in Eastern Canada, while B and C squadrons were to be recruited on the prairies, and particularly from serving members of the North-West Mounted Police, who dutifully volunteered in large numbers. The four squadrons were to form two battalions; command of the first, with 379 officers and men, would go to Lieutenant-Colonel F.L.

Lessard, an officer with twenty years' experience in the Quebec Garrison Artillery, while the second, with 398 officers and men, would be under the command of Commissioner L.W. Herchmer of the Mounties, a fifty-year-old officer who had served in the British army before joining the NWMP. Lessard's battalion was formed around a nucleus provided by the permanent force's cavalry regiment, the Royal Canadian Dragoons (RCD), and was permitted to adopt that name once it reached South Africa. The second battalion, under Herchmer, would serve in South Africa as the Canadian Mounted Rifles.

Artillery was a much more specialized branch of the army than cavalry, and it was simply not practical to recruit officers and men off the street and dispatch them to war as cannoneers. As a result, the three batteries of artillery—one each from Kingston, Ottawa, and Quebec—drew almost all their men from the permanent force and the militia. Once they reached South Africa they would come under the command of Lieutenant-Colonel C.W. Drury, who was already there.

One knotty problem for the government arose from the pay rates set for the second contingent. When the RCR had enlisted, the understanding was that Ottawa would cover the difference between the British soldier's traditional pay of one shilling a day and the higher rates paid in Canada's permanent force. This meant that an RCR private drew 50 cents a day and Colonel Otter $4.75. But when the second contingent was raised, the government authorized the same pay-scale as that of the North-West Mounted Police: 75 cents a day for a private and $7.12 for a lieutenant-colonel. The outrage of the RCRs was enormous—they had done the fighting, and this was their reward! Otter, himself furious, could not understand how a CMR colonel commanding half the men he did could draw more pay. Worse yet, Ottawa then gave married soldiers of the new contingent a daily separation allowance of half-pay plus 5 cents extra for each child. That seemed to widen the gap between the first and second contingents, though in truth virtually all the men (if not the officers) were single.

While the new units were completing their preparations, yet another cavalry unit was being raised in Canada for service as a unit of the British army. This was Lord Strathcona's Horse, completely financed by the octogenarian Donald Smith, an extraordinary man who had worked his way up from fur trader to director of the Hudson's Bay Company, and whose financial backing had been essential in the building of the Canadian Pacific Railway. Smith had driven the last spike in that railway in 1885; in 1896 he had gone to London as Canada's high commissioner, and he had been elevated to the peerage the following year. His personal regiment was to be a special corps of mounted riflemen that, like the CMR, would be formed around a nucleus of NWMP officers and NCOs. The commander was to be Sam Steele. A legendary figure in the West, Steele had no trouble finding volunteers. He had his pick of the Mounties for his unit, and took 32 officers and men to be his officers and NCOs; he got his full complement of 537 from more than 2,000 who tried to join up. "The men enlisted," he boasted, "are composed of the very pick of the cowboys, cowpunchers, rangers, policemen, and ex-policemen of the [Northwest] territories and British Columbia." Half his men were ranchers or farmers, and half had been born in Great Britain.

Raising the regiment cost Lord Strathcona a total of $550,083, a sum that included $48,000 for arms and ammunition, $60,000 for equipment, and $95,000 for horses and harness. Half a million dollars is a large sum in our time; it was a huge one in 1900, when a dollar was worth at least thirty of our own, and it gives some indication of the emotional appeal of imperialism in those heady days.

One additional Canadian unit was raised in the winter of 1900. To release the British regiment garrisoning Halifax for war service, Ottawa agreed to take over responsibility for the great port's defence. For this task the Militia department recruited, and Canada paid for, a unit of 1,004 men, naming it the 3rd (Special Service) Battalion of the Royal Canadian Regiment. Its two and a half years of service in Halifax were uneventful, and ended in September 1902 when a British regiment relieved it.

The initial experiences and reactions of the new contingent were much the same as those of their predecessors in the RCR. Private Jack Heron of A Squadron of the Royal Canadian Dragoons enlisted in Toronto early in January 1900, and drew his equipment and his horse at Stanley Barracks, in the Exhibition grounds. His first letter to his parents noted that his lieutenant was "all right. He is not so rotten as some of the officers around here." Heron added that he had drawn "a fiery little horse" for his first training ride "and did not get along very well at first but in the afternoon I kept him up all right. My legs were a little sore at first"—perhaps he was not quite the cowboy that some of his regimental comrades were—"but they don't bother me now."

Heron and his unit left Halifax on board the ss *Milwaukee* on February 21, along with C Battery of the artillery. The other two batteries, 365 officers and men and 263 horses in all, had sailed on the *Laurentian* on January 20, and the CMRs had followed on January 27. The Strathconas left Halifax on March

16 on the ss *Monterey*, which also carried 100 reinforcements to replace casualties and refill the ranks of the Royal Canadian Regiment.

While the second contingent and the Strathconas were getting ready, the government had one piece of business to clear up. The ministers had never overcome their suspicion that the GOC, General Hutton, had been the source of the leaks about the first contingent that had so embarrassed the prime minister in the fall of 1899. Moreover, Hutton had learned nothing from that experience, and had continued preaching for a national army and for military reform in numerous public speeches. As he wrote in a letter, he had tried to take "the Public into confidence to enlist Public Opinion & the Press in favour of reform, and leaving the Government to follow upon the turn of the tide in popular feeling". Generals, and especially British generals, simply could not do that in Canada, and in mid-January 1900 Prime Minister Laurier told the governor-general, Lord Minto, that because of the poor relations between the GOC and the Minister of Militia, Frederick Borden, the Cabinet wanted the troublesome Hutton recalled to Britain.

Foolishly, Minto countered by suggesting that Laurier should instead replace Borden, not the most competent administrator and a notorious tippler, with another minister. The prime minister refused, as he had to, and Minto then compounded his foolishness by saying that if Laurier insisted on the GOC's recall, he would write an official memorandum to the Cabinet outlining his view and, moreover, would tell London his opinion. Laurier countered with the statement that, if Minto acted so inappropriately, he and his government would feel obliged to resign. In other words, to defend his maladroit general, Minto had turned the affair into a constitutional crisis.

For three weeks matters stayed at the boil. Minto seemed unconcerned that the government might resign, and even argued forcefully, if stupidly, that the Minister of Militia had no right to interfere in the administration of the militia, as executive control of the Canadian military rested in the hands of the GOC. That outraged the Minister of Justice, who maintained that if that was true then Canada was no longer a dominion but merely a crown colony. Fortunately, cooler heads in London could see that a major crisis with Canada might have untold consequences for imperial and dominion unity. The way out was found when Chamberlain saw to it that Hutton was offered a post in South Africa, a plum that led the GOC to offer his resignation immediately, much to the relief of the Laurier government.

Hutton's successor would be General Lord Dundonald, a successful Boer War commander. When Dundonald came to Canada in 1902 he promptly demonstrated that he had learned nothing from Hutton's experience. He too wanted reform of the militia—which remained a nest of patronage and incompetence—and he too made his case in public speeches that embarrassed the government. This was the last straw for Laurier, and in 1904 he pushed a new Militia Act through Parliament. Now Canadian officers could take command of the militia (though British officers would fill most of the senior posts for another fifteen years); now Canadian officers would be equal in status to imperial officers of the same rank; and now the royal authority over the Canadian forces would no longer be exercised by the governor-general. In other words, the Minto–Hutton–Dundonald interference in domestic issues could never happen again.

Laurier's concern for the proprieties breached by Minto and Hutton was soundly based on Canadian political realities. Few Québécois had enlisted for service in South Africa—over the course of the war no more than 3 per cent of the Canadians who joined up were French-speaking—and he understood how this exercised Anglo-Canadians. The last thing he wanted was a major crisis that would focus on the question of the war and Canadian military preparations. That would inevitably raise the old questions about French Canada's attitude towards the Empire, which could only be dangerous for a French-speaking prime minister facing an election.

But the issue could not be suppressed. In March 1900, after news came of the relief of Ladysmith, students from Montreal's McGill university demonstrated in front of the city's French-language newspaper offices, and at the gates of the Université Laval. When the Laval students inevitably mounted a counter-demonstration and tore the Union Jack off the flagstaff in front of the *Montreal Star*, rioting erupted that was severe enough to lead to the mobilization of the city's militia.

Parliamentarians and newspapers across the country were quick to pontificate. One Tory MP blamed the riots on "paid emissaries of the Transvaal Republic". The *Ottawa Free Press* focused on "the insults offered to the British flag last night by Frenchmen" and called the whole affair "The War in Montreal". More calmly, the Toronto *Globe* denounced "the anti-French campaign conducted by a number of Conservative newspapers for months past" for inflaming "thoughtless minds". Montreal's *La Presse* discounted the fears of those who saw in the riots "a long drawn out plot with sinister intentions on the part of our English fellow citizens" and seemed prepared to accept the "suitable excuses" made by the McGill students and their professors. The last word belonged to the *Globe* when it quoted an official of the court who heard (and dismissed) the charges against five of the English-speaking rioters, none of whom, it turned out, was a McGill student:

> French-Canadians and English-Canadians were fighting side by side in the Transvaal. French-Canadian gallantry was amply shown by those who had died and been wounded in defence of the empire.... on the occasion of the next victory or when the war was over, a grand demonstration [should] be made by Laval and McGill together.

IN THE FIELD

After the triumph at Paardeberg, the Boers were in disarray in the Orange Free State. The opportunity to finish off Christian De Wet's army seemed at hand when Roberts learned that the enemy were waiting for them at Poplar's Grove, on the road from Paardeberg to Bloemfontein. Even more important, the Free State's president, Martinus Steyn, and the Transvaal's leader, Paul Kruger, were both with De Wet's army, desperately trying to stiffen the resistance of their demoralized men.

The RCR had passed an uncomfortable week since the Paardeberg victory. The weather was wet and miserable, there were flash floods that threatened the unwary who camped in dry creek beds, and there was still very little food. They were hardly ready for the battle that seemed to be in the offing. As it turned out, it was not to be; the long-range Boer artillery hammered at the advancing imperials and the Boers quickly left their positions in full retreat, virtually unhampered by the British cavalry. De Wet got away; so too did Steyn and Kruger.

For the British forces, the way to Bloemfontein was now open. For the RCRs, the next week was one of almost continuous marching on short rations. Albert Perkins' diary tells the story:

> March 9th. We marched twenty miles.... Haven't washed for nearly a week.

> March 10th. We have had a hard march and have at last stopped.... Still on one half rations.

March 11th. This march is fierce.... Were up at four A.M. Wish we had some meal or flour.

March 13th....had a hard day's work. Numbers fell out. Mules and horses dropped dead in their tracks...learned that we were eight miles from Bloemfontein....

March 15th. After a march of about five miles we arrived at Bloemfontein.... Lovely day and evening.

The RCRs, like all the rest of Roberts' army, showed the strain of the hard campaigning. The Canadian regiment had lost a quarter of its men to wounds or sickness since landing in South Africa three and a half months before, and when its 740 survivors marched into the Free State's capital, observers noted that they "were in rags; between the heat and the rain their shoes were falling to pieces. Indeed, some were actually barefooted, some had bound their puttees around their bruised and swollen feet, others had bound them up in pieces of sheepskin." The ragged band of victors nonetheless played the part expected of them, and the next day Perkins happily wrote that he was not "hungry for once. Bought bread at 1 and 6 a small loaf and had a small piece of cake." The spoils of victory were modest indeed.

For almost five weeks, the imperial forces stayed put in and around their base at Bloemfontein. Undoubtedly it was essential that supplies be brought up and that the "poor bloody infantry" and the mounts of the cavalry be given time to recuperate. The difficulty was that the respite allowed the Boers to restore their nerve and galvanize their leaders back into action. Christian De Wet had begun to work out in practice the principles of guerrilla warfare. The commando leader understood that it was unlikely his Boer fighters could resist a British army in the field for very long. What they could do was capitalize on their own advantages: mobility, familiarity with the country, and the knowledge that they were fighting for their freedom, their lives, and their homes.

The war was changing its form. There would still be set-piece battles, but now De Wet's men began to harass Roberts' huge army with lightning raids, some of which caught supply columns unaware. Other raids took key objectives—the Bloemfontein waterworks, for example—and then lured the British into ambushes. Roberts' responses were those of a conventional general. Infantry columns were sent on long, fruitless marches during which the men never saw a Boer, and the RCR did its share of this futile chasing of shadows. As Perkins wrote his mother, "These trips are hard, getting up early, and [we] are up late marching all day." And as the Boers hit the supply lines, food once again became scarce. On April 7, G Company had only 60 men ready for duty out of the 125 who had left Canada. Of the rest, 21 were in hospital, most with typhoid. Not until the end of April did the 100 reinforcements recruited for the RCR in Canada reach Bloemfontein and begin to restore the ranks towards full strength, and the replacements were as untrained as the whole regiment had been in December, and just as susceptible to disease.

So bad were matters that in May the *Globe* correspondent wrote confidentially to Toronto that "Our regiment has shot its bolt. That's volunteers—good as the best for 6 months—after that, not so good. The men are fervently homesick. When a fight occurs, nonetheless, they go ahead in a way which arouses the praise of imperial officers." While that was unquestionably true, Hamilton could also point to "a peculiar disease known locally as Mauseritis", from the Boers' standard rifle, the Mauser. Mauseritis, he said, possessed "many & diverse symptoms & one cause". In other words, some of the troops had become gun-shy.

The war was going on nonetheless. Lord Roberts decided to march on Pretoria, the capital of the Transvaal, almost five hundred kilometres to the north, and the army set out on April 21. For the Boers, retreating northwards, the object was to fight delaying actions, and they were skilled at their task. On April 25, at Israel's Poort, the RCRs ran into an ambush.

Instructions were for the Canadians to advance in open order at the Boer lines, to draw their fire, while the rest of the brigade sought to outflank the enemy position. The RCRs moved forward in silence in the hot late-afternoon sun and came within some six hundred metres of the Boers' firing line before the enemy opened up. The RCRs wavered, some starting to break ranks and flee to the rear. Colonel Otter, up with the forward companies, stopped the flight with shouts and curses, leading the men to cover in a drainage ditch, but not before he was hit in the face; the bullet passed through his neck very close to his jugular vein. Finally, the sound of firing from the flanks alerted the regiment to the success of the rest of the brigade, and the Canadians moved forward once more. "Boers could be seen in a cloud of dust in the distance," Perkins wrote.

While the RCRs continued the advance and fought small skirmishes under Major Buchan, Otter suffered the usual agonies of the wounded. He was carried by ambulance wagon twenty jolting kilometres towards

Bloemfontein before he managed to get a Cape cart and cover the last forty kilometres "sitting up and like a Christian", as he said. Once there, he refused to allow himself to be treated in a military hospital, so dreadful was their reputation. The British army's medical arrangements were primitive, especially in Roberts' army. The treatment methods and even the instruments were so old-fashioned that one distinguished surgeon who went to South Africa told a post-war investigatory commission that the Royal Army Medical Corps used "instruments which I should have thought would only be found in museums". This was not for Otter. Instead, he found a room in a private house and allowed the RCR's surgeon to treat him. It was the first time in five months that he had slept under a roof.

The advance on Pretoria now continued at a fast pace as the resistance in the Orange Free State began to melt away. South of Kroonstad, President Steyn's provisional capital, the enemy mounted an effective delaying operation on the Zand River, but though this cost the RCR two dead and two wounded in an engagement of nine hours, it scarcely delayed the main advance. Kroonstad fell on May 12, followed by Lindley, Steyn's next seat of government, and Heilbron, the one after that. At Heilbron one of the RCR's surgeons, Captain Eugène Fiset, lay ill in the makeshift hospital with fever, and fell into a deep sleep one night. When he awoke the next morning, he was astonished to discover that the town had been briefly retaken by De Wet's commandos after the advance had moved on, and that he was a prisoner. "At first," the *Globe* reported, the Boers "were amazed to find a Frenchman in the British uniform, and when they grasped the fact that he was a French Canadian great interest was shown." De Wet himself came to talk with Fiset and "inquired with the greatest interest about the Canadian constitution and...how the French were treated, whether their language was allowed, and on a variety of other points bearing upon the relations of the races." As the *Globe* concluded, "Evidently De Wet...is looking ahead to a future co-operation between two races." Fiset, who would later serve as lieutenant-governor of Quebec, was liberated from his friendly captors when the Highland Brigade forced the Boer commandos to depart Heilbron post-haste.

By May 26 Otter was finally well enough to resume command of his little band, fewer than five hundred strong despite the reinforcements sent from home. Good thing Otter was back, the *Globe* correspondent privately told his editor, "for Buchan is a coward and Pelletier, while brave enough & a particularly fine fellow, loses his head & has no judgment." For the reporter to praise Otter was a marked change. The colonel led his Canadians across the Vaal River at the head of the invading force and Roberts' army at last entered the Transvaal itself.

In England and in Canada people sang "We're marching to Pretoria," and indeed it was almost an unopposed trek to Johannesburg and the Boer capital. There was one brief but stiff engagement at Doornkop, close to Johannesburg, on the afternoon of May 29, when the 19th Brigade, including the RCRs, faced the strongest point in a Boer position. The Canadians, the Gordon Highlanders, and the Cornwalls advanced in line, moving across a dry streambed towards the enemy about two and a half kilometres away. Suddenly the Boers set the veldt grass on fire, obliging the attacking troops to jump through the flames—and to be silhouetted against the charred ground. As so often was the case, the attack was muddled, with the Gordons climbing Doornkop ridge under fire and suffering heavy casualties while the Canadians stayed at the base and fired at the Boers above them. By 5:00 P.M. the ridge was clear, but not before the RCR had eight more men wounded.

The way to Johannesburg was open now, and the city fell. Pretoria itself, ringed by impressive forts, capitulated without a shot a few days later, on June 5; the *Manitoba Free Press* headlined the news "Rats Leave the Sinking Ship", a reference to the flight of the Boer leaders. More politely, the *Halifax Herald* shouted that "The Transvaal's Capital Is Now Ours", showing a drawing of the Union Jack and Queen Victoria ("Empress of Africa, too, God bless her") prominently on the front pages. The RCR entered the city as the advance guard of the infantry on the 5th. There were only 27 officers and 411 men on parade the next day.

In Toronto bonfires were lit, fireworks were set off, and crowds roamed the streets in full-throated emotionalism. In Quebec City, too, church bells pealed out the news of victory while newspapers issued special editions. "Flags and decorations," said *Le Soleil*, "were at once put up on all public buildings.... The whole good city of Quebec, the old French city, always loyal, exhibited in this spontaneous fashion its exuberant joy at the announcement of this great success for British arms." No one could doubt that "the capture of Pretoria brings to a final end the bloody tragedy...of Southern Africa." In Parliament, Sir Wilfrid Laurier's motion to congratulate the queen on the approaching termination of the war received all but unanimous consent. Only Henri Bourassa, recently re-elected to the Commons as an independent, rose to oppose it.

The war was over—so said *Le Soleil*, so said the House of Commons. The enemy's capitals had been occupied, his armies bested in the field.

There was satisfaction in the ranks of the RCR at the result, and at the way the Canadians had stood up to the rigours of the campaign. But there was no blinking at the price of victory, and certainly not by Colonel Otter. He said privately that the war had been "blood and sand and everything that is disagreeable all for a bit of riband and a piece of silver", and to a relative who gloried in the RCR's part in avenging Majuba he replied bitterly, "Yes, we avenged Majuba and a d—d nasty job we had of it—not many of us are likely to forget that morning during the remainder of our natural lives." A splendid little war? Not for those who fought it.

THE SECOND CONTINGENT

But the war was not over. Although many of the Boer leaders and commandants were close to capitulation after Pretoria's fall, they were given new heart by the success of De Wet's commandos. That able general had cut the railway line between Bloemfontein and Pretoria, scooped up seven hundred British prisoners, and almost singlehandedly prolonged the conflict another two years.

The war was now a straight guerrilla conflict, a forerunner of the kind of war that would later bedevil the British in Malaya and the French and Americans in Vietnam. The Boer commandos lived off the land, drawing their supplies and their strength from the people. They struck hard, blew up rolling stock and rail lines, disrupted the British supply lines, and caused casualties everywhere; then they retreated before a counter-attack could catch them. It wasn't sporting, it wasn't war as it was known at the turn of the century, but it was effective.

To counter the raids, the British developed counter-insurgency tactics. When word was received of a commando operation in a specific locale, the whole area was sealed off with barbed-wire fencing and blockhouses linked by telephone and manned by infantry; mounted units then moved out to force the Boers towards the blockhouses, where they would be easy prey. To reduce the support the commandos had from Boer farmers and other civilians, crops and farmhouses were burned, while families of Boer fighting men, women and children both, were interned in concentration camps.

For the most part, this was the kind of war the second Canadian contingent found itself engaged in. Some of the Canadians had already gone far afield. C Battery of the artillery had participated in the four-hour battle that led to the relief of Mafeking on May 16, after a siege of 217 days. D and E batteries had served around De Aar for some time, the former moving east of Bloemfontein as futile efforts were made to mop up surviving Boer fighters. E Battery had participated in a punitive expedition against the Boer rebels in Griqualand that lasted a month and involved some heavy fighting, most notably at Faber's Farm on May 30, where the Canadians saved the day when a sudden night attack on the British camp produced near panic. "The calm tenacity with which the Canadians stuck to their guns and brought them into action under the steady shower of lead," T.G. Marquis wrote, "turned the tide of battle." One gunner was killed and eight were wounded in the vicious little fray. Serving with the Griqualand force as an intelligence officer was Colonel Sam Hughes, the vain and colourful militia man, who had come to South Africa on his own and was, he firmly believed, well on the way to earning at least one and possibly two Victoria Crosses. He may even have deserved them. Hughes led a counterattack during the fight at the farm, after which he walked up and down the Canadian gun lines encouraging the men. Urged to take cover, Hughes is said to have replied, with the common touch that often endeared him to soldiers, "Never mind me, boys, give them beans."

The mounted rifle battalions, inevitably hampered by equipment and clothing problems (the khaki uniforms turned white when washed, Colonel Lessard complained) and difficulties with the "Argentine ponies" they had received in South Africa, had also seen some heavy fighting in April and May. B Squadron, operating in the Dewetsdorp area near Bloemfontein, had run into a false white flag raised by Boers at a farmhouse. Moving forward to accept the surrender, a patrol found itself under fire for the first time. With assistance the patrol managed to disengage, and the farmhouse was burned to the ground as punishment. It is "hard for an Anglo-Saxon to think any man capable of such depravity," Marquis wrote of this improper use of a white flag, and after that the troopers were cautious about surrenders. B, C, and D squadrons had also played a notable part around Kroonstad, one of the few times the two Canadian contingents came together in action. The horsemen, as the *Quebec Telegraph* put it, "formed part of the advanced guard of the main army, and fought daily...." The war was in many respects like that experienced earlier by the RCRS. Certainly the supply of rations was no better; Jack Heron wrote home that "We don't get very much issued to us, in fact if we lived on Government rations we would starve in about a week but we manage to make up by commandeering from the Boers."

Heron had participated in all the actions that led to the capture of Pretoria. "I don't know what the people of Pretoria thought of us," he wrote, describing the scene as the two mounted rifle battalions rode into the capital, "but if Toronto had seen us then they would have wondered what was coming. I don't believe any of us had washed for about a week & the dust was thick on us, our clothes were full of holes & the stuff we carried on our horses was enough to kill the poor animals." He added that "It isn't the marching or the fighting that bothers us it's the lice & the noncoms & the officers & its hard to say which is the worst...." If the lice weren't "chewing you all night so that you can't sleep the noncoms & officers are chewing at you all day so that you don't get any peace at any time." The lice—"lobsters", Heron called them—drove the men to distraction.

One notable action for the RCDs on the march to Pretoria was the swimming of the Vet river, under fire, by lieutenants Borden and Turner and five men, who then put thirty Boers to flight. Harold Borden, the son of the Militia minister, was killed in action on July 21; Richard Turner, who won the Victoria Cross some months later, would be a senior Canadian commander in the Great War.

The first VC of the war won by a Canadian, however, went to a member of Lord Strathcona's Horse. The Strathconas had spent six weeks in Cape Town after their arrival, drilling and bewailing their fate at not getting into action. It would come soon enough. One squadron of the regiment was shipped north by sea on May 24 to cut the Boer supply line through the Portuguese port of Lourenço Marques, in an operation that was aborted when the British command realized the enemy had too much strength in the area. The squadron then rejoined its unit at Durban and pushed forward to join up with General Buller's army at Sand Spruit in the Transvaal. The regiment's first fighting came on July 1, Dominion Day, when a small party of the Strathconas, deceived by a white flag, walked into an ambush. One trooper, a cowhand from Pincher Creek, died and two others were taken prisoner; the Strathconas would henceforth deploy in skirmishing order whenever they approached a white flag. From that day on the regiment was in almost continuous action as part of General Lord Dundonald's 3rd Mounted Brigade, exchanging fire with Boer rearguards, often divided into penny-packets as small as twenty or so men. It was one such minor action that won the Victoria Cross for Sergeant Arthur Richardson, one of the Mounties Sam Steele had brought into the Strathconas. At Wolve Spruit on July 5, in a brief encounter with Boer horsemen, one of Sergeant Richardson's men was badly wounded in the arm and thigh and had his horse shot out from under him. Although his troop had been forced to retire, Richardson rode back through the cross-fire to within a few hundred metres of the enemy to reach his comrade and carry him to safety.

The award of a VC to a Strathcona was immensely gratifying to Colonel Steele, who was proving himself a highly effective battlefield commander. He tried to rein in the high spirits among his largely undisciplined men by preaching caution. He stressed discipline on the march and in bivouac, repeatedly telling his men that bonfires drew enemy shelling and warning that a cup of tea was not worth dying for. He sacked the incompetent, he promoted the able—and he led from the front.

By the fall, the Strathconas had created a formidable reputation for their ferocity. Rumours that they lynched Boer prisoners likely grew out of colonial bravado, but there was something frightening in their nickname among the British: "The Headhunters". The war was turning savage as guerrilla depredations exhausted the British armies, and as the strain mounted, every Boer man, woman, and child became a potential enemy to be hated and feared. In such an atmosphere, acts of barbarism became almost the accepted norm.

Lieutenant E.W.B. Morrison of the artillery, who had earned a Distinguished Service Order in the fight at Leliefontein in November 1900, reported one typical instance of repression after a minor engagement at the Transvaal village of Dullstroom:

> On the steps of the church were huddled a group of women and children.... The women were white but some of them had spots of red on either cheek and their eyes blazed. Not many were crying. The troops were systematically looking the place over and as they got through with each house they burned it. Our Canadian boys helped to get their furniture out, much as they would do at a fire in a village at home. If they saw anything they fancied they would take it.... I went into a very pretty little cottage standing in a rose garden on a side street. The C.M.R.'s and R.C.D.'s were looting it, but really helping the woman out with her stuff more than sacking the place.... I certainly was sorry for her—we all were—until the house began to burn and a lot of concealed ammunition to explode and nearly killed some of our men.... all the same it was a sad sight...the pathetic groups of homeless women and children crying among the ruins as we rode away.

General Kitchener's policy of devastation and depopulation was a brutal one. Women and children were rounded up and lodged in appalling conditions, in filthy and disorganized camps. An estimated twenty thousand, about one-fifth of those put into the camps, died. Thousands of children succumbed to measles epidemics, and David Lloyd George, the Welsh politician, foresaw "a barrier of dead children's bodies...between the British and Boer races". The term "concentration camp" quickly acquired its special ignominy.

Yet there were acts of kindness that cut across the lines of war. When Colonel Steele fell ill with food poisoning and almost died, he was carried by ambulance to Potchefstroom, where his batman hired a room for him in the house of a Boer woman. Although her husband was serving as a commando, Steele wrote later that "I shall never forget her kindness and that of her daughters, whose husbands were also in the field. I have never felt worse in my life; but there was nothing that those kind people could do that was left undone to bring me back to health." Before the colonel returned to the Strathconas, and with his blessing, his batman married a Boer woman—one of the first Canadian war brides.

The effort to recruit experienced outdoorsmen was paying off in the battle against Boer guerrilla tactics. One notable example involved the Royal Canadian Dragoons in a sharp engagement at Leliefontein in November 1900. As part of a large force under General Smith-Dorrien that included CMRs and Canadian gunners, the RCD and two 12-pounder guns had the task of providing the rearguard. Out of nowhere, two hundred mounted Boers charged the small party of Canadians, coming within seventy metres. Lieutenant H.Z.C. Cockburn put his small party between the main body and the Boers, deliberately sacrificing his command. Cockburn got away with a wound, but all his men were killed, wounded, or captured. Later the same day, the Boers again hit at the rearguard, desperately trying to seize the guns. Lieutenant Richard Turner, already wounded, got a dozen of his troopers dismounted and deployed and held off a hell-for-leather charge by the Boers. He was wounded once more, but not before shouting, "Never let it be said the Canadians had let their guns be taken!" His sergeant, Eddie Holland, worked the RCD's Colt machine-gun with great effect from the left flank of Turner's little band, and when the enemy were nearly on him he seized the hot gun by the barrel, wrenching it off its carriage, and rode to safety. Turner recalled that "The Boers thought they had captured the gun and tried to turn it" on the retreating Canadians. "When they found the gun was gone they were so angry they burned the carriage." All three RCDs were awarded the Victoria Cross.

THE RETURN OF THE RCR

For the Royal Canadian Regiment—the first contingent—the war was anti-climactic after the capture of Pretoria. The battalion was sent off to the little railway town of Springs, west of Johannesburg, to protect a long stretch of track. The Boer armies had been defeated but the commandos were still fighting hard, blowing up railway engines and cars and cutting the line. Otter and his men, like an increasing part of the British army, were now on counter-insurgency duty: there were occasional alarms and excursions, but most days were simply boring. The one compensation was that for the first time since their arrival in the war zone, Otter was able to get his men under shelter in the town's homes and sheds.

The regiment was sent back to the field in August 1900, as the Canadians participated in yet another futile attempt to catch Christian De Wet and his 1,500 men. Why the British command persisted in trying to trap the fleet Boers with plodding columns of infantry puzzled every man in the RCR, and the footsore troops were delighted to be sent to guard the railway from Delagoa Bay later that month.

By late summer, Otter had become obsessed with the fact that his battalion's term of enlistment was soon to expire. Operating with virtually no terms of reference from Ottawa, he had tried to get the government to tell him what to do, but without success. The colonel understood all too well that the war's new phase was straining Lord Roberts' manpower. He also knew that his men were sick and tired of South Africa and desperately anxious to return to Canada. What to do?

Field Marshal Lord Roberts asked Otter on September 8 to get his men to extend their service, and to the professional soldier that Otter was, that seemed tantamount to an order; without canvassing his troops, he replied at once that "your wishes will be gladly complied with", though he suggested that a few men might be allowed to go home for compassionate reasons. So pleased was Roberts that he called on Otter to congratulate him. That made the colonel's embarrassment all the greater when almost every one of his men, and some of his officers, flatly refused to stay one day longer than their promised year. Humiliated, Otter had to report this news to Roberts, apologizing that "my own zeal led me to judge too hurriedly of that of my officers and men...." Another, more desperate appeal from Roberts and much pleading by Otter persuaded nearly 300 RCRs to change their mind, though even this led to dispute; the British general assumed the Canadians would stay for the duration of the war, or at least for three months; the RCRs thought they had agreed to help out for a few weeks. The RCRs won, but Otter was so embittered by the whole affair that he refused to bid the first draft of returning RCRs farewell. Roberts showed more class, thanking the 17 officers and 385 men for their service under him.

For Otter's now tiny battalion of 13 officers and 229 men, there was a final stint of garrison duty and participation in a gala pageant in Pretoria on October 25, as Britain proclaimed its annexation of the Transvaal. Then, as soon as transport could be found, the RCRs were on their way to Cape Town. On November 7 they boarded ship for England.

Why England? Because Roberts had promised those who stayed in South Africa past their term of enlistment that they would be reviewed by the queen, and he delivered. The little battalion landed in England to a warm welcome and the aged queen reviewed them at Windsor Castle, addressing them "in a strong, clear voice". Then she had the officers to lunch, leading the ecstatic Otter to write, "My heavens, this is the hardest yet, we are simply deluged with kindness...."

On December 12, after further celebrations and a full dose of imperial pageantry, the RCR boarded ship for home. The battalion arrived in Halifax on December 23, the men were paid off at once, and the companies marched to trains hurrying them home for Christmas. The Toronto men, with Otter at their head, arrived in the city on Christmas morning to find a dutiful crowd of cheering dignitaries and militia men and the compulsory speeches of welcome at the armouries, but it was clear that the city's C Company, which had arrived seven weeks before, had received the lion's share of the credit and glory. Some of that credit had been squandered by widespread public drunkenness as the returning veterans let down their hair, and complaints about Otter had been bruited about. Thus for Otter and his men there was a slightly bitter taste to it all—something that summed up the entire South African experience, and was magnified when Otter continued to come under attack in the press.

The RCDs, the CMRs, the artillery, and the Strathconas were also hailed warmly on their arrival home in January and March 1901. Soldiers were paraded through the streets of their home towns, fêted with speeches and dinners, and given gold watches. Sam Steele's men drew special cheers when their trains reached Montreal, although the stories about their hard reputation had reached Canada and Steele spent some time denying every allegation. Later, a British Royal Commission gave the LSH a clean bill of health, and Steele himself drew praise: "There was no better commander than the rough-riding colonel from Canada."

End of a War

There were still volunteers willing to go to South Africa, however much the war had lost its glamour. Late in 1901, a second regiment of Canadian Mounted Rifles was recruited. Its nine hundred men, along with a field hospital (including eight nurses), sailed for South Africa on January 14, 1902 and served there until the Boer surrender in May. Under command of Colonel T.D.B. Evans—who had commanded the Yukon Field Force, and now replaced Herchmer as the colonel of the CMRs of the second contingent—the mounted infantrymen participated in one noteworthy engagement. On March 31, 1902, at Boschbult, the 2nd CMR was part of a British force of two thousand that came under attack from a larger Boer force. There were skirmishes and finally a major fight in which twenty-one CMR troops acting as rearguard fought several hundred of the enemy. Colonel Evans' report noted that Lieutenant Bruce Carruthers had arranged his men in a half-moon formation, shouted that there would be "No surrender," and run forward to meet the attack, killing one Boer at fifteen paces. "Before their ammunition was exhausted, seventeen out of the twenty-one [Canadians] were either killed or wounded," Evans said, adding that before they were captured the survivors destroyed their rifles so the Boers could not use them. The 2nd CMR's losses on that day were eight killed, forty-two wounded, and seven missing.

Four additional regiments of Canadian Mounted Rifles were raised in 1902, each with 509 officers and men, though by this time there was the odd rumble of discontent in Canada. The Winnipeg *Telegram* said that "unless under stress of some greater necessity, or to testify to some great principle, Canada cannot spare any more of its able-bodied workers." Neither necessity nor principle was at stake, in the newspaper's eyes. The units nonetheless sailed for South Africa in May, but arrived after the Boer capitulation, and the disappointed CMRs promptly returned to Canada. There were still more volunteers. In 1901 the South African Constabulary, a quasi-military police force being raised by the British, found 1,208 of its volunteers in Canada, and Sam Steele became a colonel in the new force. His object was to make the Constabulary the equivalent of the NWMP.

In all, Canada enlisted 8,372 men, including the Halifax garrison battalion of the RCR and unofficial units such as the South African Constabulary and the Strathconas. Of these, 89 died in action, and another 135 succumbed to disease; 252 were wounded. The financial cost to the dominion was less than $3 million, and much of that was earned back by the sale of materiel to the War Office, including $2.5 million worth of forage in one year. Most of the unit commanders, including Otter, Evans, Steele, and Lessard, were decorated, these four becoming commanders of the Order of the Bath.

It had been a small war but not one without significance, for it was the high-water mark of British imperialism. It was also the end of an era; the old queen had died in January 1901, just weeks after reviewing Otter and his men. The Victorian age was over.

When the call went out in 1899 for roughriders to counter Boer guerrilla acts, these Canadian cowboys joined Lord Strathcona's Horse—as did the dissolute son of a duke, a fugitive from U.S. justice, a journalist, and several former British officers who enlisted as privates.

Like so many soldiers heading off to war, this steely-eyed stalwart of the Canadian Mounted Rifles posed for the camera before leaving for South Africa, his riding crop in hand and his hat attached by a capline so that he wouldn't lose it in battle.

Canadian Mounted Rifles in Winnipeg, around 1901. The men are wearing Boer War service dress and the "lemon-squeezer" or "New Zealand hat" worn by many British and Commonwealth cavalry units during the war. The long Lee-Enfield rifle was used by Canadian infantry and mounted infantry. The men on the left are wearing what appears to be the South African Medal. The cavalry in the background, in the white helmets, are also Canadian.

Toronto celebrates the anniversary of the capture of Pretoria on June 5, 1901; the scene is Yonge St. south of Richmond. The celebrations were dubbed "mafficking," recalling the joy when the relief of the besieged city of Mafeking had been reported the year before.

The CMRs practise "mounted combat" during the long voyage on the *Corinthian* in 1902; tug-of-war was also popular.

The CMR camp in Durban, June 1902; bell tents like these remained in use until the 1950s. The number of horses used in the Boer War created enormous logistical problems.

Canadian scouts near Drietfontein in 1902. Note the strap keeping the rifle attached to the trooper's arm, and the rough, if serviceable, uniforms.

The CMRs had more than rifles at their disposal; this Colt machine-gun was nick-named "the potato digger" in reference to a hinged arm that was blown down-wards when it fired.

The Boers might have experience and desperation on their side, but the imperial troops had the "war cycle"—perhaps the strangest technology of the campaign. Designed and built in Cape Town, the machine could carry eight riders—scouts, messengers, or medics—over railway tracks, as fast as 50 kph.

Opposite page:A trooper of Lord Strathcona's Horse sleeps on the engine cover of a camouflaged Sherman tank guarding a possible crossing point on the Imjin River. The machine-gun with its ammunition box is ready for action; spare ammo boxes are attached to the tank hull.

PART TWO
THE AGE OF WAR

IV
THE KOREAN CONFLICT

The Boer War had shown English Canadians that their country had a part to play in the Empire, and could play it with distinction. It had shown French-Canadians that the Anglos were mired in imperialism and absolutely determined to have their own way. As for the British, most of them would have agreed with Joseph Chamberlain that the war had "enabled the British Empire to find itself; it has united the British race throughout the world, and it has shown to all whom it may concern, that if ever again we have...to fight for our very existence against a world in arms, we shall not be alone."

Chamberlain would be proved right. The "British race" in Canada was united, and its sons would march off to war in huge numbers in 1914. The dreadful conditions of trench warfare, the carnage that took the lives of sixty thousand Canadians—even these could not slake the nation's enthusiasm. Imperialism had Canada in its grip—so much so that, to the cheers of English-speaking men and women, the government of Robert Borden would impose conscription to ensure that French Canadians and other non-British Canadians were made to do their duty in Britain's war. But the cost of the 1917 Military Service Act was severe in terms of domestic peace, and the relief when the war ended in 1918 was profound. The Germans had been crushed by the weight of Allied arms in a war to end wars, and the Treaty of Versailles had restored peace and security to the world.

A major element of the peace was the League of Nations, which aimed at guaranteeing the territorial integrity and political independence of its members through such peaceful means as arbitration, conciliation, and economic sanctions. In the early years it had several successes, as well as doing substantial humanitarian work. But then one aggressor after another thumbed its nose at the League's decisions. In 1931 Japan—Asia's most powerful nation—invaded the territory of Manchuria, effectively declaring war on China, and answered the League's protests by ending its membership. In 1935 Italy invaded Ethiopia and ignored the League's feeble sanctions. In 1936 Germany—which had left the League three years earlier, under the new and sinister leadership of a virulent racist named Adolf Hitler—began rearming in defiance of the prohibitions set out in the Treaty of Versailles. The League—like the peace it was meant to secure—was no more than wishful thinking. The world was again descending into war.

What would an isolationist Canada do? The disillusionment with the fractious politics of Europe and Asia was profound, but not so great as to prevent the country from again marching off to war in 1939. When the European war was won in May 1945, the government prepared for the invasion of Japan, but the island nation was forced to surrender in August by the atomic bombs that fell on Hiroshima and Nagasaki. Canadians were spared heavy casualties in the final fighting in the Pacific; even so, more than forty thousand Canadians died in the Second World War.

However terrible the first two world wars had been, the atomic bombs that devastated Hiroshima and Nagasaki raised the spectre of a third—some said final—world war, fought with weapons that could barely be imagined. Suddenly the search for peace was a global imperative. The world needed a more powerful replacement for the ineffectual League of Nations. Countries whose economies had been demolished by the war had to have financial help, lest they fall prey to stronger nations and the cycle begin again.

With Europe drained by the war, the United States became the unchallenged leader in these initiatives, offering Europe billions of dollars in aid through the Marshall Plan and taking the lead in organizing the United Nations—and Canada identified more and more with the behemoth on its southern border. The British Empire, which had seemed so irresistibly glorious for so long, was now visibly on its last legs, while North America's post-war prosperity fed a boom in technology and consumerism that made all things seem possible. The influx of immigrants to Canada and the U.S. had diversified the populations of both nations, further weakening Canada's link to the United Kingdom and creating many family ties across the border. As communications and travel opened up, differences between the two countries seemed almost incidental to many.

In some areas the new partnership was in fact vital. Britain's desperate peril during the war years had forced Canada to seek shelter under the broad wing of the American eagle, and the Permanent Joint Board of Defence set up in August 1940 would indeed prove to be permanent; with the Soviet Union unfolding as the great rival of the West, Canada's vast Arctic became a buffer zone that it could not hope to defend alone. Economically, too, the closer ties were necessary, for the U.S. alone had the dollars to pay for Canada's products and raw materials. For better or worse, the old colonial ties had been largely shaken off.

It also seemed that the lessons of the two wars had been learned; clearly a third world war could not be risked, and the mechanisms to prevent one were being put in place. First among them was the United Nations, formed at the San Francisco Conference of 1945 as a replacement for the old League. The "Great Powers"—Britain, France, the United States, the Soviet Union, and China—would be permanent members of a U.N. "Security Council" which would also include six non-permanent members elected for two-year terms. The Security Council would have the exclusive right to act in matters of collective security, and its ability to do so would be extensive. It could take "such action by air, sea or land forces as may be necessary to maintain or restore international peace and security" and to accomplish this all members of the U.N. had to "undertake to make available to the Security Council...armed forces, assistance and facilities...." For "urgent military measures" member nations were to "hold immediately available national air force contingents for combined international enforcement action". And to advise and assist the council on the military requirements for the maintenance of peace and security, the drafters of the charter created a Military Staff Committee consisting of the "Chiefs of Staff of the permanent members of the Security Council"—again the Great Powers—"or their representatives".

In the proposed wielding of all this power, little heed was paid to lesser members of the U.N. The Canadian government protested at the idea of Canadian troops being ordered into action without Canada's consent—as Prime Minister Mackenzie King said plaintively, "I feel sure that whenever a particular member was desired to take serious enforcement action, consultation would be a practical necessity"—and the Military Staff Committee was grudgingly authorized to invite other nations to be associated with it "when the efficient discharge of the Committee's responsibilities requires the participation of that Member in its work".

But there was a fly in the ointment. Each of the Great Powers reserved to itself the right to veto any Security Council decision it disapproved of, making intervention unlikely in most parts of the world. For even as world leaders talked of peace, they were locking themselves into opposing camps. It would be only a matter of time before hostilities flared again.

POST-WAR CANADA

Canadians believed that the end of the Second World War would usher in a new era of peace, prosperity, and progress. After almost six years of war—and ten years of economic depression before that—it was time for better things. The nation's economy was robust, its factories ready to turn from war materiel to the consumer goods of a new era—cars, washing machines, radios, and soon even television sets. Men and women whose lives had been disrupted by the hardships and separations of war were marrying, settling down in new homes, and having children. The result was the greatest building boom in Canadian history, and a "baby boom" of hundreds of thousands of infants.

In June 1945, the Liberal government of William Lyon Mackenzie King won a renewed mandate on the promise of "Jobs, Jobs, Jobs" and "A New Social Order for Canada". It was the start of the welfare state. Unemployment insurance had been brought in during the war—when there was, conveniently, little unemployment. In the late summer of 1945 the first family-allowance cheques showed up in mailboxes. Young families began to buy homes financed through the government-owned Central Mortgage and Housing Corporation, while veterans attended universities, colleges, and technical schools on government allowances and tuition payments. There were even plans for universal health insurance.

Canada's contributions to the Allied war effort had gained the country new international recognition, and even a little bargaining power. Its membership in the World Bank, International Monetary Fund, and other major international agencies such as the Atomic Energy Commission attested to that. The country shared the dark secret of the atom with Great Britain and the United States, a very small and prestigious club until the U.S.S.R. exploded its own atomic bomb in 1949; it also had Barbara Ann Scott, the blonde darling of the ice who won an Olympic gold medal for figure skating in 1948 and may well have been Canada's most popular heroine ever. The early post-war years were—as one Hollywood movie dubbed them—"The Best Years of Our Lives".

There was, however, a dark side: a growing fear of the "Red Menace" of Communism. During the war the U.S.S.R. had been an essential ally, but after Germany surrendered it soon became obvious that the Russian army was not going to leave Eastern and Central Europe. Soviet secret police were rounding up and jailing thousands of non-Communist and anti-Communist political, religious, and intellectual leaders. Worse, the U.S.S.R.

was not demobilizing as the West was. As the months passed, the Soviets entrenched themselves more and more deeply in their newly conquered territories.

The Red Menace moved closer to home when news got out that a cipher clerk from the Soviet embassy in Ottawa, Igor Gouzenko, had defected and brought with him evidence of an extensive spy ring gathering information on defence research in Canada, including some minor atomic secrets. Canadians were shocked, and suddenly anyone even remotely suspected of Communist sympathies was ostracized. Radio programs, movies, and popular fiction warned that Communists lurked everywhere, and were plotting to overthrow Western civilization.

This paranoia grew hand in hand with the deepening Cold War that resulted from Gouzenko's revelations, the Soviet imposition of Communist governments across Eastern Europe, Soviet intransigence at the United Nations and in other international bodies, and the deadlock between East and West over the future of the defeated Germany. As Communist regimes cut virtually all ties of trade, travel, and communication with the West, the U.S.S.R. became a bogeyman hiding who-knew-what unspeakable horrors.

In such a polarized world, Canada had no choice but to take sides. In early 1946 the government decided to continue its alliance with the United States for the defence of the North American continent. The two countries quickly entered into a large number of arrangements covering joint operation of Arctic weather stations, cold-weather testing of military equipment, radar, and air defence, and the operation of U.S. bases in Newfoundland and Labrador.

But Canada also supported the concept of collective security—the idea that peace-loving nations must band together to maintain global peace and ensure that North America (or any other part of the world) would never be threatened. The lessons of the 1930s seemed crystal clear: if only Britain, France, the United States, and the Soviet Union had stood together, Hitler could have been stopped without a great war that killed millions. "We have all come to see that the cause of freedom in the world is a single cause," the Canadian ambassador in Washington said, "that neutrality has become a snare and isolation a delusion." As Lester Pearson put it in an internal memo in 1948: "the best defence of Canada remains collective security arrangements with other Powers who think and act as we do." This seemed even more urgent following the coup that toppled the democratic government of Czechoslovakia in February 1948, installing the Communist Party in power. With the Nazis defeated, it now appeared that all of Europe was threatened by Communist expansion instead.

It would have been ideal if the United Nations could have played the lead in organizing a world collective security system; Canadians had been enthusiastic supporters of the U.N. in the hope that would happen. But it was not to be. By 1946 the Western and Soviet sides on the committee—and on the Security Council itself—were talking past each other in the recognition that they were far more likely to fight one another than to co-operate in putting down other aggressors. That led one politician to state disgustedly in a House of Commons committee, "There is a great deal of force in the suggestion made lately that the big fellows should be disarmed and the little fellows should set up the police force."

What was left of the hopes for collective security, with the U.N. paralysed? Not much. Louis St. Laurent, the Secretary of State for External Affairs, said in a blunt speech to the U.N. in 1947, "There is a growing feeling in my country...that the United Nations...is not showing itself equal to the discharge of its primary task of promoting international confidence and ensuring national security." If the Security Council was frozen in futility, nations might have to "seek greater safety in an association of democratic and peace-loving states willing to accept more specific international obligations in return for a greater measure of international security."

In the spring of 1948, with the deadlock over Germany worsening and the Soviets blockading Berlin, Canada, the U.S., and Great Britain began discussions on the creation of a Western security pact. Later in the year France and the Benelux countries were invited to join. The result, in April 1949, was NATO—the North Atlantic Treaty Organization, which aimed to achieve collective security through a balance of power that was based on keeping Soviet Communism out of Western Europe. As St. Laurent's successor as foreign minister, Lester Pearson, put it, the North Atlantic Treaty was "more than a treaty for defence. We must, of course, defend ourselves, and that is the first purpose of our pact; but, in doing so, we must never forget that we are now organizing a force for peace so that peace can one day be preserved without force."

CONFLICT IN KOREA

In the early morning hours of June 25, 1950, North Korean troops, led by Soviet-supplied T-34 tanks and covered by Soviet-built fighter planes, poured across the 38th parallel and sent panicked South Korean soldiers into headlong flight. The invasion came as a total surprise in Western capitals but its roots lay in a series of diplomatic and political events that stretched back at least as far as the end of the Second World War.

Korea had been occupied by Japan in 1905 and annexed in 1910; from then until their liberation in 1945, the Korean people were oppressed and exploited by the Japanese Empire, despite several attempts to overthrow the usurpers. At the 1943 Cairo Conference, after Japan's entry into the war, the U.S., U.K., and China promised Korea independence. But the 1945 Yalta Conference gave the U.S.S.R. a zone of influence in Korea in exchange for its entry into the war against Japan; accordingly, the Soviet army invaded Manchuria, north of Korea, on August 8, 1945. The Soviets had waited to the very last moment; forty-eight hours earlier, the U.S. had dropped the second atomic bomb on Japan, and two days after the Soviet invasion of Manchuria, Japan sued for peace.

It was clear to Washington that the Red Army would soon occupy all of Manchuria, but how far down the Korean peninsula was it likely to go? There was nothing to stop the Russians from taking control of the entire peninsula; the closest U.S. troops were on the island of Okinawa. The Americans proposed to the Russians that Soviet troops halt at the 38th parallel and, to their surprise, the Russians agreed. In the months that followed, this informal demarcation line began to harden into a boundary. The Soviets supported the establishment of a Communist regime, to be led by Kim Il Sung, while the Americans supported the anti-Communist exile Syngman Rhee. Both sides poured tens of thousands of troops into the country, although neither was yet willing to officially recognize the political division of the peninsula.

Although the U.S. initially tried to match the Soviet military buildup, the Americans were anxious to pull their 45,000 troops out of Korea since they were carrying out massive post-war defence budget cuts. If the Soviets could be persuaded to accept a U.N.-arranged political solution to the division of Korea, they reasoned, both countries could pull out. Since the U.S. and its allies dominated the U.N. General Assembly at that time, it was easy for Washington to have the General Assembly establish the United Nations Temporary Commission on Korea (UNTCOK). UNTCOK was supposed to oversee free elections throughout the country and to supervise the withdrawal of both Soviet and U.S. troops. But the U.S.S.R. would have none of it; it objected strongly to the committee, arguing that since Korea was not a U.N. member, UNTCOK had no jurisdiction there.

Canada had been chosen as one of the eight member countries of UNTCOK, and Moscow's declaration threw a scare into Mackenzie King. He was convinced—rightly, as events showed—that Korea was one of the world's powderkegs, and he feared that if Canada did not withdraw from UNTCOK it might eventually have to send troops there to back U.N. decisions. But

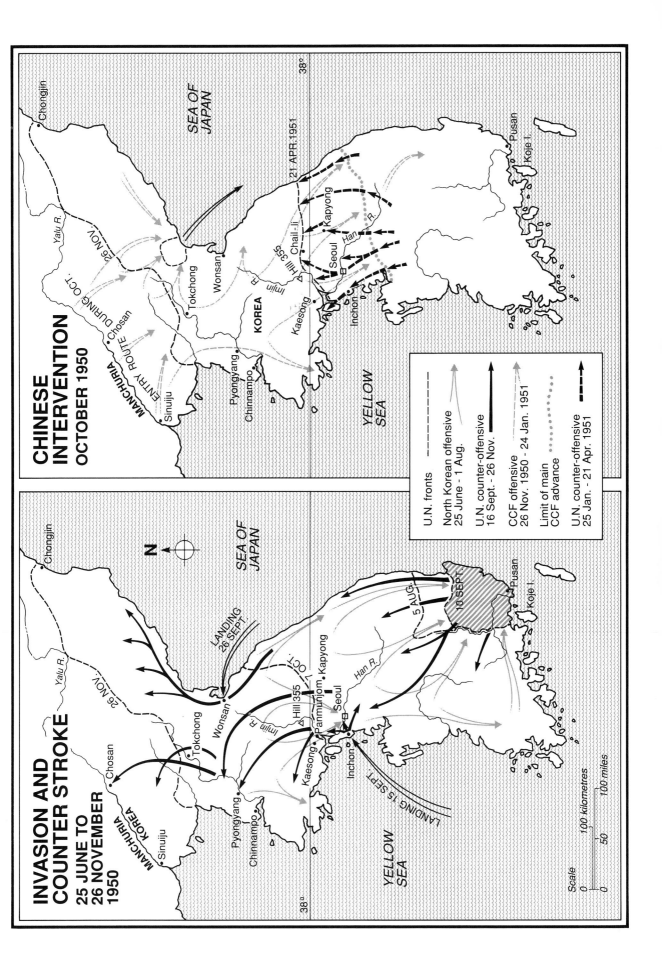

CHINESE INTERVENTION
OCTOBER 1950

SEA OF JAPAN

38°

21 APR.1951

26 NOV.

Yalu R.

DURING OCT.

MANCHURIA

ENTRY ROUTE

Chongjin

Chosan

Sinuiju

Tokchong

Wonsan

Chinnampo

Pyongyang

Kaesong

Inchon

Seoul

Kapyong

Chail - li

Hill 355

Imjin R.

Han R.

KOREA

YELLOW SEA

Pusan

Koje I.

INVASION AND COUNTER STROKE
25 JUNE TO 26 NOVEMBER 1950

N

SEA OF JAPAN

38°

26 NOV.

Yalu R.

MANCHURIA

KOREA

Chongjin

Chosan

Sinuiju

Tokchong

Wonsan

LANDING 26 SEPT.

7 OCT.

Pyongyang

Chinnampo

Kaesong

Panmunjom

Kapyong

Hill 355

Imjin R.

Seoul

Inchon

LANDING 15 SEPT.

Han R.

5 AUG.

10 SEPT.

Pusan

Koje I.

YELLOW SEA

Scale

0   50   100 kilometres

0   100 miles

U.N. fronts

North Korean offensive
25 June - 1 Aug.

U.N. counter-offensive
16 Sept. - 26 Nov.

CCF offensive
26 Nov. 1950 - 24 Jan. 1951

Limit of main
CCF advance

U.N. counter-offensive
25 Jan. - 21 Apr. 1951

Louis St. Laurent, Secretary of State for External Affairs, strongly believed in the U.N. and in the need for Canada to be active in major international issues. He threatened to resign if King insisted on a withdrawal, and it soon became clear to King that many other Cabinet ministers supported St. Laurent. The wily King relented, but only on condition that Canada take no part in any UNTCOK action unless it had the support of both the U.S. and the U.S.S.R.—which was highly unlikely.

UNTCOK travelled to Korea, confirmed the Soviet threat, and proceeded to organize elections for a constituent assembly in the U.S.-controlled sector south of the 38th parallel. An assembly was duly voted in, Syngman Rhee was elected chairman, a constitution was adopted, and on July 20, 1948 Syngman Rhee was elected as the first president of the Republic of Korea. The U.S.S.R. retaliated by establishing the Democratic People's Republic of Korea in the north, under Kim Il Sung, and arming it heavily.

In December 1948 the Soviets "withdrew" from Korea—secretly leaving hundreds of advisers, pilots, etc., and massive amounts of military equipment—and by June 1949 all the Americans had left except for a small handful of advisers. Rhee was upset at the U.S. withdrawal, especially because it was not coupled with any substantial offer of military aid. He accused the Americans of abandoning South Korea, and he was essentially correct. American military experts believed Korea was virtually indefensible; political experts felt it was only a matter of time before the Rhee regime collapsed and the Communists gained control of the whole country. In a speech in January 1950, U.S. Secretary of State Dean Acheson pointedly described the "defensive" perimeter of the free world in Asia as running "from the Ryukyus to the Philippines", which appeared to exclude Korea and reflected Washington's view that Korea was not worth defending and would not be defended if invaded. But no one considered that a probability; U.S. military intelligence consistently denied that any such thing appeared to be in the offing, and the CIA barely mentioned Korea in its weekly intelligence summaries. On June 20, 1950, U.S. Assistant Secretary of State for Far Eastern Affairs Dean Rusk declared: "We see no present indication that the people across the border have any intention of fighting a major war...." In fact, the order for invasion had already been given.

The memoirs of Soviet leader Nikita Khrushchev suggest that the initiative for the attack came from Kim Il Sung. Khrushchev wrote that at the end of 1949 Kim Il Sung told Stalin that he wanted "to prod South Korea with the point of a bayonet"; he assured him that the first poke "would touch off an internal explosion in South Korea", and "the power of the people would prevail." According to Khrushchev, Stalin eventually went along with the idea—after consulting Chinese leader Mao Tse-tung—because "no real Communist would have tried to dissuade Kim Il Sung from his compelling desire to liberate South Korea." The Soviets supplied massive quantities of arms and their pilots flew combat missions in support of the invasion, but Stalin insisted that Soviet advisers be withdrawn before the invasion so that no evidence would exist of their complicity.

THE INVASION AND THE INITIAL RESPONSE

As soon as the American president, Harry S. Truman, learned of the invasion, he sought a special meeting of the U.N. Security Council. Normally any resolution against North Korea would have been vetoed by the Soviet Union, but in June 1950 the Soviet Union was boycotting the council over the U.N.'s failure to award China's seat to China's new Communist government. Thus the U.S. had little trouble getting a resolution passed which branded the attack a breach of the peace and called for an immediate end to hostilities and the withdrawal of the North Koreans back across the 38th parallel. The North Koreans refused to heed this and on June 27 the council passed a second resolution, calling on U.N. members "to furnish such assistance to the Republic of Korea as may be necessary to repel the armed attack and to restore peace and security in the area." It was nothing less than a call to arms.

The U.S. had worked diligently to ensure that this call went out from the U.N. and not from Washington, but in truth Truman had made his decision to aid South Korea at least twenty-four hours before the Security Council resolution was passed. The act of invasion had convinced him that the U.S. had to come to the rescue of the Rhee regime. As he wrote in his memoirs: "if the Russian totalitarian state was intending to follow in the path of the dictatorships of Hitler and Mussolini, they should be met head on in Korea."

Even before Truman made his decision, USAF fighters, flying from bases in Japan, were in action over Korean battlefields. They were sorely needed; although the North Korean army was smaller than that of the south on paper, it was much better trained and equipped. Dedicated to Communism, it was also much more highly motivated. With surprise, momentum, and the shock effect of massed armour on their side, North Korean troops were sweeping all before them. U.S. fighters and bombers strafed, bombed, and rocketed the invaders, but could do little to slow their progress. Communist forces occupied the southern capital, Seoul, only four days after launching their assault. In the first week of fighting the Republic of Korea (R.O.K.) forces lost 44,000 men killed, wounded, or taken prisoner, virtually half their number. On June 30 Truman took a second key decision and committed U.S. ground forces to the battle—easier said than done because the closest forces were the occupation troops in Japan, who were used to the easy life and neither mentally nor physically ready to fight a war. When they first clashed with North Korean troops on July 5 the Americans were routed, in the beginning of what would be a long withdrawal occasionally delayed by rearguard actions.

On the day Truman committed ground forces to Korea, Canada responded to the U.N. call to action with an announcement that the destroyers HMCS *Cayuga, Athabaskan,* and *Sioux* were to be sent to the western Pacific. The destroyers were the first-ever Canadian military contribution to an exercise in international collective security, and Secretary of State for External Affairs Lester B. Pearson tried to make much of this contribution, claiming that it was "no mere token" and that the sinking of one of these destroyers would claim a considerable loss of life. Washington was not impressed; as one State Department observer put it, "Okay, let's call it three tokens."

It was easy to declare that the preservation of the U.N. was a cornerstone of Canadian foreign policy and that collective security was the only acceptable way to prevent another world war. It had taken little in the way of military or financial resources, at least at the time, to commit Canada to NATO. But when the Soviet Union had blockaded Berlin in 1948, in an effort to starve the city into surrender, Canada had refused to help with the airlift; British, American, French, and Australian flyers and ground crew had been there, but no Canadians.

In November 1948 Mackenzie King had handed leadership of the Liberal government over to Louis St. Laurent, who felt that participation in Korea was in keeping with Canada's strong support for the notion of collective security. He said just this in announcing to the House of Commons that the three destroyers were being sent: "Any participation by Canada in carrying out the U.N. resolution—and I wish to emphasize this strongly— would not be participation in war against any state. It would be our part in collective police action under the control and authority of the United Nations for the purpose of restoring peace."

There was in fact another, unmentioned reason for Canada's participation. In Washington, London, and Ottawa the Communist invasion of South Korea was seen as a Soviet act—Soviet-inspired, Soviet-planned, and Soviet-supported. It was thought of as a Cold War equivalent of the

Munich crisis of September 1938, when Hitler had tested the will of his enemies and found it wanting. If the Soviet Union was allowed a victory in Korea, Europe itself would soon be threatened with invasion; the real target was seen as NATO, and NATO's members felt obliged to respond one way or another.

On July 7, 1950 the Security Council passed a resolution calling on all countries contributing forces to the conflict to place their troops under a unified U.N. command, the commander to be named by the United States. Later that day, General Douglas MacArthur, who was already in command of the U.S. occupation forces in Japan, was given overall responsibility for U.N. forces in Korea. That same day Ottawa announced a second contribution to the fighting: 426 (Transport) Squadron, consisting of Canadair-built North Star aircraft, was ordered to fly to Tacoma, Washington to begin operations in conjunction with the USAF's Military Air Transport Service as part of the Korean airlift. Meanwhile, the British government had announced that it was placing its naval forces in the war zone at the disposal of the U.S., to fight on behalf of the United Nations.

If the press was any measure of popular feeling, the people of Canada strongly supported the United States and the United Nations in the early weeks of the campaign. Writing in *Saturday Night* magazine, Wilfrid Eggleston declared, "We must band together to oppose aggression, no matter from what source," while Michael Barkway warned that "Korea means that we've got to be ready to meet the Russians almost anywhere almost any time." The *Halifax Chronicle-Herald* commended the U.S. for its quick reaction: "against this Red aggression the answer of the United States has been gratifyingly prompt." The *Ottawa Journal* asked whether Canada should send ground combat troops to Korea and hoped "that the question is in the minds of our defence authorities and in the minds of the Cabinet."

THE CANADIAN ARMY SPECIAL FORCE

The question was very much in the minds of the Cabinet. On July 14, Canada had officially informed the U.N. secretary general, Trygve Lie, that the three destroyers were being transferred to General MacArthur's command. That same day, however, Lie had sent telegrams to the governments of the fifty-three U.N. members that had signified their support, asking for ground forces. Due to a mix-up at the Canadian mission to the U.N. in New York, the telegram was misplaced until after its contents had been released to the press by the United Nations. Lie had not intended to embarrass anyone in so open a fashion, but Ottawa was nevertheless put in a very difficult position. As one Canadian official told the press, "You don't just spring things like that on member governments."

The embarrassment was reminiscent of the early days of the Boer War, when Laurier had been caught off guard by Britain's premature announcement of Canadian involvement. When the official request did arrive in Ottawa, St. Laurent was off fishing; both Minister of National Defence Brooke Claxton and Pearson were also out of town. An enterprising reporter tracked St. Laurent to his summer home and called him on the telephone, and St. Laurent responded, "I wish reporters wouldn't bother me when I'm on holidays."

St. Laurent returned to Ottawa soon after and he, Claxton, and Pearson consulted with the service chiefs as to the feasibility of sending troops to Korea. Lieutenant-General Charles G. Foulkes, Chief of the General Staff—who also sat as the chairman of the Chiefs of Staff Committee—outlined Canada's options. If it became necessary to send ground troops, Foulkes favoured the dispatch of a specially recruited brigade-sized force that would fight as part of a Commonwealth division. Special recruiting would allow Canada to send ground troops without stripping units from the small regular army; fighting in conjunction with a Commonwealth division would allow the Canadians to use British lines of supply. That was especially important since most of the equipment available was surplus from the war, and was British by design or manufacture. Moreover, since large numbers of the volunteers were likely to be veterans, they would be used to British-style training and tactics.

St. Laurent and his ministers listened but, for the moment, did nothing. On July 19 the prime minister told the press that the Cabinet had decided "that the dispatch, at this stage, of existing first line elements of the Canadian Army to the Korean theatre would not be warranted." That caused a howl of protest from the Tory press, which claimed Canada was holding back because of the poor state of its defence establishment.

They were perfectly correct. After the Second World War, the King government had ruthlessly cut the defence budget to the point where, in late 1947, there were fewer than 30,000 men and women of all ranks in the three regular services. The onset of the Cold War spurred some additional recruiting and purchase of modern equipment in 1948 and 1949, but if forces were sent to Korea, not enough would remain in Canada for its own self-defence. The navy had almost no modern vessels, while the air force's first-line fighter jet was the obsolete British-built de Havilland Vampire.

In the midst of this predicament, Mackenzie King died on July 22. For the next few days, as the Cabinet contemplated its options, his body lay in state in Ottawa. When St. Laurent noted the passing of the "King era" he was right in more ways than one: King's death signalled the passing of Canadian isolationism. It is highly unlikely that the cautious and suspicious King would ever have countenanced participation in the Korean conflict. Now his one-time ministers argued the issue on the train home from his funeral in Toronto, with Pearson adamant that Canada had an obligation to send an army contingent to Korea.

As the hot July days passed, the pressure on Ottawa mounted. The U.S. was especially annoyed by the foot-dragging. After all, had not St. Laurent put great emphasis on the U.N. and the collective-security nature of the Korean "police action"? Had he not stressed Canada's strong commitment to both? Washington was in a state of crisis as the North Korean juggernaut rolled relentlessly on, and scratch U.S. units were being thrown into action as quickly as they could be brought to the battlefront, but in Ottawa everything seemed to be "holidays as usual".

On July 26 the U.K. announced that it would send a brigade group to Korea and the Australians promised that they too would send ground forces. Washington formally asked Ottawa to send a brigade, and London made discreet inquiries as to what size of force Canada would send and whether or not the Canadians were willing to join a Commonwealth division. Pearson made a quick trip to Washington and New York, where he sought assurances that Canadian troops would not be committed to battle without proper training and preparation and warned the U.S. that pestering Ottawa was only counter-productive, while Foulkes secretly told the army to get ready to begin recruiting and training a special force. The long-anticipated announcement came on August 7: St. Laurent told the public that Canada would raise a brigade group, a brigade accompanied by some of the supporting arms and services (tank units, engineers, a field hospital, etc.) which would normally be attached to a division. This contingent—its initial strength was to be approximately 5,000 all ranks with 2,100 reinforcements—was to "be available for use in carrying out Canada's obligations under the United Nations Charter or the North Atlantic Pact". NATO was mentioned to keep Canada's options open in the event that the conflict in Korea ended before the troops could be sent overseas.

The formation was to be known as the Canadian Army Special Force (CASF), and its core would consist of second battalions of three regular-force regiments—the Princess Patricia's Canadian Light Infantry (PPCLI), the Royal Canadian Regiment, and the Royal 22e Régiment (Van Doos). St. Laurent called on fit young men, preferably veterans of the last war, to enlist. Their terms of enlistment were to be for eighteen months or as long as the emergency lasted. They would be supplemented by regular-force members wherever possible. Eventually Foulkes recommended, and the Cabinet accepted, a ceiling of ten thousand on this initial recruiting drive, to provide a sufficient number of reserves for "wastage".

The day after St. Laurent's announcement, Foulkes telephoned Brigadier J.M. Rockingham, commander of the 9th Canadian Infantry Brigade in north-west Europe in late 1944 and early 1945, to ask him to assume command of the Special Force. The next day Rockingham flew to Ottawa and was officially installed as commander.

THE VOLUNTEERS

The day Rockingham flew to Ottawa, recruiting offices across Canada opened their doors to long lines of volunteers. In many there was chaos; the staff were ill-prepared to handle such a crush of men. Eight thousand were taken in the first three weeks alone, including a large number of undesirable and unfit men. Later Lieutenant-Colonel J.R. Stone would comment:

> They were recruiting anybody who could breathe or walk. Brooke Claxton pushed the enlistment along because he was a politician at heart and didn't really give a damn about what else was happening. He was recruiting an army....

The haste created countless personnel and morale problems. The first contingents of Canadians were to have the highest venereal disease rate of all the U.N. troops in Korea. The CASF had abnormally high rates of men "absent without leave" (AWOL), and Canadian prison stockades were usually full. More than 25 per cent of the volunteers had to be weeded out before the first contingents could be sent across the Pacific, compared to approximately 7 per cent in the Second World War. It seems the recruiters took almost anybody in the initial rush—including one man in his seventies and another with an artificial leg!

Why did these men, mostly young, want to leave peacetime Canada to fight in the far-off hills of Korea? For many of the volunteers, adventure, escape from boredom, or the lure of a steady paycheque had more to do with it than did a determination to stop Communism at the 38th parallel. Young Peter Worthington, who joined in the third year of the war, was "kicking around Europe", according to his memoirs, and running out of money. He wrote to the Malayan police, then gearing up to fight Communist guerrillas, and to Ottawa to enquire about joining the Canadian army—his father had been an officer in the PPCLI and a major-general in the last war. The Canadian reply came first and within a few months Worthington was in Korea. George Henderson of Stratford, Ontario, heard Lester Pearson talk about Korea on the radio. He later recalled that he had been "waiting for something to do" and thought "walking around Korea would be the same as walking in Canada."

The most interesting character to join the Canadian Army Special Force never lived; he was Private Jacket Coates, the fictional creation of Lieutenant-Colonel Herbert Fairlie Wood. Wood served in Korea and was afterwards commissioned to write *Strange Battleground*, the official history of the Canadian army in Korea, published in 1966. Wood's book is dull, pedantic, and thorough—everything suggested by the phrase "official history". But while he was at work on *Strange Battleground*, Wood was also writing *The Private War of Jacket Coates*, the memoir of a rogue who just wants to serve his time, collect his pay, and stay as far away from combat as he possibly can. The book has all the colour and atmosphere that *Strange Battleground* is lacking, and tells the story that Wood dared not write in the official history. And why did Jacket Coates sign up? In his words, "I have always been one to rally to king and country in an emergency, and in 1950 the emergency was that I was broke."

Soon thousands of men were making their way to train depots to travel to army camps for basic training, while veterans did their best to instil unit pride in the new recruits. One of the volunteers was Sergeant Tom Prince, a Canadian Indian who had served with the elite Special Forces of Canadian and American commandos formed to fight in Italy in the war—the Devil's Brigade. While waiting for a train in Winnipeg, Prince was overheard lecturing a small group of volunteers in a loud voice:

> You're in the Princess Patricia's now. You are hard! You drink hard! You play hard! You love hard! You hate hard! You fight hard! You can decide what you drink, how you play, who you love. We'll decide who you hate and who you fight.

It was soon clear that training in widely scattered locations would take much too long. After seeking one large central location where the bulk of the three battalions could train at once, Ottawa made arrangements with the Americans in early October to use facilities at Fort Lewis, Washington. It had ready facilities—recently vacated by U.S. troops bound for Korea—it was near a large port (Seattle) and major rail lines, and it was far enough south and near enough to the west coast to escape the worst ravages of winter. On November 10, the first elements of the CASF arrived there. Eleven days later, tragedy struck; a train carrying soldiers of the Royal Canadian Horse Artillery through the mountains of British Columbia collided head on with another train at Canoe River and seventeen soldiers were killed. A local telegraph operator was charged with criminal negligence and John G. Diefenbaker, MP, agreed to conduct his defence. At the trial Diefenbaker revealed that the railway had placed the men in a wooden car between two steel cars; when the two trains collided, the car carrying the soldiers folded up like an accordion. The jury exonerated the accused.

At Fort Lewis the designation Canadian Army Special Force fell into disuse, to be replaced by the more official-sounding 25th Canadian Infantry Brigade (CIB). The men trained hard in the cool, wet weather, and short visits to the bars and brothels of Tacoma alleviated the hard work and repetitiveness of military routine. They were assigned the northern part of Fort Lewis, which was really more like a small city than a military post. They found most American ways—and American military slang—strange, but they did welcome some of the differences. As Jacket Coates remembered:

> In the Canadian Army of those days, beer drinking was usually done sitting on a rickety bench in the oldest and crummiest building in camp, to the tune of breaking bottles and violent talk.... Our masters called this dump the Men's Wet Canteen.... In Fort Lewis the American equivalent was the Enlisted Men's Garrison Club.... There were reading-rooms and television-rooms and dancing rooms with juke boxes.

The Canadians were soon ensconced in these opulent surroundings, downing American beers and sneering at the soft U.S. soldiers who needed all this luxury!

THE PPCLI GO TO KOREA

As better troops and more and better equipment arrived in Korea over the summer, the North Korean offensive had been slowed. By the end of the first week of August, the North Koreans had been stopped along a perimeter outside the southern port city of Pusan. The headquarters of the U.S. Eighth Army, under the command of Lieutenant-General Walton H. "Bulldog" Walker, had been moved from Japan to Korea, and at that point Walker had at his disposal approximately 95,000 men along a 200-kilometre front, with troops continuing to arrive throughout the month—the 27th

British Infantry Brigade joined them towards the end of August. A stale-mate of sorts had developed, with each side probing the other. The South Koreans and the Americans had suffered dearly in the long retreat from the 38th parallel, but the North Koreans had been worn down too; from the day their attack began until the line stabilized around Pusan, they had suffered some 58,000 casualties.

On September 15, 1950, MacArthur executed one of the boldest strokes of his military career. Approximately 70,000 U.S. troops landed at Inchon, a small and barely accessible port some thirty kilometres south-west of Seoul, crushed the token North Korean defence there, and drove on to the occupied capital. The North Koreans were caught napping as the U.S. drive swept everything before it. By September 26 Seoul had been recap-tured, the North Korean supply lines to the south had been cut, and Walk-er's forces had broken out of the Pusan perimeter and were pursuing flee-ing North Korean units northward. Less than a month after the Inchon landing, U.N. troops—contingents from Britain, Australia, Turkey, and other members had joined MacArthur's forces by then—had crossed the 38th parallel. At that stage the U.N. General Assembly adopted—over strenuous U.S.S.R. opposition—a British resolution authorizing MacArthur to conduct operations in North Korea as well. In effect, the U.N. was setting out to unify the peninsula by force of arms. Throughout the rest of October and into November, U.N. forces advanced towards the Yalu River, the boundary between China and North Korea, despite increas-ing signs that China was preparing to intervene on a massive scale.

As a result of the rapid successes which followed the Inchon landing the U.S. Joint Chiefs of Staff reassessed their need for ground combat troops, and in the last week of October they informed Ottawa that most of the 25th CIB would not be needed. The Canadian government then scaled down its planned contribution and decided to send only the second battal-ion of the Princess Patricia's Canadian Light Infantry (2PPCLI). Since the Patricias were now destined for occupation duty rather than combat, there seemed no need for lengthy training at Fort Lewis, and their departure date was moved up. Towards the end of October a small advance party sailed for Pusan to prepare the ground for the battalion's arrival; on November 25, after only four days of advanced unit training at Fort Lewis, the remainder of the battalion followed. The voyage epitomized the mili-tary experience of "hurry up and wait"; it was tedious and it was depress-ing. To relieve the boredom a small group of men launched Operation Haircut and formed a "cue ball" club; everyone in it was shaved to the skull. Those reluctant to join were pounced on, their arms and legs were pinned, and their heads were shaved clean. Just before arriving in Pusan all the cooks were given the cue ball treatment—revenge for the quality of the food on the trip over.

By the time the Canadians arrived on December 18, the war had taken a dramatic turn for the worse. As U.N. troops had advanced to the Yalu, Chinese "volunteers" had begun to infiltrate across the river in great numbers. As early as the beginning of November an estimated six Chinese armies, consisting of approximately 180,000 soldiers, had been in position between the Yalu and the advancing U.N. troops. For the most part the Chinese soldiers travelled on foot under cover of darkness, carrying supplies and spare ammunition with them. Yet MacArthur seemed blissfully unaware—or disdainful—of the buildup. He assured Truman that the Chinese would not attack and told his "boys" they would be home for Christmas. He was so certain of his position that he ordered his forces in the north deployed in two large formations, x Corps in the east and the Eighth Army in the west, separated by many kilometres of mountains—a cardinal military sin.

On November 26 the Chinese launched a massive attack which brought about an almost immediate collapse of the Eighth Army and virtually cut off thousands of U.S. Marines—the bulk of x Corps' fighting strength—in far north-eastern Korea. On almost every front, panic seized U.S. units— the troops and the press soon labelled it "bug-out fever"—at the very prospect of being attacked by these Chinese soldiers swaddled in quilted cotton uniforms, wearing rubber-soled sneakers, and carrying sub-machine ("burp") guns. These were not only the embodiment of the inscrutable "yellow peril" that generations of racist whites had feared would take over the world; they were also the dreaded "Commies" who would sink to any depths to destroy democracy. They seemed prepared to attack as a human tidal wave, heedless of life and limb, to achieve their purposes. Within weeks MacArthur's troops were driven back south to the banks of the Imjin River, north of Seoul. For a brief time the Chinese regrouped. Then, in the early morning hours of December 31, they attacked again. Within five days Seoul was recaptured by the Communists, and when the Chinese reached the limit of their advance on January 24 they were some sixty-four kilometres south of the occupied capital.

Although Lester Pearson had received commitments that Canadian troops would not be sent into battle without proper training, Bulldog Walker wanted to use the Patricias as quickly as possible. He proposed to give them three days in Pusan to unpack their equipment and organize themselves, then send them to a "training area" just thirty-two kilometres south of Seoul—close to the deteriorating front. In effect the PPCLI would form part of Walker's reserve.

The nightmare of Hong Kong was constantly in the minds of Canadian leaders. In late 1941, an under-trained and poorly equipped contingent of Canadian troops had been sent to help defend the British crown colony against possible Japanese attack. When the attack came, the defenders had been quickly overwhelmed; 290 Canadians were killed in the battle, 287 (or one in five) died in Japanese prison camps, and many who did come back were broken in body and spirit. As far as Ottawa was concerned, that was never going to happen again.

The Canadians were under the command of Lieutenant-Colonel J.R. Stone. A veteran of the Second World War, Stone was a popular leader; his men called him "Big Jim" and his unit was known as "Big Jim's Patricias". Stone's command instructions had been framed in such a way as to head off the sort of action Walker was now contemplating. Nevertheless, as the situation at the front grew worse, Walker began to insist that the Canadians join the 29th British Infantry Brigade then positioned north of Seoul on the banks of the Imjin River. Walker insisted (and he was not wrong in this) that the Canadians were at least as well prepared as the bulk of the occupation troops that the Americans had thrown into battle. Stone flew to Seoul to confront Walker directly. Walker was tough but Stone was determined; he produced his written instructions and forced the American to agree that the PPCLI should have eight weeks' training somewhere near Pusan before being committed to battle. Eleven days after the meeting the full weight of the second Chinese offensive fell along the Imjin; the 29th British Infantry Brigade suffered 300 killed and wounded. If Stone had not persevered, the Canadians might have been slaughtered.

The Canadians were shocked by Korea. They knew little of the country and less of the people. They thought Koreans were especially cruel to each other, found Korean women unattractive, and recoiled from the smell and the lack of sanitation. Stone wrote Rockingham:

> Korea is a land of filth and poverty...all fertilizing of fields is done with human excreta...there will be a health problem in the spring and summer. The dust at present is germ-laden and is causing some respiratory trouble, but the sick bay has only a few patients.

One Canadian medical officer observed that the country was "crawling with vermin".

The Canadians trained until mid-February, gaining some real experience by tracking Communist guerrillas but seeing no action and neither taking nor inflicting casualties. Then, on February 15, they moved out of their rear-echelon positions to join the 27th British Commonwealth Brigade. The brigade was attached to the 2nd U.S. Infantry Division, part of IX U.S. Corps, which consisted of three American divisions and one R.O.K. division. These troops now came under the command of Lieutenant-General Matthew B. Ridgway, who had succeeded Walker when the latter was killed in a road accident, and Ridgway had ordered a counterattack all along the western portion of the front. IX Corps spearheaded the advance.

As the PPCLI joined the fight, the reality of the war hit home almost immediately. On February 19 the battalion was ordered to move out from the small village of Chuam-ni to take Hill 404. As they trudged up the road the Canadians came upon the stiffened corpses of more than sixty American soldiers laid out for a graves registration party. The men had been surprised in the middle of the night by Chinese troops and had been machine-gunned while still in their sleeping bags. Stone later remembered:

> This was the greatest lesson my troops ever had.... They saw the bodies and the sight sure made an impression. After that you couldn't *get* one of my men into a sleeping bag at the front.... The British had dug in before going to sleep and they didn't lose a man.

For the next few weeks the Canadians' war settled down into a routine of climbing hills, trudging along narrow ridges, taking cover from snipers, and launching small-scale assaults against knots of Chinese soldiers dug in on hillsides. As correspondent Pierre Berton described it, it was a war of "slow remorseless plodding from ridge to ridge, of clearing mud huts, of firing round after round into apparently empty hills, of long patrols by day and longer watches by night".

Corporal Karry Dunphy was in charge of a nine-man section in the midst of this advance. On February 21 they were awarded the dubious honour of being the first Canadians to come under fire. The men were advancing along a nameless ridge, crunching through snow, wending their way through the small pine trees that dotted the hill. Suddenly, from somewhere, a light machine-gun opened up. Bullets whizzed high above them, shaking the pine needles, cracking the air as they went by. Two or three of the men sprawled on their bellies; others went down on one knee, rifle to shoulder, or rolled into the trees, scattering. Dunphy carefully exposed himself for a few seconds to get an idea of where the fire was coming from. Then, when he realized that the gun was far away, he began to urge his men slowly forward, reminding them not to bunch up. Suddenly one man spotted a Chinese sniper, got down on one knee, and squeezed off three shots. The enemy soldier went down. Then the Canadian stood up, a strange look on his face, and began to run through the trees, screaming and shouting, "I'm in no shape for this! I got to see somebody." He was sent home for a mental discharge.

The weather seemed to conspire against the advancing troops. At night the temperature dropped to -15° C, the Canadians' first real taste of winter conditions in the field. Despite Arctic exercises held prior to the war, they were not equipped for cold weather. Their boots were quickly soaked and provided little warmth during hours of marching through the mud or standing night watch in slit trenches; the heels often pulled away from the upper part of the boot. Their parkas were badly designed, made of nylon, which did little to stop the cold wind, and were not water-resistant. Moreover, Stone complained that they were "dangerous for men at the front" because they "restricted sight and hearing". One official report pointed out, "It seems unbelievable that Canada is far behind the United States and U.K. in the design of winter clothing." On the other hand, in the daytime the sun could warm the slopes to 10°, melting the snow, adding to the mud, and making the footing even more treacherous than usual.

Nor were the men equipped with appropriate weaponry. Their standard weapon was the British-designed Lee-Enfield .303 carbine, a rugged bolt-operated rifle that needed to be cocked and reloaded by working the bolt after every shot. The Americans had long since abandoned bolt-action rifles, adopting the Garand or M1 semi-automatic carbine before the Second World War. Great for a rifle range, the Lee-Enfield was hopeless for mass, close-range fire. As one officer reported, it was "almost useless.... It has not the rate of fire to stop mass attack. It is too clumsy and slow.... It cannot produce the volume of quickly adjusted fire necessary in the sudden night patrol actions."

The Canadians did have a sub-machine-gun available: the latest version of the British-designed Sten gun, first designed during the early days of the Second World War as a cheap, easy-to-produce sub-machine-gun that could be turned out with little in the way of precision machining. It was widely used at close range by commandos and guerrillas. As a regular infantry weapon, however, it was a total failure. It did not have the precision, punch, or reliability of the American-designed "Tommygun", the Thompson .45. Its design, with its magazine protruding some thirty centimetres from the side, made it extremely awkward to carry or use. The Canadians soon left their Stens behind when going on patrol, relying on their rifles instead. They did sometimes take along the Bren light machine-gun. Brens were reliable enough but clumsy. They had to be sighted in advance, and their tripods were so large that the guns were almost useless in covered bunkers with small firing slits.

On February 21 Ridgway launched Operation Killer, intended to push the Chinese back across the 38th parallel. The 2PPCLI suffered its first casualties the next day, in attacks on Hill 444 and 419, both of which commanded the approaches to a small valley. They lost four killed and one wounded, and although they were able to capture the first objective, despite heavy attacks by U.S. fighter bombers the Chinese held out on the second. For four days the PPCLI assaulted the Chinese and for four days the enemy continued to hold out; six more Canadians were killed in these assaults. Finally a Korean deserter revealed that three Chinese battalions were dug in on the crest of Hill 419, and the Royal Australian Regiment (RAR) took a hill just to the east which forced them to withdraw.

These first few encounters began to give the Canadians some idea of whom they were up against—a tough, dedicated, and experienced enemy. In 1949 the People's Liberation Army (PLA) had carried the Communist Party to victory over the forces of Chiang Kai-shek, and many PLA soldiers had been fighting Chiang's troops—or the Japanese—for a decade or more. For much of this time they had practised for warfare without heavy weapons or air support, training to walk or even run miles at a time carrying as much as a week's rations, ammunition, and personal effects. A Chinese soldier required as little as one-sixth the rations and supplies of a U.N. soldier and had much less need of elaborate transport networks. Since the Chinese used few crew-served weapons (artillery, etc.) at the start of their intervention, they relied on a variety of tactics which almost always involved mass attacks under cover of darkness. By mid-1951, however, they had brought considerable quantities of artillery up to the front. From then on they used artillery fire to good effect, either to harass their enemies or to prepare the ground for an attack. Since they never had air cover and had to be constantly on the watch for roving aircraft, they became adept at the art of camouflage. Corporal Dunphy told Pierre Berton that he considered the Chinese "sporting soldiers" and that he was convinced that if they had wanted to, they could have "held the hills of Korea indefinitely".

The 27th Brigade continued its advance on March 7 with a co-ordinated assault on Hills 532 and 410, which dominated two important valleys running east and west across the line of advance. The Chinese were well dug in on both positions. The Royal Australian Regiment failed to take Hill 410 and, although one of the two attacking Canadian companies made good progress on Hill 532, the other came under intense machine-gun fire from the forward slopes. For the rest of the day, under a heavy, wet snow, they were forced to dig in one moment, then advance at a crawl the next, in an effort to gain the heights. During the day six more Canadians were killed and twenty-eight wounded. When the Canadians prepared to launch an all-out assault at dawn the following day, they found that the Chinese had pulled out during the night.

The Chinese had in fact begun a general withdrawal all along the front. On March 15 Seoul was recaptured by R.O.K. forces, and U.N. troops again approached the 38th parallel. General MacArthur pushed strongly for a U.N. invasion of North Korea, but President Truman would have none of it; rolling back the North Koreans was one thing, fighting an apparently endless war against the Chinese, with their unlimited manpower, was another. Backed by the Commonwealth participants in the war, Truman called for military stabilization combined with negotiations. When MacArthur publicly disagreed with his commander-in-chief he was sacked, on April 11, 1951, and replaced by Ridgway. Ridgway continued to push to the north, but his prime objective was to find a defensible line across the peninsula and then hold it against further counter-attacks. To that end IX Corps was ordered to continue its advance behind the withdrawing Chinese.

KAPYONG

The full weight of the 60th Division of the Third Field Army of the People's Republic of China fell on the Canadian troops after nightfall on April 24, 1951. The Canadians—A, B, C, and D companies of the 2PPCLI—were dug in on the slopes of Hill 677 overlooking the Kapyong River valley, several kilometres north of Kapyong village, at the junction of the Kapyong and Pukhan rivers. For several terrifying hours that night, this handful of soldiers would be all that stood between the masses of the Chinese army and the collapse of the U.N. front in central Korea.

Kapyong village is about twenty-five kilometres south of the 38th parallel and approximately forty kilometres north-east of Seoul. Just a few days before the assault, it had been a backwater of the war. By the end of the third week of April, the entire front of IX U.S. Corps had pushed an average of ten kilometres north of the 38th parallel, well past the village.

On April 18 the bulk of the brigade was relieved by troops of the 6th R.O.K. Division and went into reserve near Kapyong itself. The 16th New Zealand Field Regiment remained behind to provide fire support for the South Koreans, who continued to push slowly north. As they went, cap-

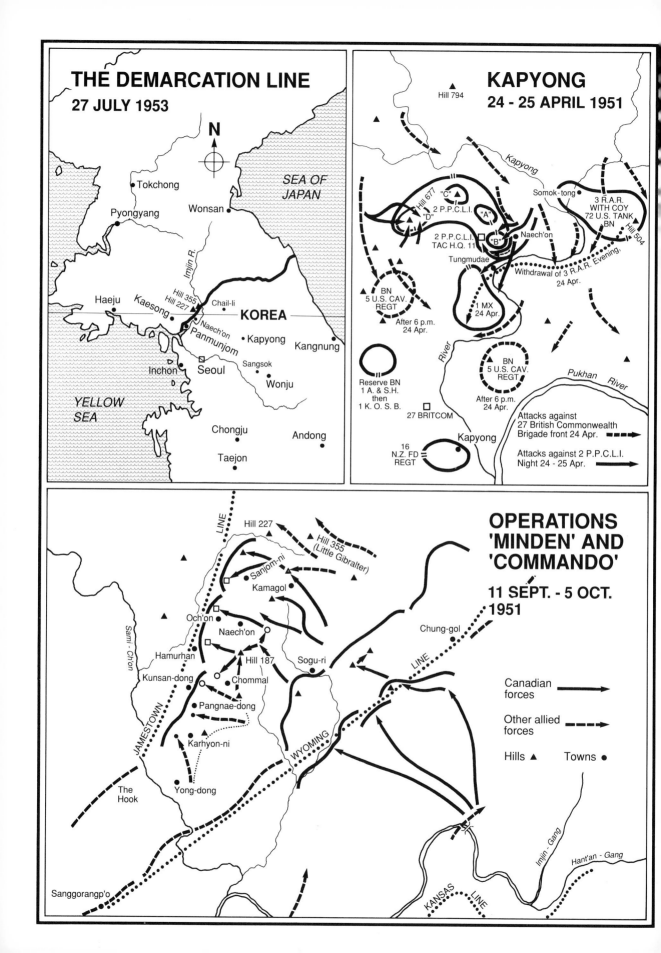

THE DEMARCATION LINE
27 JULY 1953

N

SEA OF JAPAN

- Tokchong
- Pyongyang
- Wonsan

Imjin R.

- Haeju
- Kaesong
- Hill 355
- Hill 227
- Chail-li

KOREA

- Naech'on
- Panmunjom
- Inchon
- Seoul
- Kapyong
- Sangsok
- Kangnung
- Wonju

YELLOW SEA

- Chongju
- Andong
- Taejon

KAPYONG
24 - 25 APRIL 1951

- ▲ Hill 794

- ▲ Hill 677 "C"
- 2 P.P.C.L.I.
- "D"
- "A"
- Somok-tong
- 3 R.A.R. WITH COY 72 U.S. TANK BN
- Hill 504
- 2 P.P.C.L.I. TAC H.Q. 11
- "B"
- Naech'on
- Tungmudae
- Withdrawal of 3 R.A.R. Evening, 24 Apr.

- BN 5 U.S. CAV. REGT
- After 6 p.m. 24 Apr.
- 1 MX 24 Apr.

Kapyong

River

Pukhan River

- Reserve BN 1 A. & S.H. then 1 K. O. S. B.

- BN 5 U.S. CAV. REGT
- After 6 p.m. 24 Apr.

- ☐ 27 BRITCOM

- 16 N.Z. FD REGT
- Kapyong

Attacks against 27 British Commonwealth Brigade front 24 Apr. ▰▰▰▶

Attacks against 2 P.P.C.L.I. Night 24 - 25 Apr. ━━▶

OPERATIONS 'MINDEN' AND 'COMMANDO'
11 SEPT. - 5 OCT. 1951

LINE

- Hill 227
- ▲ Hill 355 (Little Gibralter)
- Sanjom-ni
- Kamagol
- Och'on
- Naech'on
- Chung-gol
- Hamurhan
- Hill 187
- Sogu-ri
- Kunsan-dong
- Chommal
- Pangnae-dong
- Karhyon-ni
- Yong-dong

Sami - Ch'on

JAMESTOWN

WYOMING

LINE

The Hook

Sanggorangp'o

KANSAS LINE

Imjin - Gang

Hant'an - Gang

Canadian forces ━━▶

Other allied forces ▰▰▰▶

Hills ▲   Towns ●

tured North Korean and Chinese prisoners warned of an impending Chinese attack. That blow fell just after midnight on April 22 when the Chinese opened a general counter-offensive along most of the U.N. front; more than 100,000 troops attacked IX U.S. Corps and I U.S. Corps to the west of it. In the IX Corps sector, the main weight of the assault fell on 6 R.O.K. Division, which was immediately thrown back some fifteen kilometres. For the better part of a day the South Koreans tried to consolidate their positions, but just after nightfall on April 23 they broke; men and vehicles began to stream to the south, through the Kapyong River valley. The New Zealanders were quickly ordered to withdraw and join up with the 27th Brigade, which was given two difficult jobs; hold the door open so the Koreans could pass through; slam the door shut so the Chinese could not. This would allow the rest of the U.N. divisions in the area to withdraw in good order.

On the day the Koreans were attacked, the Chinese also slammed into the 29th British Infantry Brigade, attached to I U.S. Corps, which was helping to hold a line on the Imjin River. It was clear that this was no local attack; it was a well-coordinated effort to break the U.N. front at its most northerly point, thus outflanking the troops to the east—and it proved to be highly successful.

As the battle was raging on the Imjin, the commander of the 27th Brigade, Colonel Brian A. Burke, was attempting to prepare his brigade for the inevitable onslaught. He and his men were fortunate to have been in reserve when the Chinese blow fell; it had been the Koreans who experienced the full weight of the initial attack. Burke well knew that one of the cardinal principles of warfare was that to control a valley the high ground on both sides must be secured. To that end he ordered the 3rd Battalion of the Royal Australian Regiment (RAR), backed by a company of the U.S. 72nd Tank Battalion, to dig in on Hill 504, to the north-east of the junction of the Kapyong and Pukhan rivers; the Canadians were to entrench on Hill 677, across the Kapyong, about three kilometres west of the Australians.

Before positioning his companies on Hill 677, Jim Stone and his company commanders walked the slopes trying to imagine every possible Chinese approach route. Stone then placed his four companies in a rough semicircle, with A Company on the lower slopes of the hill facing the Australians, C Company on the north side, B Company just to the west of C, and D Company south of B. During the afternoon and evening of April 23 the Canadians dug foxholes and communications trenches, laid barbed wire, wired their field telephones, checked their radios, and positioned their machine-guns and mortars for the best possible fields of fire. Those on the eastern slope of the hill may well have looked across the valley to see the Australians doing the same thing on Hill 504. It was warm and dry, the best weather they had had for weeks, and on the road below them the remnants of two shattered Korean regiments went streaming past. One Canadian later recalled the sight:

> [The R.O.K. MPs] had a bunch of machine guns on either side of the road and loudspeakers that blared out that anyone going [towards the rear]...would be shot.

The threats accomplished nothing:

> These [R.O.K. soldiers] were coming out.... I've never seen such fear and disorganization like those guys piling down the road. It went on for hours.

It was not a sight to inspire confidence. A long night lay ahead.

At approximately 10:00 P.M. the Australians were hit. Blowing whistles and bugles, and preceded by a shower of mortar rounds, Chinese infantry-men rose out of the dark and rushed the RAR slit trenches. Close behind the first line of attackers came a second line hurling hundreds of grenades and carrying explosive charges to breach the wire. Chinese assault tactics were familiar by now: under cover of darkness they crept as close as they could to the U.N. positions; then, at a pre-arranged moment, the infantrymen rushed forward firing their sub-machine-guns. The object was to over-whelm the enemy by sheer weight of numbers, and at such close quarters as to deny the defenders a chance to bring heavy machine-guns and other crew-served weapons to bear. At the same time as they hit the RAR posi-tions, the Chinese also attacked remnants of the 6th R.O.K. Division, some ten kilometres farther north, and swarmed into the New Zealanders' gun lines. Across the valley to the west, the Canadians watched the sky lit by tracers and explosions and listened to the cacophony of automatic weapons fire.

For several hours no one had a clear picture of the drama being played out on the slopes and in the gun pits of Hill 504; communications with the RAR were cut off until the early morning hours of April 24, when the com-manding officer came back on the air to give brigade headquarters a situa-tion report. It was not good. The Chinese had penetrated to the centre of the Australian positions, were swarming around the foxholes, and were climbing onto the American tanks located at strategic positions on the hill. Australian and Chinese infantrymen were firing at each other at point-blank range, and Chinese mortar and machine-gun fire was raking the slopes. To further complicate matters, retreating R.O.K. soldiers were still trying to move through the area; the Australians could not tell friend from foe. At brigade headquarters Burke and his officers peered through their binoculars, helpless to intervene.

As day broke it was apparent that the RAR had held its ground; the Chinese had been cleared from inside the Australians' positions and there were even a few hours of respite as the Chinese regrouped. But then the attacks started again. In daylight it was easier to discern the Chinese intentions, and artillery fire was poured down on their troop concentrations as the New Zealanders, stripped to the waist, fed their 25-pounders like men possessed. But the Chinese attacks continued. By mid-afternoon it was clear to Burke that the RAR could not hold out another night. At 5:30 P.M. the Australians and the American tanks began to pull back. The men withdrew under constant mortar and machine-gun fire, their vehicles covered by tanks on both sides of the road. By 10:40 P.M. the withdrawal was complete. The Australians had suffered thirty-one killed, fifty-eight wounded, and three men taken prisoner. Now it was Canada's turn.

Stone had observed the battle and had decided that an attack would likely come against the east slopes of Hill 677. Before noon he redeployed B Company from its original position on the north side to a point south of A Company on the eastern slope. This move may well have saved 2PPCLI from disaster. At 8:30 that evening, just as the Australian withdrawal was being completed, about four hundred Chinese infantrymen were observed forming up in a valley near B Company's new position. The company commander called in artillery fire but the Chinese attacked *en masse*. They quickly overran one of the platoons but the others held their ground. The fighting at close quarters was deadly. One sergeant later told a Canadian war correspondent:

There's a whistle, they get up with a shout about 10 feet from our positions and come in. The first wave throws its grenades, fires its weapons and goes to ground. It is followed by a second which does the same, and then a third comes up...they just keep coming.

In one of the Canadian Bren gun pits, the situation was desperate almost from the first moment of the battle:

We sat there and held them off as long as we could until we pulled back and Wayne (Mitchell) and I got separated. I don't know how long we were there before Lt. Ross gave us the order to move out. Just as we jumped up Ross added that anyone with any ammo left should cover

the retreat of the wounded. I had three shells left so I dropped back
down and fired them off. Just as I jumped up again I fell over a China-
man who was running up the side of the hill. He let fly and got me in
the neck then ran into the end of my bayonet.

Two other Canadian machine-gunners were not so lucky. Their gun had
been sited to cover Chinese approaches towards the eastern crest of the
hill. Hundreds of Chinese swarmed around them, charging again and
again until they overwhelmed the men, who were killed where they stood.

On other parts of the hill other Canadians displayed similar courage.
Machine-gunners Ken Barwise, Jim Waniandy, and several others found
themselves in front of an onrushing tide of Chinese grenadiers. "We
opened up with our Brens," Waniandy later recalled to Canadian Press
correspondent Bill Boss, and saw them "falling all over". Barwise told a
similar story: "They kept coming in waves." He alone accounted for at
least six Chinese dead. In all, Barwise and the others fought off at least five
attacks on B Company positions. The final assault was aimed directly at
battalion headquarters, and Stone later described it:

> The mortar platoon, located with HQ, was mounted for travelling on
> twelve half tracks. Each vehicle was equipped with one .50 and one .30
> calibre machine gun.... Fire was held until the Chinese had broken
> through the trees about two hundred metres away. Twenty-four
> machine guns cut loose together. Only those who have experienced
> being under the fire of a heavy concentration of tracer bullets can
> appreciate the terror induced by that kind and volume of fire.

As the night wore on the Patricias held to their positions, but their situation was increasingly desperate. Despite the heavy fighting that swirled
around B Company on the east side of the hill, it was soon obvious that the
full weight of the assault was being mounted towards D Company on the
west. A large mass of Chinese infantry rushed 10 Platoon's position but the
platoon held. The Chinese then moved around to the north and fell upon
12 Platoon. After a few minutes of intense fighting, the beleaguered Canadians were forced to withdraw, abandoning their machine-guns. This left a
gaping hole in their lines; 10 Platoon was now cut off and surrounded on
all sides, and company headquarters was directly threatened. If D Company collapsed, the Chinese could then rush into the battalion perimeter,
wreaking havoc. In the pre-dawn darkness, company commander Captain
J.G.W. Mills made a crucial but difficult decision: after ensuring that his
men were hunkered down in their foxholes, he called artillery fire down on

his own positions. The shrapnel bursts, set to explode just below treetop height, sent clouds of hot, jagged, twisted metal into the Chinese ranks; below ground level the Canadians were protected. At daybreak they were still in position but they were cut off and, after a night of hard fighting, out of supplies. Stone called for an air drop and a flight of USAF C-119 Flying Boxcars swung over the Canadian positions as loadmasters kicked their payloads out the rear. Food, ammunition, and water floated down onto the slopes of Hill 677. It was a perfect drop.

The battle for Hill 677 was over. Ten Canadians had been killed and twenty-three wounded, and several, including Barwise and Mills, would be decorated for bravery. In the words of an American chronicler of the Korean War, "The holding action of the Commonwealth Brigade at Kapyong had been decisive. It plugged the hole left by the R.O.K. 6th Division and blocked the CCF [Chinese Communist Forces] long enough for the 24th [U.S. Infantry] Division to withdraw." In appreciation, the U.S. awarded the PPCLI, the RAR, and the U.S. 72nd Tank Battalion a Presidential Unit Citation. The PPCLI is the only unit in Canadian history ever to have been honoured in this way.

The resistance of the Commonwealth troops at the Imjin River and at Kapyong blunted the Chinese assault. A general collapse of the U.N. front at that strategic point would have made the U.N. position in central Korea untenable; it might even have led to a renewed outbreak of "bug-out" fever and an overall retreat. These two small but fierce battles preserved the U.N. position and allowed Ridgway to orchestrate a withdrawal that left most U.N. units intact, and fighting spirit high. By May 1 the Chinese offensive had petered out with the U.N. still in control of most of Korea south of the 38th parallel. The Canadians had done their part, against incredible odds.

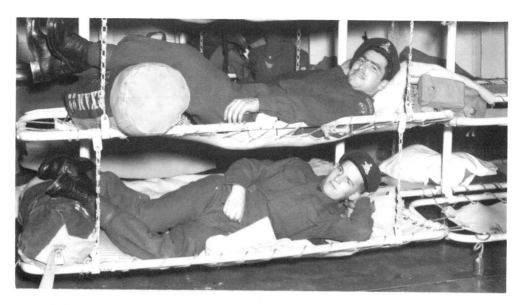

Men of the Royal 22e Régiment en route to Korea. Crammed into the holds of plodding transport ships, they were probably not quite as happy as they appear in this official photograph.

Two padres brush up their first-aid skills in Fort Lewis, Washington, before shipping out. A good padre had to be prepared to patch men up in all kinds of ways.

Brigadier J.M. Rockingham (pointing to map) confers with his officers over the hood of a Jeep. "Rocky" returned from civilian life to command the Canadian contingent during its first year in Korea; he had had an outstanding record as a brigade commander in the Second World War, and had personally selected most of the officers seen here.

After MacArthur's U.N. forces landed at Inchon on September 15, 1950, the North Koreans retreated rapidly—but they left behind evidence of mass killings of those who had opposed them. This photograph was taken by a Canadian officer.

A company of the PPCLI picks its way towards the front. The terrain is typical of central Korea—flooded rice paddies nestled among high hills covered with scrub and small coniferous trees. The men are loaded down with weapons and entrenching tools; the rifles are Second World War bolt-action Lee-Enfield .303s. The men have doffed their almost useless Great War–vintage flat-brimmed helmets, which were rarely worn.

A "dozer" (bulldozer tank) of Lord Strathcona's Horse crosses a pontoon bridge over the Han River, followed by medical and other vehicles. The dozer is a Sherman Firefly, a later version of the famous tank but with a larger gun. The twisted wreckage to the left once carried a three-lane highway, but was blown up by panicky South Korean troops as the Communists neared Seoul.

A Sherman tank of the LSH on patrol. Note that, while the tank's charge looks impressive, the path appears to have been cleared by a preceding dozer.

A PPCLI mortar crew works through the night. Every infantry platoon had at least one 2-inch mortar; it was light enough to be easily portable, and the arcing trajectory of its 2 1/2 lb bombs could bypass obstacles and even reach into trenches and dugouts.

Lt.-Col. J.R. Stone, commander of 2PPCLI, finds time for a can of cold beans while he directs action. A veteran of the Second World War, Stone was running a resort in British Columbia when the war started. At Kapyong he helped save his battalion by recognizing where the Chinese attack was most likely to fall.

Soldiers of the PPCLI trying to clean up near the front. After the lines stabilized, the men were often taken to the rear for a day for hot meals, showers, even a movie. Note the U.S. Army–style baggy pants, adopted by Canada after the Second World War.

These members of the Royal Canadian Regiment were lucky enough to hitch a ride on a Canadian half-track ambulance on their way back from patrol. Half-tracks, trucks, jeeps, and, for the first time, helicopters were used to evacuate wounded.

An RCR casualty being evacuated from a regimental aid post on the 38th parallel after the assault on Chail-Li on May 30, 1951. The RCR attack failed in the face of strong Chinese resistance and a night counter-attack.

V

TRIBALS, THUNDERBIRDS, AND SABRES

October 2, 1952. HMCS *Iroquois* had been under fire from North Korean shore batteries before, but with little effect. This day was to be different. *Iroquois* was part of Task Element (TE) 95.22, a small group of mainly U.S. destroyers operating in the Sea of Japan, detailed to bombard the railway along Korea's eastern coast. Their assignment area for the day was about halfway up the coast between the 38th parallel and the Chinese border. Since much of the coast is both mountainous and rocky, the main rail connection between Manchuria and the important port of Wonsan is carved right into the cliffs along the edge of the sea. The rail line was laid out in a fashion not much different from that of the Canadian Pacific Railway along the north shore of Lake Superior, with tunnels carved through solid rock. In their job of cutting off the supplies rolling south, the destroyers of TE 95.22 were assisted by the aircraft of Task Force (TF) 77, which consisted of the fast aircraft carriers of the U.S. Seventh Fleet.

On most days the USN's attack bombers would patrol the railway, striking at rolling stock and the many shore batteries set up to protect the rail line. Then the destroyers, lying just out of reach of the Communist gunners, would move close inshore and blast away at whatever targets they could find. Any ship that managed to destroy an entire train won entry into the "trainbusters" club. This was a most peculiar form of naval warfare, but it was all there was for the American, Canadian, British, and Australian ships which were part of the U.N. forces in Korea.

On October 2, TF 77 was refueling and reprovisioning at sea, which meant that its aircraft were unavailable; the destroyers would have to carry the ball alone. In the morning USS *Marsh* moved inshore and fired at Korean repair crews; it soon came under fire from shore batteries. Since it was best to have one ship firing on the batteries while the other bombarded the rail line, *Iroquois* moved in to join *Marsh*. Twice *Iroquois* fired at the rail line while *Marsh* stood ready to open up at the shore batteries. On the second run, just as *Iroquois* was turning away from the coast, the battery gunners opened fire. The first two shells splashed harmlessly into the sea; the third struck the Canadian ship on the starboard side, near the second gun turret. Lieutenant-Commander John L. Quinn and Able Seaman E.A. Baikie were killed instantly, and several others were critically wounded, including Able Seaman W.M. Burden. *Iroquois* hastily withdrew as shellfire hit the water around her; she suffered no more hits.

Iroquois's medical facilities were inadequate to give Burden the care he needed, but poor weather prevented a helicopter evacuation to one of the larger ships in the area. *Iroquois* was forced to leave TE 95.22 at high speed, headed for the nearest major vessel. It was to no avail; within a short time, Burden died of his wounds. The next morning the dead and wounded were transferred to the oiler USS *Chemung*, and *Iroquois* resumed its patrol duties. The three men were buried in the Commonwealth Cemetery at Yokohama. They would be the only Canadian sailors to die in action in Korea.

When the St. Laurent government had decided to make an armed commitment to the U.N. effort in Korea, it had had few resources available for immediate action. The Royal Canadian Navy was the only arm of the service that was capable of sending units without delay; *Sioux*, *Cayuga*, and *Athabaskan*—three destroyers of the RCN's Pacific Squadron—left their base at Esquimault to sail to Pearl Harbor on July 5, 1950. Captain Jeffry Brock, commanding officer of the *Cayuga*, was named Commander Canadian Destroyers Pacific and placed in charge of the small contingent.

The navy's ability to respond quickly was, unfortunately, no measure of its overall capabilities; like the army and the air force, it had been largely neglected for five years. At the end of the Second World War the RCN had boasted just over 94,000 men and women and over two hundred warships. Immediately after the war it was cut in size but still managed to retain most of the vessels needed by an all-round fighting navy: two cruisers, two small aircraft carriers, destroyers, frigates, minesweepers, and motor torpedo boats. But in 1947 the axe fell, and drastic cuts in defence spending left the RCN a shadow of its wartime self. By the outbreak of war in Korea the navy had been reduced to little more than nine thousand personnel, and only thirteen ships of significant size—none built since the end of the last war. Most of the ships were destroyers of the Tribal class.

In some ways the Tribal-class destroyer packed the punch of a small cruiser. Its main armament consisted of six 4-inch guns mounted two to a turret. Although USN destroyers possessed a more powerful 5-inch gun, many of those in operation in 1950 had only four or five guns in single-gun turrets. The Tribals also mounted eight 40mm rapid-fire weapons which could be used against either surface targets or aircraft, and had a range of anti-submarine weapons and four torpedo tubes as well. The Tribals normally displaced about 1,900 tonnes, were manned by a crew of 250 officers and men, and had a top speed of thirty-six knots. Three of them—*Iroquois*, *Haida*, and *Huron*—had served during the Second World War.

Although the Tribals matched or even outdid the USN destroyers in both punch and speed, they were far from equal in creature comforts. Canadian sailors—"ratings" in naval parlance—still slept in hammocks on thin mattresses without pillows or sheets, much as their British counterparts had done in Nelson's day! They ate where they slept, not in a separate mess, and air conditioning was unknown—a major cause of discomfort in the sweltering summers on the Sea of Japan. While the men lived, ate, and slept in crowded and unsanitary conditions, their officers enjoyed a separate mess with skilled chefs, well-stocked bars, a wardroom replete with wooden and leather furniture, and individual cabins. This disparity had helped create the conditions which had led to a number of mutinies in the years before the Korean War. The first serious incident had occurred aboard *Iroquois* in 1943, the second aboard HMCS *Ontario*, a cruiser, in 1947, and there had been others on Canada's only aircraft carrier—HMCS *Magnificent*—and two destroyers—*Crescent* and *Athabaskan*—in 1949. The mutinies had prompted Minister of National Defence Brooke Claxton to establish a three-man commission under the chairmanship of Vice-Admiral E.R. Mainguy to look into conditions in the navy. The essence of the Mainguy Report was that Canadian ratings would not accept the living conditions and treatment that were commonplace in the Royal Navy, where virtually every RCN officer had undergone his "big ship" training. A conscious effort was needed not only to improve living conditions, but to make the RCN more "Canadian" and less British. Although there was some resistance to this among RCN officers—even the Chief of the Naval Staff, Vice-Admiral H.T.W. Grant, was opposed to the thrust of the report—Claxton set about implementing the recommendations without delay. Nonetheless, little had been accomplished by the time the Korean War broke out.

The three Canadian ships steamed into Sasebo Harbour, Japan on July 30. Within twenty-four hours *Athabaskan* had left for its first assignment in Korean waters, escorting a troop ship to Pusan. For most of the war the

Canadian naval contingent—eight destroyers served in Korea, but never more than three at one time—was stationed on the western or Yellow Sea side of the peninsula, serving under the immediate command of Rear-Admiral W.G. Andrewes of the Royal Navy. Andrewes himself was ultimately responsible to the overall commander of U.N. naval forces in Korean waters, Vice-Admiral C. Turner Joy, USN. Joy answered only to MacArthur.

The Allied intent was to blockade the entire Korean coastline. The British and Commonwealth naval forces were operating primarily in the Yellow Sea, with its many rocks, mud flats, and inlets, because the fast carriers of the USN needed the open sea and deep waters of the Sea of Japan to manoeuvre in the event of enemy attack. Since the RCN was contributing only three destroyers to the naval effort, its ships were used piecemeal wherever they were needed—for shore bombardment, main-force escort duties, carrier radar picket operations, or to provide fire support for landing or evacuation operations. The three vessels rarely operated together.

Since the few small boats that had made up the North Korean "navy" had quickly been disposed of, the U.N. vessels had control of the sea. The lack of any seaborne opposition meant that they could devote most of their attention to the blockade and to destroying supply lines. On the longer east coast—rocky and mountainous virtually to the water—this meant constant attacks against shore targets. On the west coast, with its myriad small islands, U.N. ships also aided South Korean troops in capturing strategic islands held by pockets of Communists. On August 19, for example, *Athabaskan* lay off Taku Chaku island helping R.O.K. forces prepare for a landing; the Canadians lent twenty Lanchester machine carbines and showed the Koreans how to use them (despite the language barrier), provided boats, and stood ready to treat casualties. John Bovey was commander of HMCS *Crusader*, which arrived in Korean waters in the spring of 1952; he later wrote, "A blockade assignment could be either a monotonous patrol or an action-packed opportunity, depending on the initiative, ingenuity, and aggressiveness of the individual commanding officer."

One example of what could happen occurred in late May 1951, when HMCS *Nootka* was on patrol off the east coast. On that particular day the destroyer's target was a railway bridge near Songjin which spanned a gully between two tunnels. *Nootka*'s captain, Commander A.B.F. Fraser-Harris, decided to send a raiding party to check out the rail line, since there was some doubt that it was actually in use; if it was, the raiders could save the ship ammunition by simply planting a demolition charge. Lieutenant Tony Slater was ordered to take a small raiding party ashore in one of the destroyer's motor launches. As the launch neared the rocky shore, fog moved in and Slater and his party could not be seen from the ship.

In the launch, the landing party scanned the shore intently. There was no sign of anyone, and they prepared for their raid. But just as the launch grounded on the beach, a handful of North Korean soldiers who had been lying in wait in the cliffs jumped to the attack. Automatic weapons fire raked the rocky beach, bullets ricocheting off into the sea. Slater's crew fired furiously up at their attackers as the launch backed off the beach and made for the safety of the fog.

That there were no casualties was only because of the Koreans' itchy trigger-fingers. But the trip had not been unsuccessful; the Canadians now knew that the bridge was indeed a worthwhile target, and the landing party had spotted some other possible targets on their brief and eventful excursion.

Whenever the ships moved inshore on raids such as this one, a careful watch was kept for mines. With little in the way of a navy, North Korea was forced to resort to mines to protect its coastal waters; in fact, they were the chief sea weapon used by the Communist side during the war. Lookouts kept a sharp eye out when the destroyers neared shore; once mines were spotted, rifle or machine-gun fire would usually detonate them from a safe distance. Sometimes, however, the water was too shallow for the ships to get close enough. Then men had to get into motor launches or dinghies, pull up right alongside the deadly devices, and attach time-fused demolition charges. On one particular day a crew from *Athabaskan* destroyed four mines in a single morning.

INCHON AND CHINNAMPO

The two most significant operations for the RCN destroyers were the Inchon landings and the evacuation of Chinnampo.

At Inchon Brock was placed in command of TG 91.2, the smaller of the two task groups assigned to the invasion, which consisted of the three Canadian destroyers and a few Korean light-duty vessels. His orders were to provide escort for the transports backing up the invasion and to keep a watch for enemy submarines. Most RCN officers of the time had either trained with the Royal Navy or fought alongside it in the war, and were inclined to disdain the United States Navy for what they saw as its soft life, want of discipline, and lack of tradition. Brock's memoirs reflect his disgust with the Americans' apparent preoccupation with ice cream and steak, rather than good tactical planning. He was convinced that the frequent comings and goings of U.S. naval commanders were due to "the kind of paper records needed for promotion—to say nothing of the acquisition of more medal ribbons, for which there was keen competition". Liking neither the Americans nor his limited role, he approached his task with clear distaste. He was particularly chagrined when a pile of orders arrived on his desk from Admiral Joy's headquarters:

> Having no personal staff officers, I had to use my Ship's Navigator, Lieutenant Andy Collier, and my Signals Officer, Lieutenant Peter May to help me sort out this mess....we went to work examining this extraordinary example of American staffwork gone mad.... Nowhere did I discover any reference to the possible nature of enemy resistance, fog or other forms of adverse weather conditions....

> ...[but] it was comforting to know that the logistics planners had done their work so thoroughly that there would be no shortage of good food, clean water, chocolate bars, and Coca-Cola machines.

Brock was so appalled by the poverty he saw around Inchon that he came up with a rehabilitation plan, later known as Operation Comeback, which did much to improve conditions on the west coast. As part of his plan, Brock himself set up a fishing sanctuary for the islanders whose livelihood had been destroyed by the blockade.

Since there was no enemy opposition at Inchon—let alone submarines!—Brock's ships played a very minor role. They were a larger factor in the evacuation of Chinnampo, the sea outlet for the North Korean capital of Pyongyang. When the Chinese assault of late November 1950 humbled MacArthur's Eighth Army, the survivors fell back on Chinnampo; U.N. naval forces were ordered to prepare for a massive evacuation.

To seaward, Brock was in command of TE 95.12, a small mixed force consisting of one American, two Australian, and three Canadian destroyers, one American minesweeper, and a small number of R.O.K. auxiliary vessels. On the morning of December 4, he received orders from Andrewes to make ready to proceed to Chinnampo to provide cover for withdrawing USN transports and to help in the destruction of the large stockpile of food, ammunition, and fuel which could not be removed but could not be allowed to fall into enemy hands.

Chinnampo lies at the head of a treacherous estuary with many sand-bars, conflicting tidal currents, and poorly marked channels. To make matters worse, the waters had been heavily mined by the North Koreans. Not only did the main channel to Chinnampo have to be swept by minesweepers, but the ships had to be careful not to run aground or they might block the channel and present enemy gunners with a shooting gallery full of trapped warships and troop-filled transports.

Upon receiving his orders, Brock made ready to sail up the estuary at first light. He decided that his ship, HMCS *Cayuga*, and the destroyer USS *Forrest Royal* would stay out to sea at a pre-arranged spot to meet the reinforcing ships that Andrewes was sending to help with the evacuation; the rest of the force would proceed to Chinnampo.

Just after nightfall on the 4th, Brock received a message marked emergency priority from one of the transports in the harbour: "We are uncovered. Take necessary action immediately." The message was cryptic, but Brock interpreted it to mean that Communist troops had broken through U.N. lines and were rushing towards the port. Fearing that the capture of Chinnampo was imminent, he decided to risk a dangerous night passage up the estuary, although the night was pitch-black and the tide was almost at low ebb. In the course of the night HMCS *Sioux* and HMAS *Warramunga* ran aground and were forced to return to the open sea to check for damage, but the others pressed on in an extraordinary feat of night navigation. Brock remembered it well:

> "...ease just a little, Cox'n—that looks better—what's the ship's head now?"
>
> "Zero seven seven, sir."
>
> "Very good. Midships."
>
> "Midships, sir. Wheel amidships...."

And so it went—hour after hour. Weaving in and out amongst the shoals and sandbanks; depth sounder running constantly; seamen in the chains with lead and line maintaining their constant singsong chanting of depths....by 3:00 in the morning, I could see the lights of the city up ahead, glowing red on the horizon, but I could hear no sound of guns, bombs, or demolitions.

After the difficult passage *Cayuga* tied up alongside the city's main docks, where Brock beheld, to his "utter amazement and bitter anger, a whole city ablaze with lights and peacefully sleeping it off."

The menace from the north was very real, even if the panicky message had been somewhat exaggerated, and Brock was put in charge of naval defence during the evacuation. For the whole next day Chinnampo harbour was abustle with activity as transports loaded and prepared to depart, refugees jammed aboard junks and sampans, and whatever could possibly be loaded aboard ship was removed. Late on the afternoon of December 5, the last of the transports departed, escorted by part of Brock's small force. The rest of his ships then turned their guns on the docks, warehouses, and port facilities, while making every effort to avoid hitting refugees or civilian property. It made quite a sight; as Brock noted, "Whenever a fresh oil tank was hit, which was often, sprays of molten glowing metal were radiated in all directions, adding spectacularly to the show." But he had not forgotten his humanitarian concerns, and he ordered that the small craft still on the beaches should be left intact for the refugees, despite the risk that they would fall into enemy hands. Within an hour there was little else left for the enemy to use. The fires blazed all night; at first light the remaining ships in Brock's group left.

For the most part, though, the naval war was simply boring. The officers and men amused themselves with contests to see which ship could refuel the fastest at sea and who could score the most points in the "train-busters" club, but there was little to break the monotony of long patrols. It may well be that the most exciting thing to happen was the discovery that the ship's surgeon serving aboard HMCS *Cayuga*, Surgeon Lieutenant Joseph Cyr, was not a doctor at all! He was in reality Ferdinand Waldo Demara, an American who spent a large part of his life pretending to be other people—the "Great Imposter" of book, music, and film fame. When Demara's presence aboard *Cayuga* was discovered by the real Doctor Cyr, who lived in New Brunswick, Demara was quickly rushed back to Canada, released from the navy, and deported. His shipmates found it hard to believe the news; Demara had competently treated several Allied casualties, including an R.O.K. guerrilla with a bullet through the lungs, without revealing his total lack of medical training.

The RCN maintained a presence in Korean waters until September 1955. In all, eight Canadian destroyers completed twenty-one tours of duty, and over 3,500 officers and men of the RCN served aboard those ships. In comparison to the naval effort mounted by the United States, or even that of Britain, it was not a major contribution to the war effort. Given the small size of the RCN destroyer force at that time—eleven ships, of which no more than nine were ever in commission at a time—it was nothing less than remarkable.

THUNDERBIRDS

October 2, 1950. Somewhere over the North Pacific the crew of the RCAF North Star attended to their tasks as the plane droned through the darkness, leaving the base at Shemya, in the Aleutian Islands, far behind. Flying Officer Donald Payne, the pilot, kept a watchful eye on his instrument panel, while behind him the navigator did his best to plot their course along an invisible track connecting Shemya with Haneda airfield, near Tokyo. The plane was carrying a mixed load of spare parts and other supplies for the U.N. forces in Korea and was on the last outward leg of a journey that had started at McChord Air Force Base, near Tacoma, Washington, many hours before. This was the longest and most difficult leg of the journey; it normally took ten and a half hours, it was flown against strong headwinds, it was usually over thick cloud cover or through pitch dark, and there was no LORAN or other electronic navigational aid to guide the aircraft on its course. To make matters worse, the flight path passed perilously near the Kamchatka Peninsula, where Soviet fighters waited to pounce on any plane invading their airspace. The Russians filled the airwaves with music, choirs, anything they could use to jam the radio frequencies flyers used to keep in contact with the world during the long, lonely flight. Navigating here was a matter of dead reckoning, of astral shots through the plexiglass dome atop the fuselage when the sun or stars were visible, and of calculating the aircraft's drift to the left or right of its intended track. Sometimes it was also sheer blind luck.

About halfway into the flight, the North Star suddenly bucked and jerked. The instruments monitoring the right inboard engine went crazy and engine rpms climbed dangerously towards the red line. Payne tried to adjust the throttle and fuel mixture to bring the runaway engine under control; there was no response. He tried to feather the engine—to turn the propeller blades sideways to the airstream to prevent a dangerous power imbalance—but the feathering mechanism would not function. The engine began to vibrate badly, threatening to tear loose from the wing, which might rip out fuel lines and expose the wing tanks to explosion. Even if that did not happen, Payne knew, the propeller could break loose and slice into the fuselage.

Payne put the North Star into a wide bank and headed back to Shemya, his closest possible base, while putting out a "mayday" call over the radio. Reducing speed on the other engines and telling his crew to prepare to ditch in the cold North Pacific waters, he brought the plane lower over the ocean and nursed it through what seemed an endless flight—1,100 long kilometres—back to the Shemya runway. Plane and crew were saved and Payne was awarded the Air Force Cross for his "superior skill and resourcefulness", in the words of the official citation.

The Royal Canadian Air Force was the second of Canada's armed services to join the U.N. "police action" in Korea. On July 7, 1950, No. 426 (Transport) Squadron, based at Dorval Airport, Montreal, was alerted to transfer its operations to McChord and begin flying troops and supplies as far as Japan under the overall authority of the U.S. Military Air Transport Service (MATS). Administrative control would stay with National Defence Headquarters in Ottawa. On July 25, following a farewell ceremony at Dorval, six North Stars loaded with aircrew, ground personnel, and spare parts took off. They flew to Ottawa for a fly-past over Parliament Hill, where Mackenzie King's body was lying in state, and proceeded to McChord. On July 27 three of the aircraft departed McChord for Japan.

Canada's air contribution to the Korean War was limited to the operations of 426 Squadron and some fighter-jet missions flown by a handful of RCAF pilots in USAF aircraft. The fact is that at the outbreak of the war the RCAF was barely able to take on even this limited responsibility. Like the other services, it had been cut back drastically after the end of the Second World War. Its entire heavy-bomber force had been disbanded. Its first-line fighter strength consisted of a number of squadrons of propeller-driven Mustang fighters which had entered service as a stopgap measure in mid-1947, and de Havilland Vampire jets acquired in early 1948. Although the Mustang had made a signal contribution to winning the air war over Europe, it was obsolete by the outbreak of the Korean War. The Vampire, a single-seat fighter jet designed and built in Britain, was little better; with a top speed of only 850km/h, it was dangerously slow compared to the 1,075km/h Soviet-built MiG-15. Besides, there were barely enough Vampires in Canada to provide an adequate defence against the growing Soviet bomber threat—and the U.S.S.R. had tested its first atomic bomb in September 1949. Although first-class equipment was on order—the American-designed F-86 Sabre, assembled at the Canadair plant in Montreal, and the Canadian-designed Avro CF-100 "Canuck"—there was not enough of it early enough to allow its use in Korea. The first RCAF Sabres did not become operational until August 1950, while the CF-100 entered service only in late June 1951.

If an air contribution was to be made, therefore, it had to be from the RCAF's contingent of transport aircraft. Even here the selection was slim. There were several squadrons of Dakotas—the twin-engine military transport version of the Douglas DC-3—but these had neither the range nor the carrying capacity to be of any use in the Korean airlift. The main strength of the RCAF's transport capacity was the four-engine DC-4M2 North Star, designed and built by Canadair. The RCAF had ordered a number of the very first of the production run and assigned them to 426 Squadron.

No. 426 (Thunderbird) Squadron had started life during the Second World War as a Halifax heavy-bomber squadron but had been disbanded at the end of hostilities. It was made operational once again in August 1946, with elements of No. 164 Squadron, which had flown Dakotas and twin-engine Lockheed Lodestars during the war. The Thunderbirds were given the chief responsibility for northern supply operations, flying freight and personnel to the growing number of weather stations and other military facilities in the high Arctic. At the outbreak of the Korean War they were Canada's only long-range heavy-transport squadron.

THE KOREAN AIRLIFT

The Korean airlift—the massive supply line needed to support U.N. operations in the peninsula—primarily involved the heavy transports of the USAF's 61st and 62nd Troop Carrier Groups. It was based on a number of daily flights across the North Pacific following the same basic stages: from McChord to Elmendorf Air Force Base near Anchorage, Alaska (2,100 km); from Elmendorf to Shemya (also about 2,100 km); and from Shemya to Haneda (2,400 km). From Haneda, cargoes and troops were flown into Korea aboard USAF transports; the RCAF was specifically ordered not to send planes into Korea, although a number of 426 Squadron personnel did make the trip aboard MATS planes. Once unloaded, the aircraft were flown east across the Central Pacific from Tokyo to Wake Island, Honolulu, San Francisco, and back to McChord. (The different routes east and west were dictated by the prevailing winds.)

The aircraft were kept on the move almost constantly, with minimal rest periods built in for proper maintenance, but the crews could not be expected to follow such a killing pace. At Shemya, Haneda, Wake Island, and Honolulu, crews disembarked for a forty-eight-hour rest and handed their planes over to the crews that had preceded them. Thus it took the air-craft approximately eighty hours to complete the 17,600 km circuit but the crews usually made the round trip in eleven days.

Something of the flavour of the airlift was captured by journalist Pierre Berton, who accompanied one of the crews on a trip ferrying tires, machinery, generators, and spare parts in early 1951. The leg from McChord to Anchorage was routine:

> For nine monotonous hours we flew north and west with only the sea showing grey and choppy through the ragged clouds. Occasionally the far-off vapour trail of another aircraft, a chalk scrawl in the blue, served to emphasize the loneliness of the empty world of sky around us.

Berton describes the navigator doing "things with a slide rule" and the radio operator telegraphing weather reports back to McChord while the air traffic assistant served up bacon, eggs, and beans on pink plates.

But when they finally reached Shemya there were strong cross-winds, and the plane had to be diverted east to Adak, a narrow island airstrip blotted out by clouds and surrounded by high mountains. They were talked in by an air traffic controller glued to his radar screen:

> Ahead and directly below, two parallel chains of lights loomed suddenly, framed on either side by the black bulks of Adak's cliffs. A moment later we had landed. It was 5 a.m. Aleutian time, 8 a.m. McChord time. "Twenty-five hours," said [the pilot], who had been on the go steadily since 7 a.m. "Not a bad day's work."

No. 426 Squadron's original deployment of six aircraft was soon increased to its full wartime complement of twelve. The Americans did what they could to accommodate the Canadians at McChord, but as the major staging-point for the airlift, McChord was crowded to bursting. As more USAF aircraft became available for the airlift, there was less need for the 426's planes, which were sorely needed back in Canada. Towards the end of June 1951, the Thunderbirds moved back to Dorval, but they continued to participate on a reduced scale until June 9, 1954, when a 426 North Star flew the 599th and last mission.

Although the flights to Japan and back tested the crews' endurance and navigational skills, they were more boring than anything else. Nevertheless, mishaps did happen. In April 1951, a North Star descending into Ashiya, Japan was given incorrect instructions from Ground Control Approach and brushed a hilltop. The plane suffered a dented nose cone

Sabre, H.L. Soucy. Canadian pilots jumped at the chance to fly the new F-86 Sabre in Korea, although it meant being posted on exchange to the USAF. This painting was done during the war, and presented to 444 Squadron of the RCAF for Christmas 1954. (CWM 82006)

Welcome Party, Ted Zuber. As a forward platoon sergeant greets two newly arrived soldiers, a grimmer welcome is offered by Chinese corpses frozen on the ridge, their eyes pecked out by birds. Zuber was in Korea as a young soldier, and it was years before he captured his memories on canvas for the Canadian War Museum. (CWM 90026)

First Kill, Ted Zuber. When Zuber was a novice scout/sniper in Korea, his first shot at an enemy sniper moving into position was a miss—"My observer was quite disgusted"—but his second shot was a kill. The investigating patrol found an American infrared "snooperscope" on the body; "He had obviously planned to target our fellows returning from patrol in the dark." (CWM 90031)

Contact, Ted Zuber. On 23 October 1952, the Chinese attacked and overran the American-held Hill 355, leaving the Canadian Van Doos on the neighbouring saddle terribly exposed. The Canadians held the position throughout the night until an American counterattack pushed the enemy back. (CWM 90033)

"o-Group"—B Squadron LdSH (RC)—Wainwright 1983, G. G. Jamieson. It wasn't all peacekeeping between Korea and the Gulf War. Here, officers and senior NCOs receive their orders for the next stage of a NATO exercise; the canvassed space between two camouflaged vehicles is being used as a command centre. Doctor Jamieson was medical officer with the Lord Strathcona's Horse. (CWM 84040)

De Havilland DHC-4 Caribou in Repair—Lahr, Germany, Tom Bjarnason. In the years between Korea and the Gulf War, Canadian pilots carried out more prosaic tasks—like delivering observers and supplies for U.N. peacekeeping missions, and evacuating refugees and wounded. (CWM 72005)

Night Run, Ted Zuber. This eerily Arctic landscape is in fact the desert of Qatar. Terrorism was a constant concern during the Gulf War, and the Grizzlies went out regularly to check the perimeter fences. (Courtesy Ted Zuber and DND)

Gas Attack TOPP *High,* Ted Zuber. Troops rush for a shelter during a Scud alert, while yellow lighting inside and mercury vapour lamps outside create a nightmarish effect. "TOPP High" is the maximum level of alert. (Courtesy Ted Zuber and DND Ottawa)

and considerable damage to its systems, but fortunately the crew had no ill effects beyond those from the bourbon "prescribed" by the sympathetic USAF! At the end of December 1953 a North Star was landing in a ferocious cross-wind at Shemya when the aircraft started to skid sideways on the snowy runway and was literally blown into a gully, nose down, but none of the eight passengers and crew was hurt. Three days later a second North Star was climbing out of Vancouver when an engine overheated. The pilot turned back but was hampered by heavy icing on the wings, and as the plane touched down the nose wheel and the starboard wing dug into the ground. The aircraft cartwheeled, skidded across the runway, and broke up. Although aviation gas poured out of the ruptured fuel tanks, nothing caught fire and no one was killed—a miracle since a volunteer on the crash crew reported that "the passengers were lighting cigarettes as they got out"!

Despite these mishaps, 426 Squadron compiled a remarkable record in the four years it was involved in the airlift. Its twelve aircraft flew some 13,000 personnel and approximately 3,200 tonnes of freight without serious injury or fatalities, and only two planes were lost. Given the primitive state of both aircraft and navigational aids in the early 1950s, it was a record to be proud of.

SABRES

March 31, 1951. As the F-86-E Sabre jets of the USAF's 334th Fighter Interceptor Squadron of the 4th Fighter Interceptor Wing (4th FIW) moved north into North Korean airspace, Flight Lieutenant J.A. Omer Lévesque of the RCAF became especially vigilant, constantly looking back to check if enemy fighters were trying to creep in behind the formation, and peering intently overhead to spot any fighters diving from above. Just ahead and below him was his element leader, USAF Major Edward Fletcher, also flying a Sabre. Eleven other Sabres and a formation of B-29 medium bombers filled out the group.

Each fighter squadron was composed of three sections of four fighters, and each section was made up of two pairs or "elements". A section flew in a "finger four" arrangement, with the fighters positioned much like the fingertips of an outstretched hand. The "finger four" was first used by Luftwaffe pilots during the Spanish Civil War and has survived into the jet age as a formation that offers both great flexibility and mutually interlocking protection. As Fletcher's wingman, Lévesque had the job of flying above and to the left of Fletcher, sticking with him through thick and thin, keeping enemy fighters off his tail. As leader of the two-plane element, Fletcher had to decide when, where, and how to engage enemy fighters, and to swoop back if need be to help Lévesque.

The B-29s were to bomb bridges across the Yalu River at Sinuiju, North Korea, in an effort to stem the flow of men and supplies coming in from Manchuria. To avoid provoking China into widening the war even further, the U.N. command had ordered its air forces—which were made up almost entirely of fighters and bombers of the USAF—not to fly north of the Yalu. Although reconnaissance planes often crossed the line, the fighters and bombers generally obeyed this rule, and thus the Yalu became the "bombline" while the country beyond was a sanctuary for Communist aircraft. The airspace south of the Yalu quickly became known as "MiG Alley", since the MiG-15s which formed the main fighter force of the enemy rarely ventured more than fifty kilometres south of the river.

At jet-age speeds, tiny dots materialize into swept-wing fighters spitting cannon shells in the blink of an eye. On this day the MiGs hit Lévesque's formation just as the bombers neared the target. Rolling to the left, Fletcher followed one of the MiGs; Lévesque rolled right and swung in behind another, holding his fire as the pilot first spiralled downward in a tight turn, then snapped upward in a steep climb into the sun. Then, apparently satisfied that he had evaded his pursuer, the MiG pilot resumed straight and level flight. Off to the left but 1,800 metres behind, Levesque pushed down on the firing button and sent a stream of .50 calibre bullets hosing towards the MiG. Pieces flew off the enemy fighter. Lévesque then closed to less than 500 metres and fired again. Pieces blew off the left wing, and the MiG snapped violently to the right and began to descend, upside down, towards Manchuria, where it crashed and exploded. Omer Lévesque was the first (but not the last) Canadian to destroy a MiG in the Korean War.

Lévesque was no novice to air fighting. During the Second World War he had shot down four German fighters before being downed himself and taken prisoner; after the war he had stayed in the military and risen to the rank of flight lieutenant, and he had joined the 4th FIW as an exchange pilot. He stayed with the 4th FIW until March 1951, and when he returned to Canada he brought back the American Air Medal and the United States Distinguished Flying Cross (DFC).

Although no Canadian fighter squadrons were sent to Korea, Canadian pilots were anxious to get combat experience on the Sabre before it became Canada's first-line fighter jet serving with NATO in Europe. The USAF was more than happy to give them first-hand experience against the MiGs, so Canada and the U.S. worked out an agreement whereby Canada would send pilots to Korea, preferably with some prior Sabre experience, to serve for six months or fifty missions, whichever came first. Since he had been the pioneer, Lévesque was put in charge of pilot selection for the RCAF. Eventually seventeen other Canadian pilots served there; they accounted for nine MiGs destroyed, two probably destroyed, and ten damaged.

Although the Korean skies were the scene of the world's first jet-to-jet air battles, those battles followed a much more ritualized pattern than the air fighting of the Second World War. The pattern was dictated both by the weapons used and by the political limits the U.N. forces placed on themselves. In many ways the fighting more closely resembled the combat of the First World War, but at much higher speeds and greater altitudes.

The North Koreans had used a variety of propeller-driven fighter-bombers to attack ground troops at the start of the war, but those aircraft had been no match for the Americans' straight-winged jets (the F-80 Shooting Stars and F-84 Thunderjets of the USAF, and the Grumman F9F-4 Panthers of the U.S. Navy) and MiG-15s were soon deployed. With a top speed of 1,075km/h, an operational ceiling of 15,545 metres, and an armament of one 37mm and two 23mm cannon, the swept-wing fighter was far superior to anything the U.N. forces had available in Korea or Japan. The Sabre was quickly rushed into battle while the other fighters were relegated to a ground-support role.

Even the Sabre was not quite the equal of the MiG. It was about as fast but it could neither fly as high nor fight in the rarefied air above 14,500 metres. Its six .50 calibre machine-guns could pump out far more rounds than the cannon of the MiG, and at a higher muzzle velocity, but it also took a lot more .50 calibre bullets to bring a fighter down. Put simply, the MiG was better at higher altitudes, the Sabre better at lower ones.

The Sabres carried out daily fighter sweeps from their bases near Seoul into the airspace of MiG Alley in an effort to entice the Communist pilots into combat. They also flew in support of the B-29s and as top cover for fighter-bombers whenever they carried out missions deep into North Korea. But the pilots were seriously hamstrung by the official decision not to fly across the Yalu River. It gave the MiGs a number of major advantages: virtually all the fighting was done above Communist soil in northern North Korea; the pilots could count on their radar to vector them towards the U.S. fighters, whereas Sabre pilots were usually too far from home; and the Communists enjoyed a convenient refuge close at hand. All these factors, combined with the MiG's height advantage, meant that Communist pilots could pick and choose their combat opportunities. Thus most of the air-to-air combat involved small formations, usually only one or two elements, battling it out as lone knights of the skies.

It was fortunate indeed for the Sabre pilots that only a few of their adversaries were really any good. These hot pilots—"honchos" they were called by the Sabre pilots, from the Japanese for "boss"—were probably instructors and were almost certainly Russians or East Europeans. Allied pilots reported that the majority of the MiG pilots—North Koreans or Chinese—seemed to have little stomach for air fighting; some would eject at the first opportunity. With all the disadvantages they laboured under, Sabre pilots still achieved a kill ratio of approximately 14-1—mainly as a result of their superior skill and tactics.

CANADA'S TOP GUNS

If success in air fighting is measured in damage inflicted on the enemy, Flying Officer E.A. Glover and Squadron Leader J.D. Lindsay were Canada's "Top Guns" in Korea. Glover had flown Hurricane fighters and Typhoon fighter-bombers with the RCAF before being shot down and taken prisoner in May 1943. He joined the 4th FIW at Kimpo, near Seoul, in June 1952 but never even saw a MiG until late August. On August 30 he damaged two MiGs in a whirling dogfight. Nine days later he was flying wing in the second of two elements when a pair of MiGs were intercepted. The MiGs made a hard right turn which threw off the other three Sabres but Glover, flying high and to the right, pulled around and opened fire, scoring hits on the wingman. The two MiGs went into a crash dive, zooming down from over 12,000 metres to just under 5,000, with Glover close behind and firing all the way. The leader, although shot up, escaped into Manchuria, but the wingman tried to pull up, lost control, and crashed.

Glover scored his second kill the very next day, when his squadron was escorting a fighter-bomber mission; he spotted a MiG swinging in behind the tail of an F-84 Thunderjet and shot it down. He collected his third victim one week later when three Sabres attacked a force of twenty MiGs; Glover set a MiG ablaze and it went spinning out of control. He would receive both the American and the Commonwealth DFC.

During the Second World War, Squadron Leader Lindsay had flown Spitfires with No. 403 Squadron, accounting for six and a half German planes (when two Allied aircraft shot down one enemy plane, each scored a half-victory). He joined the 51st FIW in Korea in July 1952 and shot down his first MiG on October 11, while leading a flight of four Sabres near the Yalu. His epic battle, however, came on November 26, while he was flying lead in a two-plane element with Second Lieutenant Harold E. Fischer of the USAF. At close to 14,000 metres, Lindsay led Fischer in an attack on no fewer than twenty-one MiGs. As Lindsay and Fischer opened fire, two MiGs clawed around to the right and pulled into a steep climb. The two Sabres followed them, Lindsay concentrating on the leader. Suddenly two other MiGs jumped Fischer. Lindsay carved a tight turn and came to the aid of his wingman, heading into the attackers. At a distance of less than 300 metres and an angle of approximately 90 degrees, he opened fire, and the MiG pilot jettisoned his canopy and bailed out. It was no wonder Lindsay was known as the "MiG Magnet". He would take home an American DFC to add to his collection.

Not all missions were so successful. Flying Officer R.D. Carew was at 13,000 metres over North Korean territory when his Sabre's engine flamed out. As he began a long, harrowing glide towards home, the other Sabres moved in to cover him. When he was just over 2,000 metres he was still far behind enemy lines, so he headed for water before bailing out; he made a neat landing on an island and was promptly picked up and flown home.

None of the Canadian pilots serving in Korea was killed, but one—Squadron Leader Andy MacKenzie—was shot down and spent two years in captivity. MacKenzie was an experienced veteran, credited with eight and a half German fighters in the Second World War. He was posted to Korea in mid-November 1952 and flew his first four missions without catching sight of a MiG. On his fifth mission—December 5, 1952—he was flying wingman for USAF Major Jack Saunders when they spotted some twenty MiGs at just over 12,000 metres, across the Yalu River. Suddenly two MiGs peeled away from the formation and dove towards the Sabres. Cannons firing, they passed below Saunders and MacKenzie. The Canadian put his Sabre into a diving turn, to follow them, and called for Saunders to cover him, but the American pilot turned in the opposite direction. Since it was MacKenzie's job to fly wing for Saunders, he pulled back in a climbing turn. All at once, out of nowhere, a burst of fire blew off his canopy and destroyed his controls. Although the media were told that MacKenzie had been shot down by a MiG, the truth was that another U.S. pilot had mistaken him for a MiG about to attack Saunders.

His plane mortally stricken, MacKenzie bailed out. He was quickly taken prisoner and was held in a Communist POW camp for two years, enduring months of constant interrogation, isolation, deprivation, and the usual array of psychological tricks. Like a handful of other Allied flyers, he was kept in captivity long after the end of the war, with the Chinese not admitting that he was still alive. "I felt completely frustrated, defeated and helpless," he later told *Weekend* magazine. "There seemed to be a continual feeling of oppression hanging over me.... It finally reached the point where I had to burst my bonds or suffocate." Eventually he fabricated a statement in accordance with his captors' demands, saying that he had been ordered to fly over China, where he had been shot down and captured. In December 1954 he was finally released.

Canada's contribution to the air war over Korea was admittedly small, but it was high quality. The Canadian pilots shot down or damaged far more of the enemy than they themselves lost, and the pilots learned about jet-age fighting. They also learned about fighting alongside American pilots; since the RCAF and USAF were partners in the defence of North America and allies in the defence of Europe, these were valuable lessons. Fortunately the price was low enough that the lessons were worth the cost.

Canada sent six Tribal Class destroyers to Korea: *Athabaskan, Cayuga, Haida, Huron, Iroquois,* and *Nootka.* The Tribals typically had six 4-inch guns and eight 40mm Bofors guns, as well as torpedoes, depth charges, and the Squid mortar. Here, *Nootka* has been assigned to shell a bridge at Songjin; while the destroyer stands off, its cutters use a line to sweep the channel for mines.

Nootka's crew prepare to board a Korean fishing junk for inspection; such junks regularly laid mines and carried North Korean soldiers and weapons to the islands. Junks found carrying contraband were destroyed.

Nootka takes on ammunition from USS *Virgo*. Note the heavy anchor chains on *Nootka*'s deck and the twin guns in its forward turrets. American supply ships carried comforts like fresh meat and ice cream—one major reason why the RCN preferred U.S. supplies to the mutton of the RN.

HMCS *Sioux* sails through an icefield in February 1952. Note the Union Jack tied to the forward turret as a recognition signal. Although *Sioux* bore a Tribal name, it was in fact a former RN "V" class destroyer, slightly smaller than a Tribal, and sporting two 4.7 inch guns in single turrets instead of six 4-inch guns.

Inside the plot room of *Athabaskan*. The plot room is the heart of a warship; in dimmed light men watch the radar screens, monitor the RTF (radio-telephone), and attend to the ship's sonar array.

Inside the cockpit of a North Star on its way to Korea in April 1951. In essence the North Star married the fuselage of a Douglas DC-4 to the Rolls–Royce–built Merlin engine. The result was a plane with better range, speed, and carrying capacity.

Nootka bombards the enemy coast in May 1951. These night actions were usually directed at trains, as sparks from the smokestacks gave the gunners something to shoot at. In July 1952 the "trainbusters" club was formed, for ships proven to have destroyed at least one train; despite their small numbers, Canadian ships claimed 8 of the 28 trains demolished after that date.

North Stars being serviced at McChord Air Force Base. Although much of the equipment was American, the ground crews were Canadian, and they worked around the clock to keep the aircraft flying. The base was so overcrowded that a number of temporary wooden "nose hangars" had to be constructed as a stopgap to shelter ground crews carrying out major maintenance.

Flight-Lieutenant A. Lambres climbs into his F-86 Sabre; Lambres damaged two MiGs during his tour. In the background, other Sabres stand in sandbag revetments. The checkerboard pattern on the tail was for squadron recognition, and a yellow stripe around the fuselage distinguished these jets from the MiG-15s, which were also silver and swept-winged.

Ernest Glover poses with a T-33 trainer. Glover destroyed three MiG-15 fighters and damaged three others during his tour with the USAF, and was awarded the DFC. Like most Sabre pilots, Glover was a Second World War veteran—the *Top Gun* movie image of boyish young fighter jocks was not true of either Korea or Vietnam.

Squadron Leader Andy MacKenzie with his Sabre. MacKenzie was accidentally shot down by a U.S. jet and became the only Canadian fighter pilot taken prisoner. The official story was that he had been downed by a MiG, and he faithfully supported that fiction until 1980.

VI
WITH THE 1ST
COMMONWEALTH DIVISION

In July the weather in central Korea gives no hint of the cold, vicious winds and heavy snowfalls that plague the land in the depths of winter. Green rice shoots poke up through the water of rice paddies that in January are frozen so solid that trucks and jeeps can drive over them. The sun beats down on rocky hillsides and coniferous trees, and the land dries out. Thick dust swirls up in the wake of passing vehicles. The mud of spring is just a memory.

On just such a day the 1st Commonwealth Division was born, when the Australian, Canadian, Indian, New Zealand, and United Kingdom contingents were combined on July 28, 1951 under the command of General J.H. Cassells of the British army. The idea of an integrated Commonwealth division had been mooted by both British and Canadian officers as far back as July 1950, when both countries were studying the question of whether or not to commit ground forces to Korea. The plan was rooted not in any sense of Commonwealth solidarity, but in practical necessity. Canada had only one brigade group in the field; it would have been the height of folly, not to mention extremely expensive, to set up a fully functioning system of supply depots, storage, recreational and leave facilities, and transportation for such a small contingent. And it was natural for the Canadian military to want to link itself to a British formation. Canada's forces in Korea were still equipped with almost entirely British-designed weapons. Furthermore, the many veterans in the Canadian contingent were used to British tactics and British traditions.

The Commonwealth Division was one of several that made up I U.S. Corps, commanded by Lieutenant-General J.W. "Iron Mike" O'Daniel, which was itself part of the Eighth U.S. Army. In matters military, "Iron Mike" was boss and passed orders down from General James A. Van Fleet, commander of the U.S. Eighth Army, and I U.S. Corps to Cassells; it was then up to Cassells to assign tasks to his brigade commanders and support services. The division was composed of the 25th Canadian Infantry Brigade (CIB), the 28th British Commonwealth Infantry Brigade (made up of British, Australian, and New Zealand troops), the 29th British Infantry Brigade, and a number of artillery, armour, anti-aircraft, engineer, and medical units. The Belgian Battalion was also attached to it. At the time of its formation the division held a 10,000-metre section of the front line along the Imjin River, anchored between the 1st R.O.K. Division on the left and the 25th U.S. Infantry Division on the right.

If practical necessity alone had not been enough to convince Canada and the other dominions to throw their lot in with the British, the April fighting would have provided the clinching argument. During that battle, there had been a tragic breakdown in communications between I U.S. Corps headquarters and Brigadier Tom Brodie, commander of the 29th Brigade. When Brodie had told headquarters over the radio that things were getting "a bit sticky" for the surrounded Gloucesters, they had failed to grasp how desperate the situation was and had refused permission to withdraw; they had simply not understood the nuances of British under-statement. As a result, the Gloucesters were massacred.

What the Commonwealth forces needed was a divisional command insulating the fighting battalions from the Americans, who had little understanding of the subtle but important differences between the British and American way of doing things. As Lieutenant-Colonel N.G. Wilson-Smith of the 1PPCLI later put it:

> when 1st Commonwealth Division was formed...its headquarters stood between U.S. Corps Headquarters and our forces. From this time on, at the Battalion level especially, the direct effects of serving under U.S. command were fairly well filtered out.

Wilson-Smith noted that U.S. artillery support, a handful of U.S. artillery observers, visits by the odd general, and "a plentiful supply of Hershey bars and American cigarettes" were the "only tangible evidences of higher control".

That was true for almost everyone but the wounded. This was the war of the MASH unit—the U.S. Mobile Army Surgical Hospital—a prefabricat-ed complex set up as near the front lines as possible, to receive casualties by helicopter. For the first time in the history of warfare, seriously wound-ed soldiers were able to undergo advanced medical treatment, including surgery, within minutes of being hit. At the MASH unit American doctors and nurses repaired the worst of the casualties, who were then evacuated by road and air to Seoul and on to hospitals in Tokyo.

When the 25th CIB was being formed, the 25th Canadian Field Ambulance had been formed with it, and its doctors and nurses would serve with the Commonwealth Division until the end of the war. Although the American system of helicopter evacuation and MASH units worked extremely well, it was thought important, as one report noted, "to provide Canadian medical attention for Canadian casualties at all levels where such attention is necessitated." Put simply, it was important in terms of morale for the wounded to be taken care of by someone who was not a foreigner. For this reason, a Canadian Field Surgical Team—a Canadian MASH—was formed before the end of the fighting.

Medical care was extremely good in Korea. For every 1,000 Canadians wounded, only 34 died from their wounds, compared to 66 in the Second World War and 114 in the First World War. Some of this difference was due to better drugs, especially penicillin and sulfa and various drugs that lessened the effects of shock and blood loss, and some to the use of armoured vests, which became standard equipment for Canadian soldiers (as they were for U.S. soldiers) in the summer of 1952. But much of the improvement was directly due to the speed with which casualties were brought to the medical units.

Korea was a swamp of infectious diseases. Haemorrhagic fever, caused by a virus carried by a chigger mite, could kill—up to 7 per cent of the U.N. soldiers contracting it died. Malaria was more easily avoided through preventive medicines. Soldiers treated at the Commonwealth Hospital in Tokyo were more subject to jaundice than those in U.S. hospitals because of the re-use of intravenous equipment; the Americans used plastic disposables. After the war two Canadian army doctors concluded, "The Korean conflict may have been a localized war but it was a dirty, difficult one. It served as a training and testing ground and, as in the case of all wars, medical knowledge was advanced."

THE AFTERMATH OF KAPYONG

Back on May 4, 1951, not long after the Chinese offensive against Hill 677 had spent itself, the remainder of the 25th Canadian Infantry Brigade docked at Pusan and the Canadians crowded the rails for their first glimpse—and smell—of Korea. They whistled and stomped as a U.S. Army band played, "If I knew you were coming I'd have baked a cake." On the dock was the obligatory South Korean reception party and Brigadier Rockingham, who had flown over in advance of his men. He told the press that he had "never seen troops as willing and anxious to do their jobs as these fellows", but he also stressed that they would remain near Pusan for some time yet to complete their unit training. After about ten days the brigade moved north to join the British 28th Infantry Brigade (which had relieved the 27th Brigade), near the Han River. Both units were attached to the U.S. 25th Infantry Division and participated in a counter-offensive which began May 20 and was designed to push the Chinese back across the 38th parallel. One week later, the 2PPCLI joined the counter-offensive as well.

As the U.N. forces approached the 38th parallel, the previous pattern of battle was repeated. Once again small units, usually no larger than companies, assaulted the Chinese, who were invariably dug in on strategic hilltops. These were short, sharp, set-piece battles, with little of the sweep and movement that modern warfare was supposed to be all about. The flavour was well captured by Derek Pearcy, a Reuters-Australia correspondent, in describing an RCR patrol setting out at 6:00 A.M. after a night of hectic preparations:

> Keyed up with training and waiting behind the lines, they started out carefully.... Their small arms were at the ready, their eyes alert for the slightest movement ahead of them.
>
> The first shot rang out. The infantrymen ducked for cover, fanned out, and opened fire at a hill on their flank.
>
> There was a short silence, then a rattle of Sten guns, then silence again.
>
> The Canadians emerged cautiously from shelter and closed in warily on a camouflaged dugout.... A young Canadian looked intently into the dugout, laughed a little, then waved the others on.
>
> By mid-afternoon the Canadians were under heavy harassing fire.... From the gnarled mountain on their left came the continuous crack of small-arms fire....
>
> The infantrymen crossed a field to scale the mountainside from the north. Chinese entrenched on the razor-backed ridge opened up a wild barrage of machine-gun, rifle and mortar fire and the Canadians climbed up, jumping out from behind rocks and trees. For an hour the valley resounded to the crack of rifles, the crash of grenades and the thump of tank guns and mortars.

Allied fighters added to the din as they wheeled and dove to rocket and drop napalm on the Chinese.

This was the last dispatch Pearcy ever wrote; he was killed the next day.

It was an endless, frustrating type of warfare, but it had moments of high heroism. On the night of May 26 a forward artillery observer attached to the Van Doos was trying to radio firing co-ordinates back to the guns but could not get through. His driver, Gunner Arthur M. Garaughty, decided to lay a cable back to the Canadian lines. He and another soldier jumped into the jeep and drove back through the dark, spooling out telephone wire behind them. Garaughty manipulated the steering wheel with one hand, shifting gears and holding a flashlight with the other, trying to read a topographical map as he drove. Chinese fire raked the route and mortar rounds began to fall near the jeep, cutting the cable. Garaughty spent the remainder of the night patrolling the 6.5 kilometres of cable, splicing it together wherever it was cut by mortar fire. His actions earned him the Military Medal.

The Canadians stayed in the line until June 1, when they were relieved by the Americans. They then joined up with the rest of the British and Commonwealth units, and took their place in the new Commonwealth Division near the junction of the Imjin and Hantan rivers.

THE FALSE DAWN OF PEACE

The hard slog of the U.N. forces back to the 38th parallel provided proof to Western leaders—if any was still needed—that China's full participation in the war had ended any possibility that Korea could be unified by force without launching a third world war. On June 1, 1951, Trygve Lie signalled as much to the Communists in a speech delivered in Ottawa. He proclaimed that U.N. objectives would be met if a ceasefire could be arranged and the "peace and security of the area" could be restored. Several weeks later the U.S.S.R.'s delegate to the U.N. agreed to ceasefire negotiations. The Chinese endorsed the decision. General Ridgway was authorized to hold ceasefire talks and discussions began at the village of Kaesong, on the 38th parallel, on July 10.

It was clear that military victory was unattainable for either side. The North Koreans might have achieved total victory in the first months of the war, but the U.S. and the U.N. had rallied quickly enough to avert that; from then on stalemate had been inevitable. The only question was how long it would take to arrive at an agreement, and how many men would die before that happened.

In this situation, the war began to assume a predictable pattern. The lines that straddled the 38th parallel were strengthened and fortified, not unlike the trenchlines of the First World War, although no continuous trenchline was built across the width of Korea. Bunkers were deepened and reinforced, trench sides were shored up with corrugated iron, mine fields and barbed wire were laid. Field kitchens, first aid stations, and helicopter landing zones were prepared. Patrols were sent out night after night to probe enemy defences, test enemy responses, and capture prisoners, who were questioned for any small bit of intelligence they might possess.

Patrolling became a specialized craft. There were standing patrols—probes sent into no man's land to set up listening posts or night ambushes. There were reconnaissance patrols, to collect information and identify enemy positions for possible attack by air or artillery. There were fighting patrols—raiding parties which crept into position with great stealth, attacked a portion of an enemy position, and tried to carry off a prisoner or two. There were also roving patrols—designed to stir up trouble in designated areas—and nuisance patrols, to keep the enemy on edge after dark. Every now and then one side would attempt to improve its strategic position by capturing this vantage point or that river crossing. Guns would crash, tracers would light up the night sky, jets would spread napalm over the hilltops, and men would die. Much of the time, though, the men killed time in their bunkers, listening for word of progress of the peace talks and thinking of the people at home who were living normal lives.

For this war was very different from the one the nation had experienced just a few years before. Then the effort had been all out: those who were not fighting were working in war plants, collecting scrap metal or rubber, or buying war bonds. There had been rationing and rallies and radio plays exhorting Canadians to greater efforts in supporting the war, and few families had not had at least one member in uniform.

But not now. Most Canadians were getting on with their lives, almost oblivious of the fighting and killing taking place in the hills of Korea. The nation was prosperous and united as the post-war boom continued. There was no rationing; there were not even restrictions on credit or foreign exchange. A good time was being had by all—with the exception of the seven to eight thousand in Korea.

It was not long before a deep cynicism began to mark the thoughts of men all along the U.N. lines. Why were they there? What were they fighting for? The mixture of frustration and resentment was dangerous, and the officers tried to dispel it by ordering constant patrolling, some of which was useless and just wasted lives, or by more comical expedients, such as firing red, white, and blue smoke-shells at the Chinese positions on Queen Elizabeth's coronation day.

It was just that mix of boredom and mischief that provoked Lieutenant Peter Worthington into a prank that landed him in serious trouble. One morning while the PPCLI was in reserve, U.S. planes accidentally bombed a bridge over the Imjin River that was held by U.N. troops. Worthington, who was already displaying his journalistic skills as editor of the battalion newsletter, decided to write about the attack:

> It was newsletter time, so I included a sarcastic item to the effect that "Four unidentified U.S. planes with U.N. markings bombed and strafed the Teal bridge, but fortunately no soldiers were killed, only 11 Americans."

Canadian Press correspondent Bill Boss reported the item and it didn't take long for Worthington to be called on the carpet:

> I took a jeep to Seoul, apologized to some bored American brigadier general who didn't know what it was all about, didn't care, and, I felt, had only just learned by my presence that there were Canadians in Korea.

Adding to the morale difficulties was the growing contempt many Canadian and other U.N. troops felt for the Koreans. They were especially shocked by their cruelty: both sides apparently thought nothing of wholesale shootings of civilians who were suspected of supporting the other side. Mass graves seemed to be found almost everywhere. One story filed by Bill Boss proclaimed "Canadians Becoming Used to Korean Cruelty", and went on to describe the views of a Canadian staff sergeant who had just turned a North Korean civilian over to South Korean police: "They have their own methods. We don't understand the workings of the Oriental mind. They do.... We don't ask them to beat them. But if they do, we don't know anything about it." Lester Pearson wrote Claxton, "I am becoming increasingly disturbed by the growing evidence that, in their contact with Koreans, United Nations troops are behaving in such a way as to endanger the future relations of the western nations with Korea and, indeed, with all of Asia." He attributed these attitudes to ignorance and racial prejudice.

The army denied Pearson's charges and insisted that the Canadian soldier was "not only friendly towards the Koreans, but goes out of his way to help them with food, clothing, medical attention, etc.," and claimed that unit commanders had to stop their men from giving too much away or adopting too many Korean orphans. It was a harsh fact of this war, however, that civilians had to be kept clear of the immediate fighting area. It was impossible to tell friend from foe when uniforms were not worn, and there was considerable Communist guerrilla activity near and behind the U.N. lines, while Korean farmers strongly resisted leaving the little paddies cultivated by their fathers and grandfathers before them. As one Canadian officer put it, "there are some sad sights in carrying out this military necessity."

To combat low morale, the Canadians adopted a new rotation and leave policy. Each battalion was to be rotated back to Canada after one year in the line. While in the line, battalions would regularly send men back to rear areas for a day of rest, hot meals and showers, and recreation. Soldiers would be sent to a Commonwealth Division rest camp at Inchon for a seventy-two-hour leave after a hundred days in the line. After four months of service came the big payoff—five full days in Tokyo. There the division operated Ebisu Camp—a leave centre. But Tokyo had much more to offer than Australian rations and warm English beer. Jacket Coates was only following a well-established Canadian tradition when he sidled up to the bar at the Prince Haramuri Hotel:

> "Let's have a beer," I said, and beckoned to a passing waiter.
> "What will you have, sir?" he asked, in perfect North American.
> "The works," I replied with a grin. "A steam bath, some food, these young ladies, rooms for the next five days, and something to drink."

DRAWING THE LINE

The war of patrolling, shelling, and probing dragged on through the hot months of the summer of 1951. The main U.N. objective was to push its line forward to where it could be securely anchored as close to the 38th parallel as possible. Each time the line was re-established, it was given a new name—the "Kansas" line, the "Wyoming" line. And each time new bunkers, foxholes, and trenches were dug, new wire, minefields, and telephone lines were laid, new gun lines were sighted in, and men put up signs, photos, and pin-ups in a vain attempt to suggest permanence.

In early October, as the 2PPCLI was being relieved by the 1PPCLI—each Canadian battalion was relieved twice in the course of the war—the Commonwealth Division took part in Operation Commando, a push to extend the lines as far north as possible before the onset of winter. When the push ended the U.N. forces anchored themselves on the "Jamestown" line, which ran the length of a small river. It was destined to form the U.N. front line until the end of hostilities.

The portion of the Jamestown line occupied by the Commonwealth Division ran roughly northeast-southwest, to the north of the Imjin River and north of the 38th parallel, through an area of low, rocky hills that looked somewhat like the Laurentian Mountains or Gatineau hills only with fewer trees. Some of the hills had only recently been planted with young pines, but the valleys looked as if they had been farmed for centuries, with diked paddies on the valley floor and terraced plots climbing up the hillsides. In more peaceful times those plots had yielded beans, cotton, corn, and sorghum. Now the small farmhouses were abandoned.

The hilltops were held by rifle platoons, in island-like positions linked by communications trenches. A platoon position often consisted of a more or less circular trench around the very top of a hill, with bunkers at the back of the hill, away from direct enemy observation, and firing trenches dug perpendicular to the main defensive trench, pointing towards the enemy lines. Canadian diplomat Arthur Menzies visited one of these forward areas in the fall of 1951:

> Each company occupied some prominent hilltop…and completely encircled it with barbed wire and mines. The valleys between the positions were strung with barbed wire and planted with mines so that any enemy attempt to infiltrate between the company positions would be held up long enough to be spotted by searchlights and fired on. Across the valley that lay before us—perhaps a mile and a half away—we could just make out the outlines of Chinese bunker positions on hill formations like those occupied by the PPCLI.

As each unit rotated into one of these hilltop positions, it attempted to improve it in one fashion or another. This "capital investment" made it impractical to change the position of defences easily and discouraged inventiveness. As Captain J.R. Madden observed following a visit to the Jamestown positions:

> Company after company occupied the same hills, lived in the same bunkers and fought from the same trenches. A company commander was called upon to display little initiative. As long as he insisted upon the observance of certain fundamental principles he was safe.

These defences were wholly inadequate to repel a truly determined enemy—the defensive lines to the rear such as the Wyoming line were much better fortified and supported—but what was the alternative? As Madden pointed out:

> That even semi-permanent defences were not properly prepared was due to the lack of direction from above; the uncertainty produced by the truce talks; the maintenance required during the rainy season to keep even the most primitive entrenchments usable; and the initial weakness of the enemy. It was only when the Chinese had more guns, more ammunition and learned to concentrate their fire that the weakness of our field works became painfully obvious.

On Friday November 2, 1951, Chinese burp-gunners and grenadiers assaulted the positions held by A and C companies of the Royal Canadian Regiment, on Hill 187 and a nearby spur, just after dark. The RCR was right in the centre of the Canadian brigade, on the right flank of the Commonwealth Division, on the Jamestown line. Bugle-blowing Chinese infantrymen came in, wave after wave, through gaps blown in the wire by Bangalore torpedoes—essentially pipe-bombs—and quickly succeeded in cutting off a platoon. The fight that followed was a chaotic scramble. Lieutenant E.J. Mastronardi, the platoon commander, at one point had his flare pistol shot right out of his hand. When his revolver jammed, he wrenched a burp gun from a dying Chinese soldier and carried on the fight. In the thick of the battle, Private Johnny Johnson calmly field-stripped two malfunctioning Bren guns and put both of them back into action; it was Johnson's first day in the line.

Mastronardi had no choice but to pull back to the main company defence perimeter. He and two other soldiers fought a rearguard action while the rest of the platoon opened a gap in the Chinese encirclement. All the wounded were brought back to the company positions. The Chinese swarmed around the wire but mortar, machine-gun, and proximity-fuse fire eventually drove them off. In the morning, forty-three Chinese corpses were found hanging on the wire or half buried in the ground outside the perimeter.

The Chinese attack on Hill 187 was the opening act of a month-long campaign to push the U.N. line back and recapture some of the ground lost in the September and October fighting. These attacks were different in one important respect from the human-wave assaults mounted on MacArthur's forces a year earlier. Then, the Chinese soldiers had had little more than the weapons they were carrying and the packs on their backs. Now they were attacking from well-prepared positions, they were supplied with ample food, winter clothing, and ammunition, and they were supported by large numbers of field guns and even self-propelled artillery. Despite the best efforts of USAF night-intruder bombers and fighter-bombers roaming the skies by day, the Chinese were now trucking huge amounts of supplies, up to and including Katyusha rocket projectors, to their forward positions. In the words of the PPCLI's official historian, some of the barrages that preceded Chinese assaults "were as intense and accurate as any...seen in the Second World War".

The Canadians were next hit on the night of November 4, when two companies of the PPCLI, one from the 1st Battalion spending its very first night in the lines, were attacked as part of a large assault. The main attack came against the King's Own Scottish Borderers of the 28th Commonwealth Brigade; the PPCLI companies were hit after a heavy shelling that began at dusk. In the course of the night four attacks were beaten off, although not before the Chinese penetrated the wire of one of the Canadian positions. First light revealed thirty-six Chinese bodies caught on the wire or lying just outside it. The Pats had prevailed but, on their right, the King's Own Scottish Borderers had been forced to yield two key hills.

As the winter began to close in, the hill fights intensified. The nights were very cold with occasional snow but the sun melted much of the snow and left the hillsides treacherously slippery. The men were alternately warm, wet, and cold. Chinese shelling continued periodically and always intensified prior to an infantry assault. Most of the fighting centred on the 28th Commonwealth Brigade front to the right of the Canadians. There, important hills changed hands night after night as the Chinese attacked, the British counter-attacked, and the Chinese assaulted yet again. Towards the end of the month the 28th was relieved by an American unit because of the heavy casualties the brigade had suffered.

In the shuffle that followed, the 25th CIB was moved to a saddle, or ridge, connecting Hill 355 to the right, held by the Americans, and Hill 227, which was unoccupied. All three Canadian battalions were to be in the line: the RCR on the left, the PPCLI in the centre, and the Van Doos on the right. As the Canadians began moving into their positions on the afternoon of November 22, the Chinese opened a massive bombardment of the Americans on Hill 355, using self-propelled artillery. Soon shells were also bursting on the saddle held by the Van Doos—especially on the positions held by D Company, which was the farthest forward. The shellfire continued throughout the night as a steady rain turned to snow. The water and mud made it difficult for the engineers to keep the roads open to the beleaguered companies. Under cover of the shellfire, several Chinese patrols approached the Canadian positions and called out, "Hello, Canada." From the Canadian bunkers, searchlights stabbed the darkness and volleys of grenades were thrown at the enemy.

On the afternoon of the 23rd, Chinese shell and rocket fire rained down on Hill 355 and the saddle while a heavy snowfall threatened to close the supply roads to the front-line positions. Then, at about 4:30 P.M., an estimated five Chinese companies assaulted both the U.S. positions on Hill 355 and the Van Doos on the saddle. By early evening the Americans had been forced to pull back, but the Canadians held firm. In one 12 Platoon position a private was killed instantly by a shell that exploded inside the platoon wire. Several others were badly wounded and the position was in danger of falling into Chinese hands until one of the wounded, Corporal Earl Istead, grabbed a Bren gun and opened fire on Chinese troopers. Despite his wounds he kept at it for an hour, jamming new clips into the gun while he picked off Chinese attempting to cross or crawl under the wire to get at the neighbouring platoon.

The American pullback from Hill 355 was partly a result of their tactical doctrine. The Commonwealth Division held that it was better to stand and fight to hold a position; the Americans believed it best to offer lighter resistance, give ground under the weight of the assault, and then launch an immediate set-piece counter-attack in strength. In practical terms, however, the American retreat left the Canadians terribly vulnerable, as Chinese infantrymen began to stream down the hillsides towards the Van Doos. The Commonwealth troops trapped in their foxholes and dugouts did not appreciate the finer points of these different approaches, as their newsletter indicated:

> If there are two things that I can't stand,
> It's a North Korean and a Chinaman,
> We're moving on, we're moving on,
> See the Chinks coming up 355,
> The Yanks pulling out in overdrive,
> They're moving on, they're moving on.

Despite the Chinese gains on Hill 355, Lieutenant-Colonel Jacques Dextraze, commander of the Van Doos, ordered his men to hold fast. That night he would demonstrate an uncanny ability to anticipate virtually every move of the Chinese. With Dextraze directing troop movements and co-ordinating tank and artillery fire, four attacks had been repelled by morning—including one by some four hundred soldiers. Moreover, while the Canadians had been defending the saddle, a U.S. counter-attack had succeeded in retaking most of Hill 355.

But the Chinese had now taken the heights of the previously unoccupied Hill 227, and by early afternoon Canadian observers could clearly see infantrymen beginning to mass on the slopes. Artillery and tank fire were called down and many were killed, but the Chinese soon brought their own artillery to bear on the saddle. Within a short time, as one Canadian officer later reported, "it was impossible to move in the position".

After softening up the Canadian positions, the Chinese attacked again. One report described the initial assault:

> Three hundred could be seen coming down the hill north-east of Hill 227.... They came in over the top of Hill 227 and swarmed down in three rows. The first row was armed with burp guns, the second with heavy matting carpets (to throw over the Canadian wire) and the third with bayonets on sticks. As soon as one was knocked out another would pick up his weapon and take his place. They came over the wire like buffaloes over a bridge and there was no stopping them.

Within minutes one Canadian platoon had been overrun and another was surrounded. A Canadian rifleman ran up to Major Réal Liboiron, the company commander, and shouted, "We've had it, there's five hundred of them," and Liboiron ordered his men out. Under mortar, machine-gun, and small-arms fire, they crawled down a narrow communications trench to the defensive position held by the neighbouring platoon. Liboiron then ordered tank, mortar, and artillery fire onto the position. Later a counter-attack was organized, but the Canadians found that the Chinese had already pulled back. A second Chinese attempt to assault the position after nightfall on November 25 was broken up by accurate shellfire.

During these night actions, the myth of the "dragon lady" was born. One Canadian officer recalled the story:

> Although I didn't personally see the "Dragon Lady" as she was called, several of my men reported that they had actually seen her. She was described as being dressed in black or dark coloured clothing and was easily recognizable as a woman by her long black hair. She appeared to act as a guide for the Chinese and led the attacking troops right up to the platoon position.... One of my men claimed killing her on one of the last attacks.

The attacks ceased after that, but the killing continued. On the afternoon of November 26 two shells fell on one of the Van Doos' positions and a man was buried. When he was finally dug out, "there was so little left of him he looked as if he had been pulverized by the force of the explosion," his platoon commander, Lieutenant Gérard Bélanger, wrote:

> If we continue to lose men at this rate, the Battalion will be decimated in a few weeks....
>
> The snow covered the ground today; there are snow flurries this evening; it's quite a sight to see, especially when you're living in a hole without a heater to keep you warm. We're living like rats and we'll probably die like rats....
>
> It is now 0625; the day is just breaking and I haven't slept since yesterday morning. So much for the glorious life of a platoon commander.

LIFE ON THE LINE

While men died in the hills of Korea, talks between U.N. and Communist negotiators dragged on. Most of the first few weeks had been devoted to the preparation of an agenda, and the wrangling on almost every point had been tiresome and frustrating. At night a large searchlight stabbed the sky from near the site of the talks; it was easily seen by troops in the firing lines for many kilometres around, as they set out to kill or be killed.

The agenda had finally been settled on by the end of July but the talks had then bogged down over whether the 38th parallel or the current front should be the demarcation line. Towards the end of August the talks had broken off, and they had not been resumed for two months, this time at a new site, Panmunjom. The armistice-line question was finally resolved but one last major issue remained—the repatriation of prisoners. The Communists insisted that all prisoners be returned to their respective armies. The U.N. argued that prisoners should have the right to choose their destiny, because it was obvious that many thousands of North Koreans did not want to return to the Communist side. On this the talks bogged down once again. The ongoing stalemate served to increase fears that the United States might resort to atomic weapons. On November 30, in response to a reporter's question at a press conference, Truman had indicated that the United States would "take whatever steps are necessary" to win the war. When asked if this included the use of the atom bomb, he replied, "there has always been active consideration of its use."

Although the White House quickly issued a clarification to the effect that mere possession of a weapon implied that its use was under consideration, Britain and Canada were deeply concerned. British Prime Minister

Clement Attlee flew to Washington for talks with Truman, while Pearson pressed publicly and privately for the U.N. forces to limit the scope of hostilities, and for a diplomatic solution to the war. Although the use of the atom bomb was completely impractical in the Korean War—small, "battlefield" atomic weapons had not yet been developed—and the U.S. never seriously considered using it, fears of a wider war continued in Ottawa.

In the weeks following the battles around Hill 355, the men experienced the full fury of the Korean winter. They quickly learned that the cold and the snow were to be feared almost as much as the Chinese. A Commonwealth Division publication entitled "Conquer the Korean Winter" warned that "The Korean winter can be one of the most unpleasant in the world" and that "CONTEMPT of the WINTER means a CERTAIN CASUALTY." Even the Canadians, some of whom had endured Arctic exercises, had to be taught how to survive and fight for weeks in below-freezing weather with a high wind-chill factor, swirling snows that made night vision almost impossible, clogged roads and supply trails, and sometimes grounded the fighter-bombers. Men were advised to dry out their socks by carrying them inside their clothes, and warned that boots would freeze solid unless they were stored in the sleeping bag at night. And it was solemnly suggested that "Latrines sited in a warm shelter have a very beneficial morale effect"!

The Chinese too suffered in the cold weather, and their difficulties were even more serious. They had less direct contact with home—a crucial factor in keeping up morale—and their supplies and freedom of movement were even more restricted. U.N. fighter-bombers roamed the skies strafing, bombing, and rocketing trucks, trains, carts, and anything else that might be carrying supplies to the Chinese positions in the mountains. Although many of their supplies got through, creature comforts were low on the priority list. While American, British, and Canadian soldiers watched movies and drank beer just back of the line, the Chinese were forced to endure hours of political indoctrination. In the rest of their free time they listened to Radio Peking, read, played poker, and even sang and danced.

In mid-January 1952 the Canadians were taken out of the line for the first time since September, as the brigade was placed in divisional reserve on the Wyoming line for six weeks. It then returned to the Jamestown line to relieve the 29th British Infantry Brigade astride the Sami-chon river. By spring virtually all the battalions, squadrons, and other forward units that had come to Korea as part of the first contingent had been rotated back to Canada and replaced. In early April, Rockingham was replaced as brigade commander by Brigadier M.P. Bogert, a pre-war regular officer and former Director-General of Military Training in Ottawa.

In early February, as the Canadians rested and recuperated on the Wyoming line, Reverend James G. Endicott and his wife were beginning a tour of China. A former China missionary and second moderator of the United Church of Canada, Endicott strongly opposed the war and was convinced it had been started by Syngman Rhee at the instigation of the Americans. Given the anti-Communist atmosphere of the day, it was not surprising that Endicott and other left-wing sympathizers who opposed the war—most of them associated with the Canadian Peace Congress— were targets of politicians, press, and security services.

Until his visit to China, Endicott's activities had been confined to remonstrations in just about every forum that would invite him. In late March and early April 1952, however, all that changed. Following a series of guided tours to rural areas, hospitals, and laboratories, conducted by Chinese government officials, Endicott wired Pearson, "Personal investigations reveal undeniable evidence large scale continuing American germ warfare on Chinese mainland...." Following this telegram, he held a press conference and made a broadcast over Radio Peking. Endicott knew little or nothing about weapons or chemical and biological warfare, believed what he wanted to believe—that the Americans were capable of the most unspeakable horrors in the pursuit of what he thought of as their racist, imperialist objectives.

Endicott's charges caused an uproar in Parliament and the press. Conservative MP John Diefenbaker demanded to know whether or not the government intended to investigate this "dastardly statement", while Opposition leader George Drew inquired whether there was a possibility of Endicott being charged under the criminal code for making statements that had "a damaging effect upon the state of mind of many of our people". In fact, the vast majority of the Canadian people, at least according to a Gallup poll, refused to believe Endicott. Despite this, he continued to make inflammatory speeches and receive wide press coverage. Finally Justice minister Stuart S. Garson announced that the government had decided to take no action since it was "probable that the ringleaders of the Communist conspiracy" really wanted publicity to "give them the appearance of martyrs", and because the government wished to protect the principle of freedom of speech despite Endicott's abuse of it.

Meanwhile a major problem was developing for the U.N. high command in Korea. For many months there had been rioting in the huge prisoner-of-war compounds on Koje Island, off the southern tip of South Korea. There, approximately seventy thousand North Korean and Chinese POWs were held in large barbed-wire compounds that were only minimally patrolled by U.S. and R.O.K. forces. Conditions were poor. Medical supplies were lacking, overcrowding and lack of sanitation created a constant risk of epidemic, and guards seemed to be especially brutal in their treatment of prisoners. Often Communist political officers allowed themselves to be captured so that they might be sent to Koje to ensure the political "correctness" of the prisoners there. Their job was made easier by the bad conditions and by the relative freedom they enjoyed inside these compounds, where the prisoners basically ran their own affairs; prisoners fashioned rudimentary weapons, conducted indoctrination exercises, and even tried and executed "traitors", mostly those who were unenthusiastic about returning to Communist rule after the war. On May 7 the U.S. commandant tried to dissuade Communist leaders in one of the compounds from continuing to attack camp guards and destroy property. The leaders of the revolt enticed him to enter the compound for negotiations and seized him. U.N. troops swarmed around the compound, placing it under siege, and for twenty-four hours fifteen thousand heavily armed R.O.K. and U.S. troops, backed by tanks, patrolled the wire, until General Van Fleet arrived to take control of the situation. The commandant was released the following day but the world's attention was now focused on Koje.

After the incident General Mark W. Clark, who had just replaced Ridgway as U.N. supreme commander, decided to begin breaking up this large concentration of prisoners and to rotate non-U.S. units to Koje for guard duty. Two companies from the Commonwealth Division—one from the King's Own Shropshire Light Infantry and the other from the Royal Canadian Regiment—were to be ordered to Koje.

In preparation for this rotation, the Americans told the U.K. liaison officer in Japan that a transfer of Commonwealth Division troops was "under consideration", and the liaison officer duly informed Brigadier A.B. Connelly, head of the Canadian Military Mission in Tokyo. Connelly thought he should refer the matter to Ottawa but he was urged not to do so; General Clark "hoped it would not be necessary to consult governments at this time." Connelly agreed to the move provided it was cleared with Major-General Cassells, commander of the division. When Connelly next heard of the matter, the Canadians were already on their way to Koje.

The British complied reluctantly; the Canadian government, which did not learn of the move until after it had been made, protested strongly and insisted that the soldiers be returned to the 25th CIB. In the first place, the dispatch of the company had violated Ottawa's explicit instructions to the U.N. that the Canadian contingent be kept together. In the second place,

Canada had no wish to provide cover, or legitimacy, to an American operation which had clearly been bungled. Koje had received much unfavourable publicity in the Canadian press, and St. Laurent worried that the presence of Canadian troops there might undermine public support for participation in the war. Protest after protest was made to Washington, at the highest levels, along with statements in the House of Commons and in the press to assure the Canadian people that their troops were on Koje against the will of their government.

Some U.S. officials were extremely irritated by what they viewed as Canada's "holier than thou" approach to Koje; others took it as something of a joke. But by mid-July the Canadian troops had rejoined their units in the field. One result of this episode was that the military career of Brigadier Connelly was wrecked. Lieutenant-General Guy Simonds—Chief of the General Staff now that Foulkes had been appointed chairman of the Chiefs of Staff—was angry that Connelly had not done more to avoid the embarrassment, and although Connelly had served with distinction in the Second World War he was quietly brought back to Canada and "retired" at the age of forty-four. Even when the story of Connelly's "retirement" was published in an American newspaper, the government remained silent about the incident. The papers dealing with his dismissal have mysteriously disappeared from his file at the Department of National Defence's Directorate of History.

Through the spring and summer of 1952, life on the line continued in a semi-permanent routine. The men on both sides lived in their bunkers and foxholes for much of the time, trying to stay alive during the intermittent shelling, and when not underground they manned listening posts or forward observation outposts.

On the night of May 31, 1952, Corporal Arthur Irvine Stinson became a hero. Stinson was one of twenty-two men, under the command of Lieutenant A.A.S. Peterson, sent out to raid a Chinese position and take prisoners. The raiding party formed up in the RCR trenches in the late afternoon and watched as USAF fighter-bombers strafed and rocketed the Chinese across the valley. As the sun set, the patrol moved out through a gap in the wire. At double time the men jogged along a path through their own minefield and within minutes they were at the foot of Hill 113. There was a cluster of ruined farmhouses at the foot of the hill, and Peterson halted his men there and called for artillery and tank fire on the Chinese positions above. Then the men started to climb.

The first line of trenches was empty and so was the second. Peterson placed Stinson in charge of a small party of five and left them to clear the second position while he and the remainder of the patrol continued up to the top of the hill. Stinson's group worked their way around to the left, carefully examining the bunkers connected to the trench, and found one Chinese soldier hiding in a dugout. As they were starting to secure their prisoner, the hillside above and below them came alive with rifle and machine-gun fire. Four of Stinson's party were hit almost immediately, including the man guarding the prisoner, who tried to scramble away and was shot dead. As the firing continued, Stinson searched the body and discovered some papers identifying the Chinese unit. Then he too was hit. Meanwhile, knowing that a hand-to-hand fight so far from his own lines would bring total disaster, Peterson had ordered his men to dash straight down the hill. The wounded Stinson stayed long enough to cover the desperate withdrawal of his section, killing three Chinese in the process. Major-General Cassells called this patrol "a specially daring raid" but it was a clear failure. Had it not been for Peterson and Stinson—both of whom were decorated for their part in the action—Canadian lives would surely have been lost.

On June 20 the PPCLI raided Hill 133; as the patrol was nearing the Chinese positions, several mortar rounds being fired at the Canadian lines fell short and, by chance, landed in the midst of the raiding party; six men were killed, eighteen wounded. The following night the RCR went back to Hill 133; one man was killed, twenty-two were wounded. Two nights later the Van Doos raided Hill 169; one man was killed, five were wounded, two were missing. And so it went until the beginning of July, when the brigade was pulled out of the line.

The Canadians spent a month in reserve and returned to their old positions on the Jamestown line on August 10. By then the Chinese were trying something new; they were mounting large numbers of patrols into no man's land, raiding forward U.N. positions, and increasing the daily shelling. Heavy rains sometimes interfered with these probes but, even so, the rains were not welcomed by the Canadians. Between August 18 and 25, most of the bunkers and much of the trench line along the Canadian front were literally washed away by the heavy downpour. The work of digging in had to begin all over again.

The Chinese raids resumed after the August rains, and so did the shelling. In retaliation the Commonwealth Division stepped up its own raiding activity. These skirmishes cost lives on both sides, but they were only the prelude to a major attack on Hill 355, which had been fought over constantly for a year. By this time the American press had dubbed the hill "Little Gibraltar" because from the rear it bore a striking resemblance to its namesake—and certainly it was as much disputed.

The Chinese began to pound Hill 355 mercilessly on October 1, when a thousand shells were fired into the RCR positions. The heavy shelling continued for two days but then slackened off until the middle of the month; on October 21 an estimated 1,600 rounds poured down. B Company, on the left of the RCR, was the closest to the Chinese positions and it anchored the Canadian line, so it was the target for the great bulk of the artillery fire, which cut most of the telephone lines, caved in many of the foxholes, firing trenches, weapons pits, and bunkers, and buried much of the reserve ammunition. Although a Chinese patrol approached the wire in the early morning hours of October 23, it was driven off when several were shot dead from a weapons pit.

All through the day, the heavy shelling continued. The men hunkered down; nothing could live above ground as shell after shell fell into the B Company area, blowing apart what few structures remained and reducing a once-fortified position to rubble. Just after sunset the shelling intensified—more than a thousand rounds fell in the space of some ten minutes—and then shifted to the left and right of the company, sealing it off from its neighbours. Suddenly the barrage lifted and, as one dispatch described it, "the Chinese infantry came in yelling and overran the area while the defenders still were dazed". Within moments, organized resistance had collapsed in the B Company positions as small knots of men struggled into the neighbouring company defensive perimeters. Others stuck it out in what was left of their weapons pits and bunkers, firing at the Chinese all around them.

It was a moment for the heroics of desperate close-quarter fighting. One platoon commander, Lieutenant Russell Gardner, was shot three times; he collapsed over the barbed wire and kept still as the Chinese moved past him. Corporal Ellery M. Faulkner also feigned death; "A group of twelve Chinese passed within five feet of me but did not look twice," he later told a reporter. Sergeant D. Rennie watched from a shellhole as the Chinese carried a flag into one of the former Canadian positions: "One of them was going to plant it in the ground. The lads behind me cut them all down with a Bren gun." Lieutenant John Clark did what he could to hold his platoon's position. Like a man possessed he threw grenades and emptied every weapon he could find, including a rifle, a Sten gun, and a Bren gun, at the attacking Chinese. Then he led the remainder of his platoon to safety, carrying one of his wounded men on his back. Private Charles Morrison was not so fortunate. He stayed in his foxhole, firing into the mass of advancing Chinese, to let his platoon mates clear out. His body was found after the attack. Clark and Morrison were both decorated for their actions that night, as were many others.

When battalion headquarters began to form a clear picture of the disaster overtaking B Company—and was certain that Clark and the remainder of his men were out of the area—the battalion commander ordered tank and mortar fire down on the position, while divisional artillery pounded possible Chinese approach positions. At the same time a counter-attack was organized to go in from D Company. Although there was a brisk fire-fight with some dug-in infantrymen, most of the Chinese had melted away into the night. Within a few hours the RCR was once again in control of the entire hill. When they moved into the positions abandoned hours earlier they found Gardner and the others, with five Chinese bodies nearby.

In the weeks following, the boundaries of the Commonwealth Division were shifted westward, 1PPCLI was rotated back to Canada and replaced by 3PPCLI, and the Canadians were given responsibility for holding "the Hook"—a crestline running north-west of Hill 146, some twelve kilometres south-west of the Little Gibraltar area. The Hook was the easternmost of a line of hills that ended at the Sami-chon River, which cut through U.N. front lines. As such, it was a key to the security of the Jamestown line and was a continual target of Chinese probes and artillery and rocket fire. Until the end of January the PPCLI occupied the Hook while the Van Doos held the low hills across the river. In the bitter weather there was little fighting, and they spent most of their time improving their defences. At the end of January 1953 the entire Commonwealth Division, with the exception of the artillery, went into reserve. It would not return to the front line until April 8.

THE POWS

In the fall of 1952 the difficult question of prisoner-of-war repatriation was still unresolved. By this time the Communists held about 12,000 U.N. prisoners, while the U.N. held more than 120,000 North Koreans and Chinese—the majority of whom did not want to go home.

Most of the U.N. prisoners were in camps along the Yalu River. From the beginning of the war these POWs had been subject first to extreme physical abuse, then to constant psychological pressures aimed at dividing them, lowering their morale, and even converting them to Communism. For them the worst phase of the war had been the North Korean offensive.

The North Koreans regularly shot prisoners; after the Inchon landing U.S. troops found the bodies of a hundred of their murdered comrades in a railway tunnel. Although U.N. soldiers sometimes killed their prisoners too, their acts tended to be isolated, individual actions, nothing like the routine slaughter engaged in by the North Koreans.

The Chinese almost never killed prisoners; sometimes they even set them free after a political lecture! But in the early months of their involvement in the war they kept them on starvation rations, engaged in back-breaking work, in the midst of winter. There was little or no medicine or warm clothing, and sickness and death were common. Of more than seven thousand Americans to fall into Communist hands, almost three thousand died in captivity; the vast majority of these died in the first seven months of the war. After that, conditions in the camps improved, rations were increased, and there was an attempt to provide more of the necessities of life. It was fortunate indeed for the thirty-three Canadian POWs that they were taken after the worst period was over. That there were so few Canadians taken is almost certainly due to the fact that they entered the fighting at the very end of the war of movement, when the lines had more or less solidified.

Much has been made of Communist attempts to "brainwash" prisoners and convert them to Communism. In fact there was little of this. However, the Communists did make every effort to destroy the POWs' will to resist and even to enlist them to spy on other POWs, and to write letters or make broadcasts home that would embarrass the U.N. cause. They did this by destroying unit cohesion, separating officers from men, forcing the men to undergo constant political education, and playing on the normal resentment and self-deprecation that many soldiers experience when taken prisoner. To a large degree the tactics worked. Although there were many escape attempts, none was successful and there was nothing like the mass resistance that Allied prisoners had mounted against their German captors during the Second World War.

In early December of 1952, the U.N. General Assembly finally adopted an Indian-sponsored resolution that a neutral commission be formed to which all prisoners would be turned over after the ceasefire, so that prisoners could indicate where they wished to go. The Chinese and Soviets initially rejected this idea but an exchange of sick and wounded was agreed to and took place in April and May. Hopes for an early truce brightened considerably as the last snows of winter disappeared from the hills of Korea.

HILL 187—THE LAST BATTLE

On April 8, 1953 the Commonwealth Division returned to the Jamestown line; the 25th CIB's third rotation had been completed and the brigade now consisted entirely of the third battalions of the RCR, PPCLI, and Van Doos, as well as tanks, artillery, and other supporting arms. It was commanded by the newly arrived Brigadier Jean-Victor Allard and was assigned to the central sector of the Commonwealth Division, holding several hilltops near one of the more prominent features in the line, Hill 187, roughly halfway between "the Hook" and "Little Gibraltar". Hill 187 itself was guarded by the RCR, with the north-westernmost position, closest to the Chinese lines, held by C Company. The RCR had been the last of the battalions to rotate and its men had the least combat experience.

In his memoirs Allard wrote that the Chinese were aware of both the change of command and the rawness of the men. He was undoubtedly correct; the Communists patrolled no man's land heavily and missed little in their probes. After the rotation, Chinese patrols and artillery fire both increased, and Allard and his staff noticed that most of the fire seemed concentrated on the C Company position. A British staff officer seconded to the brigade because of his expertise in artillery told Allard he believed the Chinese were preparing an assault.

On the afternoon of May 2, Allard drove to Seoul for dinner and an overnight stay with U.S. General Maxwell Taylor. The invitation had come several days before, and Allard had accepted even though he was worried about Chinese intentions. The evening should have given him a much-needed rest, but he could not get rid of the nagging thought that something was about to happen. He later told a newspaper reporter, "I got hot feet about 10:30. I had an uneasy feeling and cut the evening short." Taylor tried to reassure him that his own units were constantly coming under fire but that nothing further seemed to develop, but Allard was determined to leave. As he was driving back to the front he heard over his radio that the artillery fire had suddenly intensified. He knew the big attack was coming.

In the valley that lay between the RCR's positions and those of the Chinese, sixteen members of the RCR watched and listened. They had moved out of Canadian lines at 8:30 P.M. to set up an ambush in no man's land, but at about the same time that Allard was leaving Taylor's headquarters, they spotted some sixty Chinese infantrymen moving towards the Canadian positions. Lieutenant J.G. Maynell quietly positioned his men along the wall of a rice paddy and radioed for a flare. As soon as the flare popped, the Canadians opened fire and threw grenades and the Chinese answered in kind. Maynell was shot in the head and killed. Corporal Joseph McNeil, who was second in command, began to move the remainder of his men back towards the Canadian lines. The wounded were dragged or carried while those still capable of shooting or throwing grenades tried to hold the Chinese off. They were able to break contact as they approached the Canadian minefield, but then they were ambushed by a second group of Chinese. As soon as the first patrol had been attacked, a second, stand-by patrol had been sent out from the RCR positions. It too was ambushed with heavy casualties. Lieutenant Doug Banton, commander of No. 8 Platoon, was killed; the men under him scattered to take cover as best they could.

At about midnight, while the men in the valley were struggling to survive, the Chinese artillery barrage on C Company intensified. Then, just as suddenly, it was lifted to the rear of the Canadian positions and Chinese infantrymen penetrated the 7 and 8 platoon defences. Throwing concussion grenades to make the Canadians think shells were still falling, the Chinese began to move along the trenches, firing and throwing grenades and pulling out dazed Canadians to take as prisoners. Lieutenant Laurie Côté later described the scene to Bill Boss:

In the communications trench between two Bren-gun pits we saw them. There were Chinese in the trench with me and more on the parapet. There were more up top and in the centre of the position throwing grenades into the trenches while a party worked towards me throwing grenades into the weapons pits.

Then the bombardment started and forced me to lie in the trench.... The Chinese also took shelter though some crawled along the parapet....

One was killed and fell on top of me, affording that much more cover.

The shellfire that killed the Chinese infantryman was Canadian. It had been called for by Lieutenant Edgar H. Hollyer, who had crouched in his bunker as the Chinese poured over the wire. Twice he had tried to get above ground to size up the situation; once he was attacked, the other time he was blown back into his hiding-place by an exploding shell. He tried to defend his bunker with grenades, but when he saw that the situation was hopeless he radioed for proximity shellfire on his own position. The gunners responded with about four thousand shells, some directed at the hilltop, others at approach routes in the valley along which Chinese reinforcements might come. On the hill, scores of Chinese infantrymen were blown to pieces. As the shells rained down, Hollyer and his men were given permission to withdraw to the 8 Platoon locality, and they moved out.

When the situation became clearer at battalion headquarters, Lieutenant-Colonel K.L. Campbell, commanding the RCR, began to plan a counter-attack. Allard allocated a company from the Van Doos and Hollyer led it back to the 7 Platoon position. He found the Chinese in the midst of withdrawing and radioed for reinforcements. As they clambered into what was left of the 7 Platoon positions, however, they came under concentrated Chinese mortar fire. They were not able to reoccupy the position fully until the next night.

By two A.M. the morning of May 3, the brief battle was over; twenty-six Canadians lay dead, twenty-seven had been wounded, and eight had been taken prisoner. A number of Korean troops attached to the Canadian units ("Katcoms") were also casualties. (Koreans were attached to various U.N. units for training under fire; most served with U.S. units and were referred to as KATUSAS.)

The Chinese had not broken through the Canadian lines and penetrated to the rear, but it was never clear that they intended to. In fact it was a mystery why the battle had taken place at all, given the obvious nearness of an armistice. Allard, for one, believed it had been a defeat for the Canadians in that the Chinese had inflicted casualties, taken prisoners, destroyed the defences of the 7 Platoon position, and recovered their dead and wounded from the battlefield.

One of the Canadian prisoners, Private John Junkins, was released shortly after the battle. A member of the first patrol, he had been lost from the main party when McNeil led it back towards the Canadian positions, and had taken refuge in an unoccupied Canadian bunker. He later related the strange events:

> I lost the main party. Shells and mortars were bursting all around and I was pinned down. I crawled into a bunker and after a time I heard Chinese voices outside. I...flattened myself against the wall.... Someone suddenly ripped away the poncho waterproof cape covering the doorway and sprayed the back of the bunker with a burp gun.
>
> I lay there for 15 minutes. Two Chinese eventually came into the bunker, pulled me out and told me I was a prisoner.

After searching him, the Chinese brought up three more prisoners, arranged them in single file, and began to move them off. For some reason they decided to leave Junkins behind. A Chinese medical orderly gave him a drink of water, stuffed some papers into his uniform—probably propaganda leaflets—and departed with the rest of the patrol, and Junkins crawled back into the bunker and waited for the Canadians to reoccupy the position.

The limited prisoner exchange which had taken place in April and early May paved the way for a ceasefire. On June 7 an agreement was reached at Panmunjom for the rest of the POWs to be handled along the lines originally suggested by the Indian delegation to the U.N., and India was selected as the country to decide the disposition of the prisoners. On July 27 a final armistice agreement was signed, providing for a full ceasefire twelve hours later and for withdrawal from a designated demilitarized zone within seventy-two hours. The armistice was to be supervised by a Military Armistice Commission composed of five representatives from each side.

The shooting stopped the night of July 27, 1953. The total Canadian toll was 1,550 battle casualties—312 servicemen killed in action, dead of wounds, or missing and officially presumed dead; 1,202 wounded, 33 prisoners of war (none of whom died)—and 94 dead from non-battle causes. By the end of September, 75,000 North Korean and Chinese POWs had been returned to the Communist side, and almost 13,000 U.N. prisoners, including 32 Canadians, had been released from the Yalu River POW camps. A handful of U.N. prisoners, like pilot Andy MacKenzie, were held for some period after.

Today the Military Armistice Commission still meets across a divided table at Panmunjom, and forty thousand U.S. troops remain in South Korea. That republic has known little democracy since the end of the Korean War, but its booming economy is making it an economic showplace of south-east Asia and its citizens are now demanding, and receiving, more of the traditional freedoms that mark true democracy. The Communist regime in North Korea remains one of the world's last hard-line Communist dictatorships, unaffected (as of this writing) by the winds of change that have transformed so many other countries. For these apparently meagre results some 370,000 U.N. servicemen paid with their lives. But in fact the results were *not* meagre; the U.N. had shown its teeth, and the free nations of the West had made it clear that they would not tolerate outright aggression. Divided as the world was, it had a certain uneasy balance; in the early days of the Cold War, that was about as much as could be hoped for.

PPCLI infantrymen cross the Imjin River in June 1951. At this point the Canadians were positioned on the south bank of the river, which was swollen by spring runoff, and patrols had to be ferried across by assault boats or motor launches. Their helmets and ammunition pouches mark the two men up front as Americans.

A wasp mobile flame-thrower used by the PPCLI. The weapon was mounted on a Bren gun carrier and shot out a stream of napalm. It was highly effective against troops in dugouts and bunkers, but its exposed napalm tanks made it extremely vulnerable to enemy fire.

A private of the Van Doos curls up with a comic book in a slit trench near Chail-Li. A slit trench was good protection against everything but a direct hit by a mortar round.

Rockingham at a PPCLI mortar emplacement somewhere on the Jamestown line; the mortar bombs are stacked on the left, and the ranging sticks in the left foreground are used to calibrate the mortar. Many of the defensive positions built early in the war proved inadequate later, when the Chinese had more ammunition and better firing technique, but by then it was too late to rebuild them properly.

A typical communications trench on the Jamestown line. Trench and bunker locations were usually obvious to the enemy because of the spoil piled up around them—and because of what one captain deplored as "the rather unsoldierly litter which seemed to identify our positions".

A L/Bdr of the Royal Canadian Artillery at the sights of a 25-pounder. With an effective range of 10,000 to 12,000 metres, these guns formed the backbone of the Canadian artillery from the Second World War until well after Korea.

PPCLI infantrymen clean their Sten guns. Although the Sten was known to be both inaccurate and unreliable, Canadians were equipped with them throughout the war. Note that the man on the right wears sneakers rather than standard Canadian-issue boots, which were unsuitable for Korea's often wet terrain.

Two soldiers of the Van Doos huddle under blankets on a cold June night. From the radio wire and the handset, this is probably an observation post. The man on the left cradles what appears to be a Chinese "burp" gun; his Lee-Enfield leans against the sandbags and an unloaded Sten gun hangs on the right.

Korea is a land of hot, dusty summers, seasonal monsoons, and winters so cold that soldiers who slept sitting down in trenches sometimes found their drenched trousers frozen to the ground by morning. These men of the PPCLI are burning gasoline in an old pot in an effort to dry out—perhaps trusting that the roof over them is too soggy to ignite.

Celebrating news of the armistice. KATCOMS—R.O.K. troops attached to the Commonwealth Division—are among the crowd. The man front and centre holds a Bren gun, and a U.S. helmet—pilfered or traded—is held high in the middle.

Canadian POWs are welcomed back to Panmunjon in August 1953.

Opposite page: Keeping the peace in Cyprus has been a dangerous job, as this sergeant of the Princess Patricia's Canadian Light Infantry seems to know all too well.

PART THREE
THE AGE OF PEACEKEEPING

VII
THE MID-EAST AND
INDO-CHINA

The Korean War had been an example, not of peacekeeping, but of collective security. There is a world of difference between the two. The chief object of peacekeeping is to keep two potential combatants separated while diplomatic efforts are mounted to resolve their conflict; the aim of collective security is to stop an aggressor, by force if necessary.

There were no instances of U.N.-sponsored collective security from 1953 to 1990. As long as the Cold War divided the Great Powers into two armed camps, each jockeying to expand its theatre of influence and each deeply suspicious of the other's every move, there could not be enough agreement or trust to allow a collective-security action. But peacekeeping was possible, at least in those instances where the Great Powers were not directly involved.

Over the next forty years there were many such cases, as the U.N. tried to maintain the precarious balance of peace. In a world increasingly dominated by superpowers and military blocs armed with nuclear weapons of terrifying power, the need to control small wars before they exploded into great crises was apparent, and military observers from many nations donned sky-blue berets with U.N. badges and disinterestedly tried to damp down conflict and steer feuding opponents to the conference table.

Even these peacekeeping operations might not have been possible had the U.N. not found a way around the monopoly of the Great Powers. The Security Council had been able to take steps to deal with North Korea's aggression only because the Soviet Union happened to be boycotting the council and hence did not cast its inevitable veto. The next time there was an international crisis, however, the U.S.S.R. or some other Great Power might block any U.N. action. The answer was the "Uniting for Peace" resolution of November 1950, which authorized transfer of responsibility for collective security to the General Assembly—where the West had a clear majority at the time—when a Security Council response was blocked by a veto. At last what Pearson called the "irresponsible and unprincipled use of the veto" could be circumvented. The U.N.'s member states, and not just the Great Powers, now had the capacity to act if necessary.

Curiously, Canada's Cold War rearmament, which quadrupled the size of the armed forces within a few years of the outbreak of war in Korea, provided the country with the ability to play a major role in peacekeeping in the years that followed. Because the Canadian forces thought of war in Europe as their first priority, Canada built up a balanced mix of forces. In addition to infantry, which virtually every nation could supply, there were military engineers, communications specialists, and ordnance and supply officers capable of managing sophisticated inventories and getting them to troops in the field. The air force had pilots experienced on both light air-craft and large transports, as well as skilled ground crew technicians to keep them flying. And though the navy was largely geared to anti-subma-rine warfare, the fleet could carry troops and equipment long distances in a pinch. The forces also had the capacity to function in both French and English, though that skill was less developed than it would be three decades later. These were formidable advantages, and when they were combined with the high reputation Ottawa's diplomats had built around the world for a distinctive committed impartiality, they virtually guaran-teed that Canada would be called on whenever the United Nations moved towards peacekeeping. In fact, Canadians are so used to seeing their troops as neutral enforcers of the peace that they tend to forget the coun-try's role in Korea. That is one reason why Korea remains largely an unknown war to Canadians, to this day.

THE MIDDLE-EAST MORASS

Canada's first forays into U.N. peacekeeping had come before the Korean War. A few Canadian officers had served as observers along the borders between India and Pakistan, in Jammu and Kashmir, in the bloody years after those two states became independent of Britain in 1948, in the opera-tion known as the U.N. Military Observer Group India–Pakistan (UNMOGIP). (In 1965–66 Canadians would also join the U.N. India–Pakistan Observa-tion Mission—UNIPOM—along the rest of the India–Pakistan border.) The presence of the U.N. did not bring any lasting peace—more than four decades later, hostilities and bloodshed still erupt from time to time—yet

the presence of impartial observers has lessened the violence, and has likely saved many lives.

The conflict between Israel and its Arab neighbours, and the persistent
tensions between Israelis and Palestinians, have created an equally
intractable situation—and a potential conflict between the Great Powers,
who, in varying degrees at different points, have supported their client
states. During the First World War the British had gained control of Palestine and had promised to create a Jewish national state, but by 1947
Britain was looking for a way out of Palestine, and although the U.N. tried
to establish an administration that could take over, its efforts were fruitless. Fighting between Jews and Arabs began after the U.N. passed a resolution calling for the partition of Palestine; after Israel proclaimed its independence in 1948, hostilities intensified. After the opposing sides accepted
a thirty-day Security Council ceasefire, Belgium, France, and the United
States—three nations with consular offices in Palestine's capital,
Jerusalem—sent military observers into the area, but the war carried on in
fits and starts until January 1949. Subsequently, Israel signed armistice
agreements with Egypt, Lebanon, Jordan, and Syria, and to monitor these
agreements the Security Council set up the U.N. Truce Supervision Organization (UNTSO) with fifty officers. The idea was that Mixed Armistice
Commissions (MACs) would investigate incidents. But there were far more
incidents than there were UNTSO officers to investigate them, and by 1953
tension on the Arab–Israeli borders had increased as guerrilla attacks
inevitably produced retaliatory strikes. A spiral of escalating violence had
begun.

The answer was to increase UNTSO's strength, and at this point Canada
became involved. Four army officers were seconded to the Department of
External Affairs for a one-year tour of duty in February 1954, and several
months later Canada agreed that General E.L.M. Burns, who had commanded the 5th Canadian Armoured Division and I Canadian Corps in
Italy during the Second World War and had subsequently become deputy
minister of Veterans Affairs, could become chief of staff of UNTSO.

Born in 1897, Burns had attended the Royal Military College and had
served overseas during the Great War with distinction. He had stayed in
the army between the wars, earning a reputation as an officer with an
uncommonly good mind. Able though he was, he was a stiff man, and no
inspiring commander; while his staff respected him, he won little affec-
tion. Nor was he much admired by the Israelis or the Arabs. For one thing,
he set out to learn Arabic but not Hebrew. His reason? The Israelis could

communicate with him in English, French, or German, but the Arab officers, for the most part, spoke no other language. There was practicality
there, but perhaps a lack of sensitivity.

In fairness, however, Burns' work was a task of almost unrelieved frustration. As he wrote later, the armistice agreements "contained certain
vague statements and compromises, essential to secure the signature of
both sides, given the circumstances of 1949. It was hoped then that the difficult points would be settled in peace negotiations after a relatively short
period...." But there were no negotiations—and there would be none until
after three more wars—and instead "there were disputes about the interpretation of the armistice agreements.... All the while, both sides violated
or failed to observe the agreements, in more or less serious ways." Burns
tried to be impartial, but "before I had been long in the Middle East, I
learned that no matter how hard one tried to be objective and impartial, if
one accepted the views of one side on any matter, the other side accused
one of partiality."

In this hornets' nest of suspicion, Burns and his UNTSO officers were
caught in the middle, desperately trying to keep peace amid the shooting.
In August 1955, for example, the Egyptians accepted UNTSO's requests for a
ceasefire and agreed to halt *fedayeen* raids launched by Palestinians dispossessed of their homes by the Israelis. But the *fedayeen* guerrillas carried
no radios and could not be reached once they had crossed into Israel, and
so the raids went on. In revenge, the Israelis sent an armoured unit into
the Gaza Strip, destroyed a police station and a hospital under construction, and fired indiscriminately into a village. "I had the feeling I was trying to stop a runaway truck on a steep hill by throwing stones under the
wheels," Burns said. The Egyptians said thirty-six had been killed and thirteen wounded; the Israelis claimed they had hit the police station because
that was the point from which the raids had been launched. All-out war
was averted, but only barely.

Despite complaints from both sides, Burns' impartiality was impecca-
ble. Whether that was true of all his officers was another question. Canadian diplomats were told repeatedly that UNTSO officers arrived in the Middle
East pro-Israeli but invariably departed pro-Arab. It was also said that officers and U.N. officials "spoke in openly critical terms of Israel". As for
Burns, when he wrote his book *Between Arab and Israeli* he took pains to
point out in his preface that it was possible to oppose Israeli policy without being anti-Semitic.

Normally each officer spent half his one-year term on the Israel–Syria

MAC and half on the Israel–Jordan MAC. Observers lived in fixed observation posts for four or five days and then had a day off; much of their time was spent conducting investigations or monitoring radio transmissions. As is often the case with military service, there was discomfort of a high order. One Canadian, returning to his quarters after being pinned down in his observation post by mortar fire, took his boots off and was promptly bitten by a poisonous snake.

By 1958, after the 1956 war between Israel and Egypt had screwed tensions higher still, there were fourteen Canadians, the largest national contingent in UNTSO, which included Swedish, American, Norwegian, French, Danish, Australian, Belgian, and Dutch officers. The next year, the number was increased to seventeen.

Their work often put UNTSO team members in peril. Two Canadian officers were injured in a mine explosion in 1956, and one of those officers, Lieutenant-Colonel George Flint, was killed by Jordanian fire two years later. The U.N. report said Flint had gone to the Israeli sector under a white flag in response to a complaint that the Israelis were firing at a Jordanian village. He died from a single shot fired by a Jordanian sniper.

UNTSO's worth is difficult to appraise. It could not prevent the Suez crisis of 1956, nor could it move the parties towards peace talks. The Israelis often complained that the observers did not stop incidents or protect Israeli citizens; moreover, they claimed, UNTSO's very existence inhibited progress towards a permanent settlement. But UNTSO did provide a medium that let the Israelis and Arabs talk to each other and reach local ceasefires. Useful or not, UNTSO continues to this day, and Canadians continue to serve in it.

PEARSON'S TRIUMPH

The Suez crisis began in Cairo, Paris, and London. The 160-kilometre Suez Canal, which connects the Mediterranean to the Red Sea and is critical for Europe's oil supplies, was owned by Britain and France. When Egypt's President Gamal Abdal Nasser nationalized the canal in July 1956 there was outrage in London; the French, fighting against rebellious Algerians, similarly feared the new Arab militancy, and the leaders of the two nations began planning a joint military strike that would topple Nasser and put them in occupation of the canal. In London especially, Nasser inexplicably was seen as another Hitler—much as Saddam Hussein would be thirty-five years later—and politicians and the press talked wildly of the necessity to avoid another Munich. Egypt in 1956 wasn't Germany of 1938, but none seemed to realize this. In September the French conceived the stratagem of involving the Israelis, who looked on Nasser as the major supporter of Palestinian guerrilla activities, and members of Prime Minister David Ben-Gurion's government, eager to seize the opportunity to hit their main enemy, were brought into the planning.

During the last week in October, while the United States was in the final days of a presidential election campaign and the attention of the world was fixed on the anti-Communist revolt in Hungary, Israel began to mobilize its armed forces. On October 29 the Israelis sent their armour into the Sinai desert, an action that was greeted, according to plan, by a joint British-French ultimatum to Cairo and Jerusalem for "the early cessation of hostilities to safeguard the free passage of the Canal". Israel instantly agreed to halt its armoured spearheads sixteen kilometres west of the Suez Canal, but Egypt, ordered to halt its troops sixteen kilometres east of the canal and to accept temporary occupation of Port Said, Ismailia, and Suez, naturally refused. With that as justification—exactly as planned—Britain and France began air and sea operations. The Egyptian air force was eliminated quickly, while, in the Sinai, the Israelis routed Nasser's army.

At the U.N. the Anglo-French-Israeli invasion was viewed with utter horror by other Western nations. The United States introduced a motion in the Security Council that called on Israel to withdraw and on Britain and France to stop the threats of and use of force. The motion was vetoed by Britain and France. The next day, the Uniting for Peace resolution of 1950 was used for the first time, the vetoes of Britain and France were overridden by the required two-thirds majority, and the General Assembly assumed responsibility.

Ottawa's response to the attacks on Egypt was one of shock, "like finding a beloved uncle arrested for rape", *The Economist* observed. In public the government was moderate, merely expressing "regret" that Britain and France "felt it necessary to intervene with force on their own responsibility". But in private the line was much tougher, the secret telegrams from St. Laurent to Prime Minister Anthony Eden fairly sizzling—so much so that London was said to be "aghast". The Canadians believed they had been lied to by Eden in his past promises and in his description of the reasons for the Anglo-French ultimatum, and they thought London was risking the withdrawal of the non-white Commonwealth, as India, Pakistan, and Ceylon reacted very strongly to this outright attack on a Third World nation.

But what could be done? The Cabinet discussed the idea of a U.N. police force for Suez, and when foreign minister Lester Pearson left for New York on November 1 he took with him the idea of transforming the Anglo-French invaders into such a force. But the temper of the General Assembly made this out of the question. In the early hours of November 2, the assembly passed a resolution calling for a ceasefire and the withdrawal of troops.

Canada abstained on this resolution, and when Pearson took the podium to explain his country's vote he advanced the idea that was to win him the Nobel Peace Prize—the idea of a large U.N. army made up of national contingents. This was very different from the original post-war plan for a cadre of U.N. generals deploying international armies, which had proved unworkable. As Pearson said,

> I regret the use of military force...but I regret also that there was no more time, before a vote had to be taken, for consideration of the best way to bring about that kind of cease-fire which would have enduring and beneficial results.... I therefore would have liked to see a provision...authorizing the Secretary-General to begin to make arrangements with Member Governments for a United Nations force large enough to keep these borders at peace while a political settlement is being worked out.... My own Government would be glad to recommend Canadian participation in such a United Nations force....

Meanwhile the fighting continued, and Britain and France were now demanding a U.N. force as a precondition to a ceasefire. After hasty consultations in Ottawa and with representatives of other countries, Pearson introduced a resolution asking the secretary-general, Dag Hammarskjöld, to submit a plan for establishing "with the consent of the nations concerned" an "emergency international United Nations force to secure and supervise the cessation of hostilities", and it passed in the early hours of November 4. At home, many newspapers portrayed Pearson as selling out Canada's friends and pandering to petty dictators. "Canada chose to run out on Britain," the *Calgary Herald* said, "at a time when Britain was asserting the kind of leadership the world has missed, and needed."

Nonetheless, bolstered by the support of his prime minister and convinced that he was acting in the long-term best interests of all, Pearson persisted. He had extraordinary capacities for hard work and endurance. He was persuasive, and willing to use his powerful charm to make a point. Before noon a scheme was ready, improvised by an informal planning group of Canada, Norway, India, and Colombia. There would be a U.N. Command headed by General Burns, still chief of staff of UNTSO, and infantry would be sent by contributing countries as soon as possible. At the General Assembly that night, this resolution passed without objection. The U.N. was going into Suez.

So were the British and French. On November 5, Anglo-French troops landed from the air and sea at Port Said. But the attack only served to demonstrate the weakness of the invaders. Why had they needed a week to get troops from their staging areas on Cyprus to Egypt? Clearly Britain and France were no longer great military powers with a worldwide reach. And then a new menace appeared in this most appalling week in post-war history: the Soviet Union, its hands still running with the blood of the people of Hungary, threatened the attackers with nuclear weapons. To Washington, Moscow proposed "joint and immediate use" of Soviet and American troops to resist the "aggression against the Egyptian people".

Though Dwight Eisenhower, the newly re-elected American president, was furious with London and Paris, he immediately rejected the Soviet suggestion. Meanwhile, Pearson and Hammarskjöld were putting the finishing touches on a report to the General Assembly. No members of the Security Council were to be permitted to contribute troops; thus the Anglo-French invaders could not suddenly put on blue berets, nor could the U.S. or the U.S.S.R. send in armies. Political control was given to the secretary-general, and the force was to be politically neutral. Furthermore, it was recognized that Egypt's consent was necessary before the U.N. could function on Egyptian territory. The General Assembly accepted the report and the United Nations Emergency Force (UNEF) came into administrative existence. To turn it into a force in being was still to be achieved.

The immediate need was for infantry, and the 1st Battalion of the Queen's Own Rifles (QOR) was picked as Canada's contribution. In addition there would be "ordnance, army service corps, medical and dental detachments to ensure that the battalion group is self-contained and can operate independently from a Canadian base". The initial plan was to fly the QOR to Egypt on RCAF aircraft and use the aircraft carrier HMCS *Magnificent* to ship the vehicles and heavy equipment—and also, as General Charles Foulkes, chairman of the Chiefs of Staff Committee said, to provide "a firm base to which we could evacuate quickly" in the event of trouble.

While the Queen's Own scurried to get ready, Ottawa sent a trio of experienced military planners to New York to sit on Hammarskjöld's newly established Military Advisory Group. How would troops get to the Middle

East? What would they eat and how would food reach them? How could they communicate with New York and their home countries? What facilities were needed for transport, for supply, for maintenance? Could the United States be asked to assist in getting UNEF under way? No one had answers, but the Canadians stood out because of their experience: they were accustomed to sending troops abroad, they had unusually balanced forces, and they were scrupulous in their administration and staff work. Thus they were taken seriously when they suggested that UNEF should be a buffer force, large enough to be noticed but not one that could intervene militarily; that the U.S. should be asked to help with stores from its large stockpiles in the area; that the headquarters and support units for all contingents should be consolidated and should function in English; and that Hammarskjöld should get Egypt to agree to let UNEF in.

The latter proved more difficult than might have been thought. Its forces had been routed, but with the ceasefire in place Egypt now wanted to see its sovereignty infringed as little as possible. The secretary-general tried to ease matters by accepting troops only from non-controversial countries—Colombia, Brazil, Indonesia, Yugoslavia, India, Denmark, Sweden, Norway, Finland, and Canada. But was Canada truly in this category? Hammarskjöld thought so; Pearson had turned his back on Britain by proposing the creation of UNEF.

Not true, the Egyptians argued. Yes, Pearson had been helpful in New York, but there were practical problems. Canada belonged to that imperialist alliance, NATO. Besides, its infantry looked like the British infantrymen still exchanging shots with snipers in Suez; they wore the same uniforms, and Canada's flag included the Union Jack in one corner. Even the name, the "Queen's Own Rifles", sounded hopelessly British. No, the QOR could not come into Egypt.

While the objections were not unreasonable, they were excruciatingly embarrassing for Pearson. His role in New York was being denounced at home, and now the Egyptians, though defeated on the battlefield, were imposing conditions and slighting a regiment with battle honours extending back to the Fenian raids. Worse yet, the Queen's Own had been moved from their home in Calgary to Halifax with the full accompaniment of public relations fanfares. If they were rejected, the humiliation to the government would be acute.

But rejected they were, and Canada's pride was salved only slightly when General Burns found a compromise. On November 19, Burns wrote to Pearson to say that "the most valuable and urgently required contribution that Canada could make to the Force at the present time would be to supply an augmented transport squadron of the R.C.A.F." to carry troops to Egypt, and that "if the administrative elements of the army contingent could go forward at an early date" this would help get UNEF operating. With Burns' letter in hand, Ottawa could claim that military necessity alone was shaping its contribution. Whether the voters agreed was less certain; seven months later they would put Conservative leader John Diefenbaker into power. By November 21, in any case, three hundred administrative troops were on their way.

As soon as the Canadians arrived, General Burns asked them to take hold of the UNEF rear area. This was a hard task for they were housed in squalid huts, slapped under a curfew, and obliged to adhere to a blackout. As one private put it, "I thought we was here to clear the Egyptians out of the Canal Zone. Instead damned if they aren't treating us like prisoners of war." Still, they did their prosaic but essential jobs well, and by the next month Burns was asking for more of them. Once the British and French withdrawal had been completed and a demarcation line between Israeli and Egyptian forces had been defined, UNEF's problems were administrative, and no other remotely acceptable country could be found to tackle them. What the general now wanted was a signals squadron, a field workshop to handle electrical and mechanical maintenance, two transport platoons, and an RCAF communications squadron. To make this more palatable, he also asked for a (somewhat more glamorous) reconnaissance squadron equipped with armoured cars. Meanwhile the QOR returned home to Calgary, morale much depleted; *Magnificent*, carrying 405 soldiers and a hundred tonnes of stores and with its decks crammed with 230 trucks and other vehicles, as well as a helicopter and four light aircraft, finally sailed on December 29. When the carrier arrived in Egypt on January 12 the Canadian representation in UNEF exceeded one thousand men, or more than a sixth of UNEF's total strength.

The Canadians' tasks in UNEF were not all that dissimilar to the work they would have done with NATO or in Canada. Their administration was handled by the euphoniously named CBUME—Canadian Base Unit Middle East. The signals squadron was spread over four sites and had responsibility for communications within UNEF, using radio, telephone, teletype, and dispatch riders, and its commander was chief signals officer to the force commander. The field workshop maintained 1,250 trucks, the Royal Canadian Army Service Corps transport company hauled supplies from the docks to the troops in the field, and other Service Corps officers ran the

Cherif quay at Port Said. The Ferret scout cars and jeeps of the reconnaissance squadron, initially formed from officers and men of the Royal Canadian Dragoons and Lord Strathcona's Horse, patrolled the sand dunes along the desert armistice line, in serious danger from Israeli and Egyptian mines. And the RCAF's 115 Air Transport Unit, flying old Dakota transports and newer Otters, shared a desolate airfield with a squadron of MiG fighters of Egypt's air force.

Despite all the difficulties of heat, disease, and boredom, their one-year tour of UNEF duty was an education for the Canadians. There was a generalized contempt for the bribery and corruption endemic among Egyptian officialdom, but there was also sympathy for the civilians caught in this territorial impasse. In a personal letter in 1962, a lieutenant with the recce squadron of the Royal Canadian Dragoons would observe of the Israelis:

> ...there is only one kibbutz available for general study.... The leaders are pleasant to talk with, polite and half apologetic about their younger members who on the whole are inclined to be a bit arrogant and know it all. I think this is probably because they have not had to do any fighting but would like to prove that they are just as good as their elders. Unfortunately because of the rules it is impossible to have a good bull session.... I have the impression that they have a feeling that the 1956 war was a little too easy and they are wondering what would have happened if it had been a little tougher. Still, they are willing to do it again and they will go all out because they can't afford to lose.
>
> The Palestinian Arab who lives in the Gaza strip is between the Devil and the deep blue Med. Jimmy Nasser is pushing on one side and Israel stands on the other waiting to kick him in the teeth at the first sign of hostility. They're an unsettled group who are afraid Jimmy will use them for shock troops if he goes after Israel and right now there is no hope of smashing Israel and taking back the land they believe is theirs.

He added that it was a "funny thing coming off the desert—everyone feels like a big party and has a tremendous itch to shoot up the local police post." In other words, the frustrations of UNEF service were severe.

Still, there were compensations. There was leave in Beirut—then a warm city of great loveliness, although in 1958 it too needed a brief peacekeeping mission—the U.N. Observation Group in Lebanon (UNOGIL)—to patrol its Syrian border. There was the chance to talk with other U.N. troops and to watch their operational style. A captain with the transport company noted that "the gun-toting Brazilians" had a "distinctive method:

if they are not making headway on the local market they simply draw a .45 Colt and point it in the general direction of the shopkeeper. Very effective. Prices come down quickly. They are the bane of good Egyptian–UNEF relations." He was later made commander of the Port Said garrison, which included a movement-control detachment, a frozen-food storage depot, and a guard platoon of Indian soldiers. "I am senior U.N. officer in the Port so I am also sort of a mild 'big effendi'." That soon palled; he wrote a few months later, "Boredom is a place much like Port Said." Still, "Whatever else this force may be it does foster the belief that the U.N. is a working reality and that editorialists are both wrong and foolish to forecast its demise. Gaza HQ is a hodgepodge of more than two dozen countries. It's quite a sight on Sunday nights to see saris, turbans, business suits, fezzes, etc. A very good feeling. The brotherhood of man...."

THE SIX-DAY WAR

A sense of the brotherhood of man remained notably lacking between Egypt and Israel and between Israel and Syria. There were regularly military provocations between the nations, and in 1967 the Middle East once more blew up.

Tension had been rising since 1966, with snipings, raids, terrorism, and counter-terrorism forming the daily diet. In April 1967 there were serious clashes along the Israeli–Syrian border, and President Nasser, the acknowledged leader of the Arab world, could not afford to be left behind. When Israel issued a warning to Syria, Nasser responded by moving troops into the Sinai desert on May 15 and asking UNEF to withdraw from its sites along the Israeli–Egyptian border and to concentrate at Gaza. Secretary-General U Thant's reply was that UNEF would leave Egypt altogether if it had no useful role to play and if it was asked, and on May 18 Nasser made that "request"; a few days later Egyptian troops occupied UNEF posts overlooking the Gulf of Aqaba, Israel's only outlet to the Red Sea. By that time Ottawa had already sent out three RCN warships to bring the Canadian contingent home. After hurried consultations in New York and with U.S. President Lyndon Johnson, and after Israel had begun its own mobilization, Prime Minister Lester Pearson said that Canada supported "the right of access to and innocent passage through the Gulf of Aqaba". Nasser's response was to call Pearson an "idiot" and then, at 1:00 P.M. on May 27, to order Canadian troops out of Egypt within forty-eight hours.

This forced improvisation on National Defence Headquarters. The sea evacuation plan was scrapped and the RCAF's Air Transport Command was called in instead. By May 30 all the Canadians, except for a small rear-guard preparing the heavy equipment, had flown out of Egypt in eighteen flights on Yukon and C-130 aircraft, along with over 100,000 kilos of equipment. As a result, Canada was spared the casualties that fell upon the Indian (fourteen killed and twenty wounded) and Brazilian (one killed) UNEF units when Israel sent its forces against the Arabs on June 5. Massive air attacks wiped out its neighbours' air forces, and then Israel destroyed Egypt's army in the Sinai. Jordanian troops were pushed out of old Jerusalem and back over the River Jordan, and finally Syria was whipped on the Golan Heights. It took barely six days and left Israel the supreme military power in the Middle East, its forces sitting on a large expanse of territory extending from the banks of the Suez Canal to the Jordan River and the Golan Heights.

UNEF's ten years of peacekeeping had ended in war, confusion, and embarrassment. In Canada the reaction against the humiliation of Canada's representatives, and against the United Nations and peacekeeping in general, was very sharp—for a time. In the guidance notes sent to its missions abroad, the Department of External Affairs noted that "The lesson which we must draw from this is that a peace-keeping operation such as UNEF is not an end in itself but a practical adjunct to peace-making. Hand in hand with peace-keeping there must be continuous efforts to work assiduously for a settlement and not to regard a truce as a satisfactory long-term settlement."

It would take another bloody war between Israel and Egypt, in 1973, to force those two antagonists to the peace table, and there would eventually be another UNEF and then the Multinational Force and Observers (MFO), an American-sponsored peacekeeping force outside the aegis of the U.N. On Israel's other borders, however, there would be no peace, only a constant series of guerrilla skirmishes and air attacks interspersed with larger actions. The U.N. would be involved in these further futile pacification attempts, always with Canadians playing their usual quiet and competent role.

INDO-CHINA

By the early 1950s, peacekeeping had become an accepted form of international action. And it was not only the United Nations that found the concept attractive. When, for example, the Great Powers and the other countries concerned with the war in French Indo-China met at Geneva in the summer of 1954, an international commission to supervise a ceasefire, monitor the transfer of populations, supervise free elections, and keep watch on subsequent developments seemed a natural idea.

Indo-China, once a federation of a French colony and several French protectorates, includes the present-day countries of Vietnam, Laos, and Cambodia. When the area was liberated from the Japanese at the end of the Second World War, the French hoped to keep these countries as virtual colonies. Laos and Cambodia accepted the idea but in Vietnam a coalition of nationalists and Communists, the Viet Minh, demanded complete independence. The result was years of bitter fighting, with the French losing ground—and heart.

In 1954, at a conference in Geneva called to resolve both this and the Korean situation, it was decided that, pending elections, a provisional line would be drawn at the 17th parallel, separating "North Vietnam" (with its capital at Hanoi) from "South Vietnam" (with its capital at Saigon). A ceasefire would allow the French to withdraw, while the Viet Minh would pull back to North Vietnam.

Although Canada had participated in the discussions that wound up the Korean War, Ottawa was unrepresented at the Indo-Chinese talks. There was, as a result, enormous surprise and not a little concern when Canada, along with India and Poland, found itself asked to be a member of an international commission to supervise the ceasefire. Ottawa learned of the request from the press, and Canada's representative at the U.N.'s Geneva headquarters told Ottawa that "The suggestion made by the Chinese delegation at yesterday's meeting that members of the Commission be India, Canada and Poland came as a complete surprise." Apparently Krishna Menon of India had suggested Canada's name to China's Chou En-lai, and the choice had seemed acceptable. The reasons were almost exactly the same as those that had made Canada palatable to India and Pakistan when UNMOGIP had been set up a half-dozen years before: it was a disinterested, non-colonial power without military commitments in the region. But there was one additional factor: the commission was to be balanced, with one Western democracy, Canada, one Communist nation, Poland, and one neutral, India. Though it was a formula for deadlock, this troika represented the reality of power in South-east Asia in a way that a wholly neutral commission could not.

One immediate complicating factor was that the United States, though it had participated at Geneva, was unhappy with the concessions made to the Communists and was trying to dissociate itself from the plan. Another was that Ottawa had little familiarity with the background and complications of the area. Still, the request could hardly be evaded. As Lester Pearson said, "Just as local conflicts can become general war, so conditions of security and stability in any part of the world will serve the cause of peace everywhere." But in view of the Americans' disapproval, Arnold Heeney, Canada's ambassador to the United States, felt obliged to mollify the State Department and assure them that "we would wish to keep the United States Government informed privately of the course of events. This we felt we could do quite properly without impinging on our international responsibilities as members of the Commission." Much later down the road, the way Canada carried out that undertaking would cause substantial embarrassment.

The Cabinet agreed to participate, but questions remained unanswered. What was the legal basis of the Geneva agreements? Which countries were committed to maintain them? How many personnel would be required of the armed forces and from External Affairs? And how many commissions would be created?

The last question was the easiest to resolve. After discussions with the Indians and the Poles, there was agreement that three separate commissions should be formed and each of the members would pay its own personnel costs, while the Great Powers would share all but the local costs, which would be borne by the parties to the agreement. Like the U.S., South Vietnam dissociated itself from the agreements, an ominous hint of difficulty to come.

By August 11 the first Canadians had arrived in Indo-China. External Affairs had provided three officers of ambassadorial rank, some eleven or twelve political advisers, and office staff. The armed forces, primarily the army, contributed eighty-three officers, including three major-generals, and thirty-one other ranks. As most of the diplomats and officers were bilingual, this was a serious drain on the officer resources of the army and on External Affairs.

The records indicate that Canada hoped to carry out its work on the three commissions, soon to be dubbed the International Commissions for Supervision and Control (ICSCs) but always known as the International Control Commissions (ICCs), with impartiality. Still, the set-up of the ICCs left no doubt that each member was expected to represent a point of view, and before long the Canadians came to the conclusion that impartiality did not work. As External Affairs told its main posts overseas, "an impartial approach on the part of the Canadians combined with the partisan attitude of the Poles and the middle-of-the-road policy adopted by the

Indians did not lead to just decisions. Since early 1955, there has been an increasing tendency in the Canadian Delegation to apply pressure against North Vietnam and to defend South Vietnam when it was considered Commission action...was unduly harsh."

As that comment suggests, the real problem for the ICCs was in Vietnam. In Laos and Cambodia there was progress; the Cambodian government took hold of its territory with some speed, the Communists were persuaded to withdraw, the resettlement of refugees and political partisans proceeded calmly, and there were free elections in September 1955. With so little work, the members of the ICC had time to grow to dislike one another. As one Canadian officer wrote, everyone agreed not to discuss religion or politics or other topics liable to bring out deep prejudice. Language kept the Poles isolated, he added, and although initial efforts were made by Indians and Canadians to socialize, those soon foundered, and both kept to themselves. By 1956 the Cambodian ICC was essentially out of work, and it existed in only token form until complete withdrawal at the end of 1969.

In Laos the ICC supervised the release and exchange of prisoners, and teams stationed around the country investigated a number of military skirmishes. The conditions were appalling and the work was ordinarily boring, so much so that the Canadian ICC commissioner, Léon Mayrand, had time to report on the Polish contingent:

> Generally speaking our members get along quite well with the Poles in off duty hours, playing games together, entertaining on a team basis, loaning each other periodicals and books. However their dress, deportment, cleanliness and observations of local customs leaves much to be desired by our standards. Their table manners and consumption of food and drink are atrocious.

What the Poles reported about Canadian intelligence and table manners regrettably remains unknown.

By 1958 the opposing factions in Laos had formed a coalition, and the new government called for the ICC's withdrawal. But in 1961 the coalition collapsed and the Great Powers began to fight out their rivalries there. The next year the Laos ICC had to be re-established, and Canada provided a delegation of nine diplomats and nineteen military personnel. In 1969, although the Laos ICC continued, Canada withdrew its delegation; instead a member of the Vietnam ICC attended the sporadic meetings. This state of affairs lasted until 1973, when the Laos ICC was briefly revived before being finally wound down the next year.

If Laos and Cambodia were relative successes, Vietnam of course was not. In 1954 the country was divided between a Communist regime in the north, under the able Ho Chi Minh, and a "democratic" government in the south, and although elections were supposed to create a single government throughout the country, the South Vietnamese—with American encouragement—disdained the 1954 settlement and simply refused to hold them. The north, equally unwilling to see a free, supervised election, similarly ignored the Geneva accords, and both countries began arming themselves with the aid of their Great Power patrons—China, the Soviet Union, and the U.S.—again in violation of the accords. Thus the Vietnam ICC, the largest of the three from the beginning, had a hopeless task. With the co-operation of the departing French administration the ICC did supervise the regroupment of civilians, as French colonials left the north for Saigon or to return to France and as Roman Catholic Vietnamese in large numbers moved southwards. At the same time 80,000 Viet Minh troops moved north, leaving behind large cadres, soon known as Viet Cong, to begin a guerrilla war in the south. By April 1955, although the north had put obstacles in the way of the ICC and although Pearson had complained in Parliament of bureaucratic obstruction and intimidation, over 700,000 people had been moved from one zone to the other—an astonishing emigration handled in relative peace—while 75,000 prisoners of war had been exchanged.

Still, the Canadian frustration was growing. The Poles were openly partisan, winking at North Vietnamese violations of the accords but protesting even minor South Vietnamese breaches. The Indians bounced first to one side and then to the other, in a parody of neutrality. As long-time Canadian diplomat John Holmes wrote, because there was more freedom of movement in the south the ICC "was in a position to prove Southern but not Northern violations. The Southerners and Americans inevitably complained and increasingly insisted that the known if not proved disregard of the arms control provisions by the Communists not only justified but made essential their doing likewise." Moreover, the mounting tempo of the guerrilla war in the south, largely indigenous but undoubtedly supplied from China and North Vietnam, led the Americans to step up their military involvement in the early 1960s and to demand ICC action to control subversion.

By 1963 the Vietnam War was in full swing, and the United States was pressuring its allies to contribute. Australia, South Korea, and other nations sent troops, but Canada refused, citing its ICC membership as the reason: how could a country monitor a ceasefire, even a sham ceasefire, if its troops fought beside one of the belligerents? The logic was unassailable, and the ICC at least served one useful purpose for Canada.

There was precious little utility anywhere else. One analysis of ICC voting found that Poland and India had voted together forty-three times between 1954 and 1965 while Canada and India had cast similar ballots forty-two times; Canada and Poland had never voted together against the Indians. Even so, only 53 per cent of Canada's votes had been cast for South Vietnam, against Poland's 84 per cent for the north. Impartial Canada was not, but compared to the Poles the record looked reasonably balanced.

The commission lost all trace of usefulness as the intensifying war made the gathering of evidence more and more difficult. The mobile ICC teams that had operated in the aftermath of the Geneva accords had been disbanded, and the teams monitoring the flow of arms at major ports of entry were allowed only limited freedom. Squadron Leader Hugh Campbell, an RCAF officer who did a tour in Vietnam, talked freely to the press on his return, admitting bluntly that the Canadians had thwarted investigations of American violations of the arms provisions exactly as the Poles had earlier blocked investigations of northern violations. If the ICC team spotted jeeps being unloaded from a ship, the Canadians would claim the vehicles were South Vietnamese exports to the United States—and as long as the ICC was on the scene, the winches would dutifully load jeeps back into the hold.

In Saigon, as the New York *Times* reported in 1967, the ICC team drove each day to the airport to "look for foreign military aircraft, their type and number of engines, takeoffs and landings". Sometimes, the paper quoted one ICC member, "we stay minutes. Other days we stay hours but that is rare." In Hanoi the teams faced more sobering conditions. There was the threat of being killed in American bombing raids, food was scarce, and the suspicion of the North Vietnamese was palpable. The only entertainment possible was poker and the occasional old movie. The boredom and futility were mind-numbing.

What is significant is that virtually all the Canadian diplomats and servicemen who served on the ICC came away firm supporters of the American intervention. A whole generation, many destined to rise high in their country's service, had their anti-Communism reinforced by Indo-Chinese service. Information collected in the north quickly found its way to the Americans; diplomatic dispatches on North Vietnamese leaders and events similarly went to Washington. Charges that this was going on were made by Squadron Leader Campbell as early as 1965 and were repeated with details by the CBC in 1967, but Ottawa's denials of impropriety were always prompt: "Members of the Canadian delegation in Viet Nam are not engaged in clandestine or spying activities," Prime Minister Pearson said in May 1967. "The Canadian delegation reports to the Canadian government and the Canadian government only; it is for the Canadian government to decide in the case of these reports...what use is to be made of them in the course of normal diplomatic exchanges...." In other words, the ICC officers were clean but Ottawa was passing things on wholesale.

In fact Ottawa had been doing more than this. In 1964 and 1965 the Canadian ICC commissioner, Blair Seaborn, had made repeated trips to Hanoi. While doing ICC business Seaborn, a senior and able diplomat, had acted as an intermediary for the United States, or so telegrams published in the "Pentagon Papers"—a top-secret U.S. study leaked to the New York *Times*—indicated. For example, the U.S. government, though worried about Canada's increasingly negative attitude to the escalation of the war, nonetheless wanted Seaborn to warn the north that it would be "punished" if its infiltration into the south was not checked. Seaborn dutifully conveyed the message, in slightly different terms, telling North Vietnam's prime minister that the "USA did not RPT not want to carry war to north but might be obliged to do so if pushed too far by continuation of Viet Minh–assisted pressures". The responses were typically stubborn and unyielding and soon the Americans began bombing targets in the north, and the war escalated further.

Technically there was nothing improper in Canada acting as it did. The role of diplomatic intermediary is one of long standing. Still, for a member of the ICC, presumably expected to play a monitoring and supervisory role, to carry messages, sometimes bellicose messages, from one warring state to another was surely not what had been intended in the Geneva accords. The Vietnam War, vicious and corrupting as it was, had begun to infect everything it touched.

By 1972, as the war went on without let, the ICC role had become completely pointless, but there was still no easy way for Canada to escape its commitment. Then South Vietnam refused to allow Indian ICC personnel to operate there, and ICC headquarters shifted to Hanoi. The rancour between the participants increased and in 1973, after the Paris peace accords had more or less ended the war, the ICC wound up its operations. In Vietnam, at least, peacekeeping had been a lost cause.

However, that did not prevent the establishment of a new ICC. This one—known as the International Commission of Control and Supervision (ICCS)—was a creation of the Paris peace talks, concluded in January 1973, between the United States, South Vietnam, the Viet Cong's provisional government, and North Vietnam. To monitor the new "ceasefire" in South Vietnam and to supervise the latest exchange of prisoners of war, the parties called on Canada, Hungary, Indonesia, and Poland—for this ICCS was evenly balanced between two Communist and two non-Communist nations.

Canada's contribution was reluctantly granted by the government of Pierre Trudeau. After nearly two decades of unhappy and frustrating experiences on the ICC the government had few illusions about the possible success of the new commission, and agreed to join only if, as External Affairs minister Mitchell Sharp put it, "the provisions for the operation of the new Commission appear workable and offer some prospects for success." The minister and his officials knew that the peace being established was largely a sham, but their view was that participation was worthwhile because it would help extract the United States from the Vietnam quagmire. Therefore, Ottawa agreed to participate for only a two-month period, and the ambassador to the ICCS, Michel Gauvin, adopted what was called an "open mouth" policy. Canada was no longer playing games—if there was interference and obstruction, Gauvin would say so. Under the ambassador were 50 officials from External Affairs, and a military team of 240 headed by Major-General Duncan McAlpine; he and most of his men were on site by late January 1973.

Like the old ICC, the ICCS operated with both fixed and mobile teams, its headquarters located in the ICC's former building in Saigon. There were seven regional headquarters throughout the south, twenty-six smaller teams which monitored the inflow of war materiel and supervised POW exchanges—the most important aspect of the operation for the United States, and hence for Canada—and fourteen point-of-entry teams. The ICCS had access to twenty-one helicopters and four fixed-wing aircraft—ironically chartered from Air America, reputedly a Central Intelligence Agency front.

The pattern that had prevailed on the ICC very quickly reasserted itself as the ICCS bogged down under a flood of complaints, the great majority filed by South Vietnam. The Poles and Hungarians proved unwilling to criticize North Vietnamese violations of the ceasefire accords. In fact the ceasefire was an illusion, with both sides fighting major engagements. The main use of the Paris accords was to accelerate the withdrawal of American forces by providing, as an excuse, the story that the war was over.

The phony peace did not satisfy Gauvin. When he was chairing the ICCS he flatly refused to call meaningless meetings that would go on endlessly without reaching agreement; either there would be agreement, he said, or there would be no meetings. As the leading student of Canada's role noted, "A competent ICCS was anathema to the communist side. Investigators might 'discover' [North Vietnamese] troops." The ambassador, of course, knew they were all through South Vietnam, and in April he lent strong support to American charges that North Vietnam was infiltrating troops into the south. The Poles and Hungarians were most unhappy with Gauvin and went public with denunciations of his "arrogance".

Nor was Ottawa pleased when Viet Cong forces kidnapped some of its peacekeepers (they were later freed) and another was killed when his helicopter was shot down. True to its word, the government—which in March had reluctantly extended its participation for a further ninety days—announced that Canada was going to withdraw on June 30, 1973. After direct representations by American Secretary of State Henry Kissinger, the Canadians remained an additional month so replacements could be found. The decision to withdraw was Canada's toughest action ever in a peacekeeping role, the first and only time that Ottawa refused to continue its participation in a charade.

Except for a skeleton team, the Canadians duly left by the end of July. The war went on until North Vietnam's victory over the south at the end of April 1975, when—with the victors at the outskirts of Saigon—the Canadians' office and personal possessions, including the official car, were flown out. North and South Vietnam were reunited under Hanoi's control on July 2, 1976, twenty years after the Geneva accords. The Vietnam War was at last over.

Lt. David Baker, the UNMOGIP pilot who took this picture of one of the "better" landing strips in the mountains of Pakistan, noted that Himalayan valleys look much alike. "All the wrong valleys we named after pilots who turned into them by mistake."

The arrival of Baker's de Havilland Caribou (DHC-4) drew such a crowd in this Indian village that a travelling bear-trainer rushed out and started a performance under its wing.

The peace-loving Buddha in the background lends an ironic touch to this view of two Canadian captains on the International Control Commission hoping to bring peace to Laos in 1955.

A corporal of the Royal Canadian Dragoons serving with the ICC buys cigarettes from a street vendor in Vientiane, Laos, in 1955.

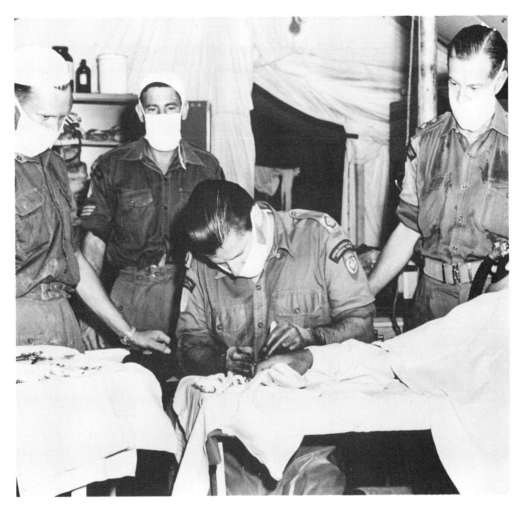

Canada always sent medical teams with its peacekeepers. These army doctors and attendants were operating in primitive conditions in the early days of the U.N. Emergency Force in Egypt.

The arrival of a de Havilland Otter (DHC-3) brings the children of El Arish running. The Otter was developed in the 1950s for work in Canada's north, but it has also served well for transporting observer teams, troops, and supplies to remote and primitive areas of desert and jungle.

Members of the RCAF's No. 115 Air Transport Unit look over the remains of an obsolete Egyptian Spitfire shot down during the 1956 war, just off the El Arish runway.

Canadians in the UNEF force in 1958 check out an Egyptian anti-aircraft gun near Signal Corps headquarters at Sharm El Sheikh, at the southern tip of the Sinai peninsula.

A Canadian major serving as a military observer with UNTSO in 1959 confers with a Jordanian police corporal at a checkpoint between Jerusalem and the Red Sea.

The first elements of the second UNEF arrived in Egypt in October 26, 1973—the day after the resolution setting up the force was officially adopted. Here, members of the 1st Signal Regiment test their radio equipment at UNEF headquarters in Ismailia, near the Suez canal.

UNEF II included contingents from Austria, Canada, Finland, Ghana, Indonesia, Ireland, Panama, Peru, Poland, Senegal, and Sweden. This Canadian captain is helping the Panamanians tune a high-frequency dipole antenna in the Sinai.

VIII
THE CONGO, CYPRUS, AND BEYOND

The Middle East and Vietnam were not the only troubled areas of the world. Everywhere colonial powers had been, there was difficulty as new nations struggled to be born. In the process, tribal and economic antagonisms burst forth to threaten the peace, often fed by outside nations pursuing their own interests.

One such area was the Belgian Congo (now Zaïre). Until 1960 a Belgian colony, the great, sprawling territory of mountains and equatorial forest had been ruled with stern and brutal paternalism from Brussels. Only the Roman Catholic Church and the giant mining cartels that had developed the mineral resources had had a share of power, and Belgium had governed as if its rule would be unquestioned for ever. It wasn't. Nationalism developed apace after the mid-1950s, and there were serious riots in 1959 in Léopoldville, the capital (now Kinshasa). In a panic lest the Congo turn into another Algeria, where France had fought a costly and ultimately unsuccessful war against a nationalist guerrilla movement for years, Brussels hastily promised independence for June 30, 1960.

Elections duly followed and a government headed by Patrice Lumumba took power on the transition date. Within a week, however, the army mutinied against its white officers and chaos broke out. The Belgian men and women who had remained fled, one step ahead of mobs—if they were lucky. Public services collapsed and Brussels responded by flying in troops to protect its nationals. Soon, the province of Katanga, site of most of the minerals, declared itself independent, and the Lumumba government appealed urgently to the U.N. for assistance, even though the new state was not yet a member.

Secretary-General Dag Hammarskjöld was quick to act. He summoned the Security Council on July 13 and asked it to provide military assistance to the Congo to help establish order and ensure withdrawal of Belgian troops. The force he proposed would be limited to self-defence and would not participate in internal conflicts. No troops from permanent members of the Security Council would be used, and units from African states would be sought first. Over the next weeks, Hammarskjöld developed the guidelines for his force. He drew on the experience of 1956 and UNEF, of course, but he also took care to ensure that the Congo force, already being called the Organisation des Nations Unies au Congo (ONUC), would be under his "exclusive command".

To take charge of ONUC, initially intended to be a small advisory force, New York named Carl Von Horn, the Swedish general who had succeeded General Burns at UNTSO. Von Horn persuaded New York that the force would have to be a large one—the country was so huge, the chaos so great. As a result, by mid-August there were more than fifteen thousand troops from twenty-four states; at its peak ONUC would muster twenty thousand from thirty-five countries.

In Ottawa there was no evident enthusiasm for participation in ONUC. Although the Progressive Conservative government had a battalion of infantry on standby and there was a list of a hundred officers from various technical services on alert, the fiscally hard-pressed Department of National Defence had no overwhelming interest in joining in; Prime Minister Diefenbaker told the House of Commons that, while a few Canadian officers from UNTSO had been seconded to Von Horn's staff, nothing more was contemplated. But U.N. requests increased, for more UNTSO officers, food, and RCAF aircraft for the evacuation of refugees and for a Congo–Europe airlift. More important, there were rumblings in New York that Canada might be asked to send signallers and logistics personnel. This alarmed the army, then in the throes of major cutbacks and acutely short of trained signals officers and men. Once word of the U.N. interest and the government's reluctance leaked out, the press got into the act. The legacy of Suez—now seen as one of Canada's finest hours—was made much of, and editorialists were sharply critical of Diefenbaker's unwillingness to assist the U.N. Under pressure Ottawa caved in, and the first group of signallers left Canada on August 9. By September 2, No. 57 Canadian Signal Unit was on the ground with some 280 officers and men.

That this was not going to be a triumphal march was immediately clear. The total disorder of the Congo was stunning to see: public services had collapsed, mobs roamed the street, and the ill-trained and brutal Congolese police and army were probably the greatest barrier to the restoration of order. One Ghanaian officer told a Canadian journalist that he had

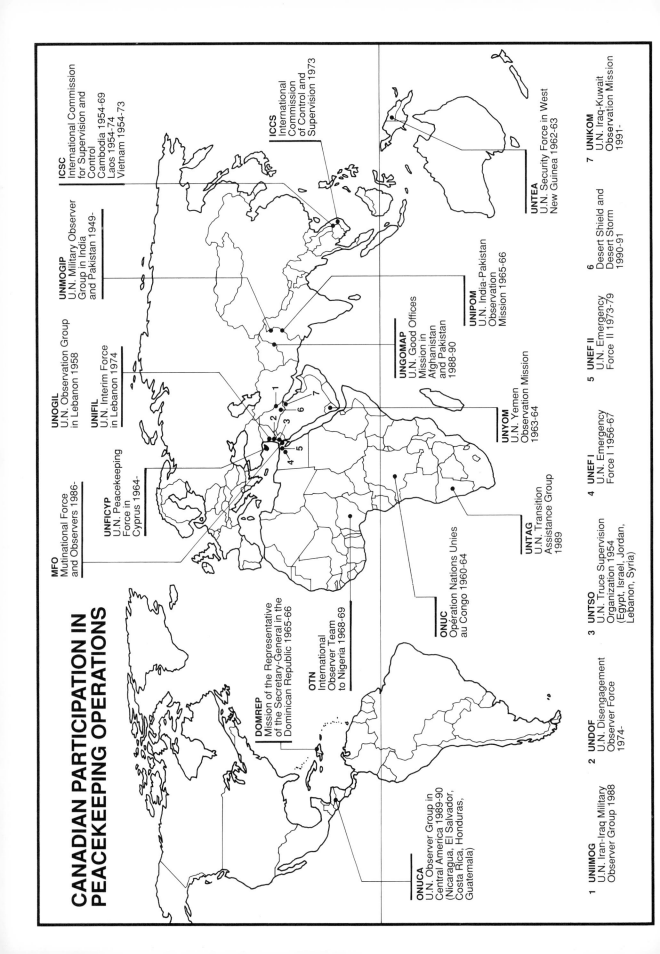

CANADIAN PARTICIPATION IN PEACEKEEPING OPERATIONS

ICSC International Commission for Supervision and Control
Cambodia 1954-69
Laos 1954-74
Vietnam 1954-73

ICCS International Commission of Control and Supervision 1973

UNTEA U.N. Security Force in West New Guinea 1962-63

UNIKOM U.N. Iraq-Kuwait Observation Mission 1991-

UNMOGIP U.N. Military Observer Group in India and Pakistan 1949-

UNIPOM U.N. India-Pakistan Observation Mission 1965-66

UNOGIL U.N. Observation Group in Lebanon 1958

UNIFIL U.N. Interim Force in Lebanon 1974

UNGOMAP U.N. Good Offices Mission in Afghanistan and Pakistan 1988-90

UNYOM U.N. Yemen Observation Mission 1963-64

MFO Mutinational Force and Observers 1986-

UNFICYP U.N. Peacekeeping Force in Cyprus 1964-

UNTAG U.N. Transition Assistance Group 1989

DOMREP Mission of the Representative of the Secretary-General in the Dominican Republic 1965-66

ONUC Operation Nations Unies au Congo 1960-64

OTN International Observer Team to Nigeria 1968-69

ONUCA U.N. Observer Group in Central America 1989-90 (Nicaragua, El Salvador, Costa Rica, Honduras, Guatemala)

1 UNIIMOG U.N. Iran-Iraq Military Observer Group 1988

2 UNDOF U.N. Disengagement Observer Force 1974-

3 UNTSO U.N. Truce Supervision Organization 1954 (Egypt, Israel, Jordan, Lebanon, Syria)

4 UNEF I U.N. Emergency Force I 1956-67

5 UNEF II U.N. Emergency Force II 1973-79

6 Desert Shield and Desert Storm 1990-91

7 UNIKOM U.N. Iraq-Kuwait Observation Mission 1991-

longed for the complete withdrawal of Britain from his country, but after being in Leopoldville and viewing the chaos, "I hope the English stay with us for ever."

This was the mess that awaited the Canadians. On August 18, two of the first signals detachments to arrive at Leopoldville airport were accosted by Congolese troops, accused of being Belgian paratroops, and stripped and beaten; their lives were likely saved by a Danish officer who delayed the Congolese until enough Ghanaian U.N. troops could be found to confront them. Protests were fired off by Ottawa and eventually drew a mollifying reply from the Congolese "authorities". That, however, did not prevent another incident at Stanleyville several days later, when Congolese troops beat and jailed another signals detachment. The detachment commander, Captain J.B. Pariseau, invited the local Congolese commander to dinner, explained that there were no hard feelings, and agreed that it had all been a ghastly error—but, Pariseau said, in future his troops would fight and the Congolese would be answerable to the Canadian army. That ended the difficulties. Even so, the editorialists who had been so critical of Ottawa's reluctance now began to change their tune. Too late—Canada was in the Congo, and its role was so critical in the absence of a functioning civilian communications net that it had to stay.

No. 57 Canadian Signal Unit's heart was the communications squadron that had its headquarters in Leopoldville and detachments scattered throughout the country. Detachments were ordinarily ten strong, and were responsible for maintaining communications with ONUC headquarters. At headquarters, which operated in both French and English when sufficient bilingual officers could be found, the Canadians handled everything from telephones to codes to dispatch riders. Indeed, to read Canadian messages to Ottawa, it often seemed as if the Canadians were running everything. Von Horn and most of his staff spoke no French, and he was described by Canadian officers as "confined to quarters and...in fact non-effective". By 1962 Canadians held sixteen positions on ONUC's staff, where they were the only officers able to speak to the Congolese employees and government officials, and Von Horn's successor as chief of staff told one Ottawa visitor that "the Canadian officers were vital to his organization and shouldered far more than their fair share of the work."

This military efficiency was not reflected in the Canadians' uniforms. Journalist Peter Worthington reported that they had a reputation for being friendly and capable but also "the scruffiest in appearance of all U.N. troops. In olive green bush pants and shirts, the Canadians resemble ill-clad refugees. The only creases the trousers hold in the steambath climate are wrinkles...." So unmilitary did they look that Canadian civilians were actually apologizing for the appearance of the signallers. Since "the bush trousers fade with every washing, no two Canadian soldiers have the same-coloured uniform." On the other hand, the Canadians seemed relatively unprejudiced: "At Leopoldville night clubs Canadian soldiers can be seen escorting Congolese damsels and creating inter-racial harmony."

The RCAF was also in the Congo, with a unit that at its peak had fifty-eight officers and men. Initially Ottawa had considered establishing a squadron of Caribou, the twin-engined workhorses that could take off from almost anywhere, but those plans fell apart. Instead the air force operated obsolete North Stars between the Congo and Pisa, Italy, and provided planes for U.N. transport duties within the Congo. The ONUC air staff was also well sprinkled with RCAF officers, including the commander, chief of air operations, and communications officer.

The Congo situation continued to exist in near-chaos. The erratic Lumumba's government ended up in a virtual war with the province of Katanga, the latter assisted by mercenaries and covertly aided by Belgian mining companies while Lumumba's government received Soviet military aid. Lumumba himself was murdered early in 1961 in mysterious circumstances, and Secretary-General Hammarskjöld died soon after in a plane crash while on a visit to ONUC.

Late in 1961, U.N. forces invaded Katanga in an attempt to end the province's secession, and there were heavy casualties. So serious did the situation become that the Canadians were ordered to shoot to kill if anyone tried to disarm them. When Colonel P.D. Smith, the Canadian commander in ONUC, told his men of the new order, "The unit's reaction to this announcement was an immediate outburst of clapping and shouting which lasted a full ninety seconds."

In March the detachment at the port of Matadi was overrun by Congolese troops after five hours of fighting. The Canadians, their villa riddled with fifteen to twenty large holes, surrendered after first destroying their cipher equipment. The Sudanese infantry guarding the villa suffered five casualties but the signallers fortunately sustained no loss. It was unclear who had fired first, and a Canadian officer reported to Ottawa with casual racism that "when two groups of excited and jittery Africans face each other at short range with their weapons loaded and cocked, someone is certain to open fire."

Individual Canadians had exciting experiences. Lieutenant-Colonel Paul Mayer and Sergeant J.A. Lessard, both of the Van Doos, won the George Medal for their part in rescuing more than a hundred missionaries at

Kisandji in early 1964. Mayer wrote that he had found himself surrounded by a crowd:

> There was much waving of arms, yelling and jabbing and spitting at me but I kept insisting that we go to the Mission to carry on the talks. The Chief then suddenly demanded to know what the ring on my right hand represented. As one of the Jeunesse [militant young men responsible for attacks on missionaries] indicated that he wanted it and was motioning that he would cut it off, I explained that it was a wedding ring.... The result...was that the Chief embraced me whereupon the Jeunesse tried to pull us apart. It was during this moment that I was hit from behind with the flat of a machete.... The Jeunesse were now arguing as to who was to kill me.... The man put the pistol against my stomach, thumbed back the hammer and pressed the trigger but the pistol did not fire since I had forgotten to put a round up the chamber.

Mayer escaped unscathed but shaken. Another officer, Lieutenant Terry Liston, was decorated for rescuing a Congolese soldier lying wounded in a minefield; Liston prodded his way through the mines with a bayonet for twelve yards "at the risk of his life".

For most Canadians the Congo was a prosaic if unpleasant posting. Even so, incidents happened frequently enough that Ottawa was not eager to help ONUC any further. A request for assistance in establishing a security service was rejected in November 1961, as was a call for more military police. The army in fact hoped to reduce the signals commitment, the chief of the General Staff claiming in early 1963 that he was at the limit of his ability to find enough men.

By then, fortunately, ONUC itself was beginning to be cut back. The war had petered out, the secessionist Katangese were back in the fold, and the U.N. was desperately short of money to pay the spiralling costs. In February 1963 there had been 317 Canadians there; on June 30, 1964 the last 56 left aboard an RCAF Yukon.

As for the Congo, the country had emerged from the chaos of 1960 into the all-too-common condition of African nations. While the regions were nominally united, their divisions remained fierce. Government services were inefficient at best, and officials saw their sinecures as licences to enrich themselves. The army, increasingly well trained and equipped, was the only force for stability, and the new president—inevitably—was a general. The U.N.'s role had bought some time, but at best, ONUC had been a partial success.

CYPRUS

While some U.N. operations have a defined lifespan, others seem fated to go on for ever. That is certainly the case in Cyprus. The small Mediterranean island has a population of some 700,000, with a large Greek majority and a substantial Turkish minority of about 20 per cent. Cyprus became independent from Great Britain in 1959, after a long guerrilla struggle by Greek islanders. Under the terms of the Treaty of Guarantee, Britain, Greece, and Turkey recognized and guaranteed Cyprus' security; each power, however, had the right of unilateral action to restore the conditions established at the time of independence. Moreover, Greece and Turkey were to station troops on the island, while Britain would retain large areas as sovereign bases.

This delicately balanced constitution needed only the lightest of pushes to send the whole structure toppling to the ground. In 1963 President Makarios, a Greek Orthodox archbishop and one of the major leaders of the guerrilla war, proposed constitutional revisions that appeared to threaten the Turks. Riots resulted, the U.N. Security Council failed to act, and a conference called by London produced no results. Britain then called on a number of NATO countries to contribute troops—something that might have been thought appropriate as both Greece and Turkey were members of the alliance—but Makarios objected; he would accept an international peacekeeping force, but it should be under U.N. control. In February 1964, after fruitless suggestions from Britain for a Commonwealth force, the issue finally came back to the Security Council.

Ottawa had been asked to participate in both the NATO and the Commonwealth forces and Prime Minister Pearson was apparently willing to contribute a battalion of infantry. He was similarly receptive to the idea of a U.N. force but, he told Parliament, there were conditions: it would have to contribute to the peace on Cyprus and its mandate would have to be for a fixed period; moreover, a mediator had to be appointed to search for peace. Experience had taught that peacekeeping without peacemaking was not enough, and Ottawa wanted no more operations that went on for years.

After clashes in New York between Greece and Turkey, with the Soviet Union supporting the Greeks, Secretary-General U Thant got the power to establish the size and composition of the U.N. Force in Cyprus (UNFICYP) on March 4, 1964. Canada, Ireland, Sweden, Brazil, and Finland were asked to supply troops but Ottawa now delayed, objecting to a lack of clarity in the force's mandated role and duties. On March 12, however, Pearson said Canada would join if a force was formed, the sole pledge of troops U Thant had received.

Pearson's pledge may have been spurred by Turkey's threat the day before to intervene if attacks against Turkish Cypriots continued. Greece responded by promising resistance, and suddenly the entire NATO position in southern Europe was jeopardized by the prospect of a war between the two countries. At this point Paul Martin, Secretary of State for External Affairs, stepped in. Working the telephones as only he could, Martin talked to the Nordic countries and wrung a promise of troops out of Sweden as well, and told U Thant that the force was a reality. That night Parliament approved the commitment of a battalion of the Royal 22e Régiment, the country's designated standby unit, and the armoured reconnaissance squadron of the Royal Canadian Dragoons. The hope was that the commitment might be for three months only.

The first Canadians of the advance party landed at Nicosia on March 15, followed two days later by infantry of the Van Doos. Their prompt arrival forestalled any Turkish invasion. The rest of the infantry, airlifted by RCAF Transport Command, arrived in a few days, and the aircraft carrier HMCS *Bonaventure*, carrying the RCD's scout cars and other vehicles, drivers, and supplies, pulled up to the dock on March 30. On April 14, Ottawa decided to supply a brigade headquarters of some 150 officers and men, and Canada's contribution reached 1,150.

By this time Finland, Denmark, and Ireland had promised infantry units. By June all the national contingents had arrived and UNFICYP had its full strength of 6,500, collectively known on the island as "Blue Berets".

The Canadians, being first on the scene despite their foot-dragging, got the hot spots to patrol. The force commander, General P.S. Gyani of India, said that Canadians could "create a more favourable atmosphere in the Nicosia area which is considered to be the most sensitive". As a result the Van Doos had the task of patrolling the Green Line, a buffer zone established by the British and so named because the senior officer involved had drawn a line on a map with a green pencil, dividing Greeks and Turks in Nicosia's crowded streets as well as the road between Kyrenia and Nicosia. After shots were fired at the troops, Makarios agreed that the Green Line should become a cleared and neutral zone and the Van Doos moved into empty homes, stores, and factories, physically interposing themselves between the fractious islanders. The policy to be followed was diplomatic toughness, as UNFICYP tried to establish its moral authority. That was not easy. As Brigadier Norman Wilson-Smith, commander of Nicosia Zone, wrote in 1965, UNFICYP had no authority to arbitrate a local quarrel or to make or enforce a decision. Force could not be used to intimidate or pun-ish, but only as a last resort. When infantry came under fire from both sides near Kyrenia in mid-April, for example, the company commander told his machine-gunners to fire sixty rounds in the general direction of the Turks. By August the Department of National Defence had decided to send powerful 106mm recoilless rifles; this was not a place where Canadi-an troops could afford to be outgunned.

The position was delicate, and not unlike that of a policeman called to break up a domestic dispute: the constable's first task is to separate the combatants, but then, all too often, both man and wife turn on the cop. In Cyprus, diplomacy and negotiating skills would be demanded of corporals and colonels alike.

By the end of 1964, matters had eased and the Canadians had begun rotating troops every six months. The island duty had much to recom-mend it. The patrolling skills that infantry and armoured car personnel had to use were good training, the weather was usually wonderful, there were good beaches, and leave could be taken in Beirut. There was also a high venereal disease rate that, one soldier remembered, led to top-level discussions at UNFICYP headquarters: "The Finns, Danes and Austrians were all for inspection of certain 'houses' by detecting and treating those involved. The British and Canadian representatives nixed the idea because of political implications. The Irish resisted on religious grounds." There was, as a result, no resolution, and VD continued rampant.

By 1969 the force's strength had been reduced by half, and Ottawa with-drew two infantry companies and the reconnaissance squadron, leaving a strength of about 480 officers and men. But there was still no resolution of the basic issues. In July 1974 the "colonels' government" in Greece attempted to bring about *enosis*, or union with Cyprus, and provoked a coup that overthrew Makarios and installed a former guerrilla gunman as president. The Turks, nearer to Cyprus than the Greeks and with highly efficient military forces, responded by sending 40,000 troops in by sea and air, effectively seizing control of almost half of Cyprus. Some 200,000 Turkish and Greek Cypriots were displaced, each communal group fleeing to the safety of its enclave. The Turkish invasion led to the fall of the Greek government and to new difficulties for UNFICYP. There was no help from New York; the force commander was told, in effect, to do the best he could.

What that meant was to minimize casualties to its troops, carry out humanitarian tasks with non-combatants and, where called for, with the opposing forces, and try to watch events so the U.N. could eventually react. But it quickly became clear that the U.N. flag had no inhibiting effect whatsoever: if necessary, either side would go right over a U.N. position to achieve an objective.

The Canadian peacekeepers, by this time paratroopers of the Airborne Regiment, came under fire, took some casualties, and dug themselves in. The contingent commander, Colonel C.E. Beattie, found himself trying to rescue women and children held hostage and to preserve Nicosia airport as a neutral zone. (He was probably helped, as one officer recalled, by the rumoured assistance available from a squadron of Phantom jets at the Royal Air Force base at Akroteri.) Beattie was highly praised for his leadership and the concern he showed for both troops and civilians, and was made a commander of Canada's new Order of Military Merit.

Beattie's efforts were matched by other officers who managed to keep the Ledra Palace Hotel, Canadian headquarters in downtown Nicosia, as U.N. territory. What had been a comfortable billet had suddenly become a hotbed of danger. A Canadian officer trying to escort stranded Turkish Cypriots back to their lines came under fire and was seriously wounded. When one of his men tried to give him first aid, he too was shot. Attempts to rescue the pair met with more fire, and the Canadians had to knock out a Greek Cypriot machine-gun post to free their men. After arranging for covering fire, Captain Alain Forand crawled out to the two, singlehandedly dragged the more seriously wounded to cover, and then directed the rescue of the second. His bravery won him the Star of Courage. But two other Canadians were later killed and seventeen were wounded.

The fighting led to renewed efforts to find a solution, but none produced results. The U.N. then requested an increase in the size of UNFICYP, and Canada doubled its contingent; armoured personnel carriers, scout cars, and infantry weapons came with the reinforcements. The task now was to create and preserve a buffer zone (BZ) running the entire 180-kilometre length of the island to separate the Greek Cypriot and Turkish Cypriot sectors. Within the BZ, UNFICYP controlled all military and economic activities, a task that it continues to carry out to this day. The difficulty with the BZ is that the Turks consider it a dead zone, open only to UNFICYP, while the Greek Cypriots consider it to be under their jurisdiction but temporarily covered by UNFICYP's mandate. The result is that the BZ is a porous barrier with both sides trying to impinge on it.

Elsewhere, incidents still abound. On July 31, 1989 a Turkish Cypriot soldier shot a Greek Cypriot national guardsman in an area patrolled by the 3rd battalion of the Princess Patricia's Canadian Light Infantry. Two privates heard the shots, ran to investigate, and summoned medical help, and the Cypriots went to the ready while the Canadian soldiers tried to deal with the wounded man and monitor events at the same time. The man died (the Turk who had shot him offered apologies) and the Canadian battalion commander ordered engineers to clear out the brush along a twisted section of front line. Now straight and clear, the roadway has been named "Patricia Way". A minor incident, an almost everyday occurrence in Cyprus.

As of 1990, twenty-seven Canadians had died in UNFICYP, most in accidents. The only certainty is that inevitably there will be more fighting; the Greek Cypriots are spending vast sums on weapons purchases, at least $325 million U.S. a year. They have acquired French AMX-30 B-2 main battle tanks, armoured personnel carriers, and helicopters, and the Greek Cypriot National Guard, officered by Greeks, numbers ten thousand. The Turkish Cypriot forces are smaller but the Turkish military presence remains large and is readily reinforced. In other words, only foolish leadership would set the Greeks against the Turks once more. Unfortunately, there is every indication that the leaders on Cyprus more than meet that requirement.

The costs of UNFICYP—and its deficit of $179 million U.S. as of 1990—only exacerbate the U.N.'s perpetual budgetary crisis. Financing of the force is by voluntary contributions rather than through assessments on all U.N. members, and that inevitably places the largest burden on the powers contributing troops, not least Canada. The annual cost of the peacekeepers is about $100 million U.S. and the total cost since its inception in 1964 amounts to $2 billion.

The Cyprus crisis has demonstrated that Pearson was correct in the conditions he tried for in 1964: a mediator was needed and peacemaking had to be part of the process. Unfortunately nothing came of those points, and Canada has been trapped in UNFICYP for more than twenty-five years. Undoubtedly the U.N. has stopped the constant sniping from escalating into open war; undoubtedly it is good field training for the soldiers. The difficulty is that some senior NCOs have done six-month stints six or seven times, or more. Virtually every regular-force soldier from armour, artillery, and infantry has served in Cyprus, and as manpower began to pinch in the Canadian forces in the late 1980s, reservists were used to flesh out the units. As Brigadier Wilson-Smith said a quarter-century ago, "Peacekeeping is no job for a soldier, but a job that only a soldier can do."

THE IRAN–IRAQ WAR

By now the Cyprus deadlock ought to have put paid to the whole idea of U.N. peacekeeping. That it hasn't suggests that there is still a role for the honest broker, someone who can step between warring factions and provide a face-saving way for them to back off.

In 1974, for example, a Canadian logistical unit was asked to join the U.N. Disengagement Force (UNDOF) along the Israeli–Syrian border, to help supervise the ceasefire and deployment of troops after the Yom Kippur War and to maintain an "Area of Separation" between the two armies. The Canadians are still there, maintaining vehicles and all kinds of electrical and electronic gear and providing supply and communications links. The posting remains a difficult one; the sweltering summers bring out poisonous snakes and spiders, whereas the winter snows are so deep that the Canadian mess hall once collapsed under them. But UNDOF is regarded as a highly successful peacekeeping operation.

As Soviet forces withdrew from Afghanistan in May 1988, the U.N. sent in a small corps of experienced peacekeeping officers called the Good Offices Mission in Afghanistan and Pakistan (UNGOMAP). Their tasks were to confirm the withdrawal, assist in repatriating refugees, and ensure that Pakistan and Afghanistan refrained from interfering in each other's affairs. It was a peculiarly complex operation because of the limited role of the U.N., the heavy U.S. and Soviet involvement on opposing sides, and the inaccessibility of the Mujahideen resistance; only the experience and good sense of the peacekeepers saw them through.

In August 1988 the Security Council authorized the formation of the U.N. Iran–Iraq Military Observer Group (UNIIMOG). Iran and Iraq had been engaged in a massive war of extraordinary ferocity since 1980 and both were near exhaustion. The U.N. had been trying for some time to get the parties to accept a ceasefire but its efforts had met with little success. A resolution of the Security Council in 1987 was initially rejected by Iran, but in July 1988 Tehran indicated that it was prepared to reconsider. A technical mission visited the war zone and it was determined that the force size should be 350 observers with communications and logistics support. After long negotiations in New York, Canada agreed to provide 15 observers and a 525-man signal and support unit until such time as the U.N. could recruit and train signallers and purchase the necessary equipment for them. The first Canadian troops arrived in mid-August.

UNIIMOG was to be divided in two, headquartered in Tehran and Baghdad, with approximately 160 observers on each side of the ceasefire line. Each detachment of observers was to be supported by 88 Canadian Signal Squadron with its 170 vehicles and radios. The Iraqis were quick to make arrangements for the UNIIMOG deployment, but Tehran was balky in a number of ways. The Canadians insisted their troops carry personal weapons, something that upset the Iranians. Communications in the Iranian forward zones were limited, yet Tehran insisted on forty-eight hours' notice of all flights—likely because USAF c5 Galaxies had to be used to transport some of the signal equipment. There was a residue of tension left from 1979, when the Canadians had harboured and then spirited away American embassy officers hiding in fear for their lives after the U.S. embassy had been seized by revolutionary militants.

There were more difficulties than usual in the operation. The obsolete radios the signallers had brought with them proved ineffective in the mountainous terrain along the ceasefire line. The radio vans had no air conditioning, a critical factor in the 45°c heat of Iran and Iraq. Maps were in short supply. And suspicion between the two sides had not been eased by the ceasefire. The U.N. was not seen as impartial by anyone, and there were serious fears for the safety of its troops.

Even without all that, life would have been unpleasant. The accommodations, fetid barracks or tents, were unsatisfactory. There was too much work for too few hours. "There is no entertainment," one officer wrote in an article published in a military journal, "except for the singing of the Koran from towers throughout the city. The troops can't even leave the compound to take a walk. And more culture shock—no local pub, and drinking is forbidden." The Iranian liaison officer whispered that even card games should not be played where they might be seen—"It is against the law to play cards in this country"—nor could the soldiers wear short-sleeved shirts: "It may offend the local women." For some of the Canadians, the officer said, "It's a bit like being in prison—working, eating, sleeping and no freedom to come and go...."

On the Iraqi side of the line, things went much better—in 1988 Iraq was seen as far more pro-Western than the fundamentalist Iranians. The troops had arrived expecting the worst. "On the aircraft," one officer remembered, "everybody had a plasma bottle on one leg, nuclear biological chemical warfare kits, flak jackets and weapons." The reality was very different. Accommodations in Baghdad were first class and the food was good. Water was readily available and the sixteen-hour days, while exhausting, could be compensated for with occasional restaurant meals. The signallers and support troops in Iraq had drawn the long straw. As for the others, the U.N. managed to set up its signals net fairly quickly, and all the Canadians, except for some fifteen observers who remained through 1990, returned home without mishap before Christmas of 1988.

NAMIBIA AND CENTRAL AMERICA

At the end of the 1980s, an unusual Canadian force served in Namibia, the former South West Africa. Although the United Nations had officially terminated South Africa's control over the region in 1966, and the International Court of Justice had supported the resolution in 1971 and ordered South Africa out, South Africa had for years refused to give up control. In January 1989 free elections were finally being planned and the U.N. began establishing its Transition Assistance Group (UNTAG). UNTAG would combine police, military observers, and infantry to supervise South Africa's withdrawal from its war against the guerrillas of the South West African People's Organization (SWAPO), and to oversee elections. There were the usual difficulties in finances, and serious problems in deploying the UNTAG forces—circumstances that led to repeated breaches in the ceasefire and to South African demands for UNTAG to leave within days of its arrival. By November, however, South West Africa was stable enough for elections to be held.

Much of the work would come down to supervision of the local police, and so UNTAG included police contingents from twenty-four countries. Among them were a hundred Royal Canadian Mounted Police—selected from two thousand volunteers—who were dispatched in October. The Mounties, as Secretary of State for External Affairs Joe Clark told the U.N., had helped to "establish by their presence the rule of law in the Canadian west. They brought order, not force, and by their conduct, established a respect that endures to this day...."

Very quickly, the RCMP had the same impact in Namibia. Wearing khaki cotton army uniforms (their own woollen uniforms would have harboured parasites) and blue berets, the Mounties accompanied local police, staffed polling stations, and helped the elections take place with surprising peace. One sergeant spent seven nights guarding ballots in the country jail—the safest spot in town—and when another spent a night in a thatched hut he was advised to ignore the lizards crawling through his uniform, as they would conveniently eat the insects out of it! The U.N. was more than pleased with the Mounties: "In their first week," one official said, "they did more organizational and public relations work in the communities—both black and white—than police from other countries did in six months.

They're clearly professionals." But accompanying South West African Police on the job and recording complaints against them was a delicate task. One constable who had come fresh from drug duties in St. John's reflected that "I really don't know if I'd like having a policeman from another country following me around while I'm doing my job. But we've established a good rapport."

Thanks to that rapport, the Mounties' first operation outside Canada ended with substantial dispatch. The elections were deemed democratic and certified "free and fair" by the U.N., with SWAPO the winner; South Africa withdrew completely; and UNTAG wound up on schedule.

Even as Namibia was entering a new era, so too was Central America. The Sandinista government in Nicaragua, like Castro's Cuba before it, was seen by the United States and its client states in the region as a focus of subversion. Certainly there were guerrilla movements in El Salvador and Honduras aiming to topple the pro-American governments. At the same time the Americans were sponsoring the Contras, a guerrilla force that threatened the Sandinistas. Prolonged efforts, strongly supported by Ottawa, by the Contadora group of four Central and South American nations to start a peace process had foundered—even though a peace treaty had been negotiated and signed in August 1987—thanks to Washington's hostility. Then, in March 1989, the presidents of El Salvador, Nicaragua, Honduras, Guatemala, and Costa Rica asked the U.N. to establish a peacekeeping force in the region.

In mid-October, U.N. Secretary-General Pérez de Cuéllar produced plans for ONUCA, the Spanish acronym for the U.N. Observer Group in Central America. Initial plans called for a six-month mandate and looked to participation from Canada, West Germany, Spain, Colombia, Ireland, and Venezuela. ONUCA was to be an observer group with logistical and air support to a total strength of 625, and its primary task would be to monitor Nicaragua's borders with Honduras, Costa Rica, Guatemala, and El Salvador. The Canadian contribution was expected to be some 40 officer observers and 100 air and ground crew to service eight helicopters. But the Canadian government's position was that Canada would only participate if a ceasefire was in place from the outset.

With that condition fulfilled, an advance team of nine left Canada on December 3 for Honduras under Brigadier-General Ian Douglas, part of an eighty-member advance party. Douglas was second-in-command of the whole force, and he was not noticeably sanguine about ONUCA's prospects; he told the press that it might last as long as the Cyprus operation. By the beginning of February there were twenty-two Canadians with ONUCA, a fifth of its strength, and the thirty-three observer posts had still not all been sited. One pilot told the press that this was the most challenging of all peacekeeping operations: "It's exciting, meeting with the Contras one day, going to see the Sandinistas the next day to try to get things arranged."

The prospects for peace improved mightily on February 25, 1990 when the Sandinista government was driven from power in a stunning election defeat. The new government persuaded the Contras to lay down their arms and began to take control of the Sandinista army. The U.N. observers turned their attention to disarming the Contras and by June, with that delicate task largely completed, ONUCA staged its "demobilization" ceremony and went home.

PEACEKEEPING AT HOME

Canadians tend to assume that problems will arise somewhere else in the world—never in Canada. The idea that troops might be needed to restore order here at home seemed virtually unthinkable until the summer of 1990.

Then militant elements on a Mohawk reserve at Oka, Quebec came into confrontation with the town council, which had authorized a golf course to expand on land claimed by the natives. A simple dispute escalated quickly, and masked Mohawk "Warriors" dressed in camouflage gear, armed with AK-47 automatic rifles, and suspected of having heavier weapons put up barricades and began to dig trenches and site anti-tank ditches. The Sûreté de Québec—the notoriously inefficient provincial police, whose racial biases towards the Mohawks were a source of constant grievance—mounted an abortive and ill-planned armed assault on the Oka barricades. One officer was killed, apparently by Mohawk gunfire. Within hours, another Mohawk group at Châteauguay had blocked the Mercier bridge joining Quebec's south shore to the island of Montreal. Soon the police were finding their manpower strained as they held back angry crowds of white commuters and protesters at the bridge while trying to maintain pressure on the Warriors at Oka. At last, on August 7, Premier Robert Bourassa made use of the National Defence Act, which authorizes a province's attorney-general to call in the military.

The army, and notably the 5th Mechanized Brigade, based near Quebec City, moved its troops and armoured personnel carriers into the two affected areas. At first the Mohawks were relieved that the hated Sûreté was off the confrontation line. But on August 27, with negotiations between the

Mohawks and the provincial government at a standstill, Bourassa asked the army to remove the barricades. The army began to exert a steady pressure and, by combining negotiating skill with a judicious use of bluff and the threat of force, succeeded in clearing the Mercier bridge. Then it was Oka's turn; by the same methods the Warriors were slowly pressed back into an ever-diminishing perimeter, and finally obliged to surrender.

All this was done under the eye of the television camera and with the print media looking on. There was extraordinary raw footage on the TV screens each night, with the public in Canada (and around the world) seeing Warriors and their supporters in face-to-face confrontations with young soldiers from the Royal Canadian Regiment and the Royal 22e Régiment. There was regular verbal abuse, occasional physical confrontations, and a continuing air of high tension. But what came across most clearly was the professionalism of the Canadian Forces.

The Oka and Mercier bridge affairs were classic examples of peacekeeping. Many, perhaps a majority, of the troops involved had served in Cyprus or on other U.N. operations; virtually all the officers above the rank of lieutenant had done so. They had learned how to handle hostile crowds, how to resist provocation, and how to carry out their mandate fairly, firmly, and without the loss of face or, more important, life. Columnist Peter Worthington wrote that the Canadian army "is, literally, the world's expert in easing tense, volatile situations", pointing out that for years Canadian "soldiers have been quietly solving tense situations without fanfare or fuss, mostly on their own judgement and initiative". Canadians who might have had doubts about the worth of their army's peacekeeping experience were largely converted by the scenes they watched nightly; Canadians who might have believed that their country could make do without armed forces watched the army save the Sûreté's bacon—along with that of the governments of Quebec and Canada. There was criticism of the provincial government's decision to send in the troops, but there was scarcely a whisper of complaint—except from the Mohawks and their supporters—about the way the soldiers did their trying job in the face of great provocation.

In 1974—when U.N. peacekeepers had been on Cyprus for a decade—a coup on the island led to a Turkish invasion and renewed violence. Above: a Canadian soldier helps evacuate refugees under fire; below: troops take refuge in an armoured vehicle.

After the 1974 hostilites, U.N. troops took on the additional task of supervising the ceasefire and patrolling the buffer zone. This M-113 armoured personnel carrier is patrolling Cyprus' "Green Line", dividing the Turkish and Greek enclaves.

By 1988 the Cyprus peacekeeping force had put in almost 25 weary years, with no end in sight. Here, members of the Princess Pat's work out on an obstacle course.

After the withdrawal of the Belgian army, the U.N. agreed that its troops would help train the Congolese army. Here, a sergeant of the Van Doos trains an officer in the use of a Canadian light machine-gun.

In contrast, the 1960 U.N. intervention in the Congo lasted just four years. These Congolese paratroopers await orders as a Swedish pilot consults with Canadian Lt.-Col. Paul Mayer, directing a mercy mission to evacuate missionaries.

A sergeant with 57 Canadian Signal Unit copes with a less glamorous but essential aspect of duty in the Congo—a mountain of outgoing Christmas mail.

By the 1960s the de Havilland Buffalo (DHC-5) was replacing the smaller Caribou. In 1974 a Buffalo flying from UNEF II in Ismailia to UNDOF HQ in Damascus was shot down by Syrian missiles near the Syria–Lebanon border, and nine Canadians lost their lives—the worst incident involving Canadians since the Korean War.

Canada took part in two international truce commissions in the course of the Vietnam War. Here, Canadian and Indonesian officers of the second commission question the sole survivor of a South Vietnamese patrol caught in a Viet Cong ambush, in 1973.

Another team views the body of a Viet Cong fighter killed in a skirmish with the South Vietnamese army at Xuan Loc, 100 kilometres south of Saigon.

A staff officer in the truce commission checks a boobytrap made of two anti-tank rockets, found near his office at Phan Thiet, not far from Saigon. Though Canada claimed neutrality, its truce commissioners' sympathies were clearly with the Americans.

In 1989, 100 RCMP officers volunteered for U.N. duty in Namibia, to oversee police elections. Among the perils they faced were poisonous snakes, scorpions, and a herd of elephants that stampeded through a tent camp.

In the standoff at Oka the army practised its hard-learned peacekeeping skills at home, keeping cool heads in the face of taunting native Warriors (above) as well as other groups like these war veterans (below).

If they missed themselves on the evening news, these Van Doos could catch up on the Oka furor in the next morning's headlines.

IX
THE FUTURE
OF PEACEKEEPING

The tearing down of the Berlin Wall and the stunning move towards democratization throughout Eastern Europe and in the Soviet Union at the end of the 1980s brought hope to a world that was desperately weary of almost a half-century of continuous war and Cold War. For forty-five years the Soviet Union and its satellites and the Western democracies had glared at each other; for forty-five years both sides had poured billions of dollars each year into armaments and into winning the support of uncommitted states by fair means or foul; and for forty-five years the risk of nuclear confrontation and annihilation had kept the world on tenterhooks.

The prospect of an era of world peace, however, verges on the illusory. Racial, religious, and economic tensions continue to fester—not least in Eastern Europe, where, with the heavy hand of Moscow removed, countries such as Romania and Hungary are rekindling their historic racial and territorial antagonisms. In the Far East the two Koreas continue to jostle each other, while Cambodians persist in destroying their country's chances of life. India and Pakistan keep tension high on their borders, while Israel and the Arab states that surround it on three sides watch the Palestine Liberation Organization and *intifada* and ponder the prospects for any kind of lasting peace. In South Africa blacks and whites seem to be moving towards an accommodation, but that troubled process is caught up in a deadly race with Zulu–Bantu antagonisms that threaten to destroy anything peace may bring. And everywhere, the poor and dispossessed are restless and angry, their near-hopeless lives battered by official corruption, rising oil prices, and declining crops.

242

The War in the Gulf

The fragility of order—both foreign and domestic—became all too clear to Canadians in August 1990. No sooner had the Oka incident demonstrated that Canada had no magical immunity to armed violence, when the Iraqi invasion of Kuwait brought the prospect of war home with startling force. The Cold War might have come to an end, but the prospects of peace really were illusory.

When President Saddam Hussein's huge army occupied the tiny emirate of Kuwait at the beginning of August, the world was unaccountably shocked. Saddam had invaded Iran in 1980, and in the vicious war that followed the Iraqis used chemical and nerve gases against Iranian troops in the field and against rebellious Kurdish villagers in Iraq. Saddam, in other words, was an especially ruthless tyrant. Now he had control of the immense oil reserves of Kuwait, while his tanks were poised on the border of Saudi Arabia, the source of much of the West's oil. Would he stop?

The Soviet Union had been Iraq's primary source of modern weaponry, but Moscow, now absorbed in its own internal difficulties, had little desire to assist Saddam in digesting his conquest. The United States had supported the secular Moslem Iraqis during their war with the fundamentalist Iranians, but President George Bush was outraged by the Kuwait invasion: Saudi Arabia's oil was essential to the industrialized world, and the Saudis were the major prop in America's position in the Arab world. Marshalling support at the United Nations, the Americans quickly and skilfully put together a huge international military, naval, and air force that ultimately totalled some 750,000 men and women from thirty-seven countries. The Soviet Union appeared as offended by the invasion as every other nation. Worried about its own oil supplies and desperate for Western economic aid, Moscow pledged its assistance to the Americans. So too did a number of Arab and Moslem nations fearful of Iraq for a variety of reasons. Syria sent troops, as did Egypt, Morocco, Pakistan, and others, and the Iranians, still recovering from their war with Iraq, lent a positive neutrality to the American-led coalition's efforts. The U.S. itself began to move more than half a million personnel into the area to defend Saudi Arabia, in an operation dubbed "Desert Shield", and to exert economic and military pressure to force Iraq to retreat. One of the first measures was a naval blockade.

When asked by President Bush if Canada could contribute to the international force, Prime Minister Brian Mulroney promptly replied that it could. On August 10, just a week after the Iraqi invasion, Mulroney declared that Iraq had "flagrantly violated international law and offended against the most basic human values everywhere". Canada's expertise and reputation were based on its peacekeeping role, he said, but that "does not remove from us the responsibility" to respond to attacks and threats against Canada's friends and allies. The country "must do everything it can" to restore Iraqi respect for international law. To that end the prime minister ordered two destroyers, HMCS *Terra Nova* and *Athabaskan,* and a supply ship, HMCS *Protecteur,* to the Persian Gulf.

In Iraq, Saddam's government quickly seized resident foreigners as hostages, while in Kuwait the embassies, including Canada's, were ordered shut. But despite Iraq's aggression and these violations of international law, in Canada there was immediate and almost reflexive criticism of the government's action. The press and spokespersons for the country's peace movement announced that this was only the second time since 1946 that Canada had sent troops abroad other than under the United Nations—the first being the multilateral force in the Sinai—clearly implying that Canadians should serve abroad only under U.N. auspices. (In fact the critics were forgetting Canada's two forays into Indo-China in 1954 and 1972.) Others argued that Canada was, as a writer in the *Globe and Mail* put it, becoming involved "in an adventure that has nothing to do with respect for international law, but everything to do with U.S. interests and domestic politics...." In other words, by supporting the U.S. in its "gunboat diplomacy" in the Gulf, Canada might jeopardize its hard-won status as the pre-eminent supporter of United Nations peacekeeping. A Security Council decision on August 25 to slap economic sanctions on Iraq and to allow a limited use of force to maintain the blockade eased that concern somewhat. And as an editorial in the *Globe and Mail* also pointed out, "failing to defend our interests"—meaning the national interests of preserving peace and deterring aggression—"would be the gravest folly".

The true folly in the affair could not escape notice. The three navy ships ordered to the Gulf were rust-buckets ranging in age from eighteen to thirty-one years. As the Iraqi forces had modern missiles and the three warships lacked anti-missile defences of any kind, ships under construction or in refit had to be cannibalized to fit them for possible action. One gun was actually removed from a museum display to be fitted on one of the ships. As a *Toronto Sun* columnist said, "the fact that they were already supposed to be 'warships' is beside the point, I guess." For a humiliating two weeks the country watched while the ships were readied for service, and when the trio began its long voyage to the Persian Gulf the navy made it clear that the length of the journey would conveniently allow time to train the officers and ratings in how to use their new weaponry. None of this was the navy's fault; the

crews were highly skilled and professional. They had, however, been con-
demned to serve in a government-neglected force that had seen its equipment rust away and had seen new ships on order delayed again and again.

While the *Terra Nova*, *Protecteur*, and *Athabaskan* and their 934 sailors
(27 of whom were women—the first time women had gone on active service with the navy) made their way to the Gulf, the tension continued to
mount. At the end of August, Saddam Hussein relented and agreed to
allow his women and children hostages to leave Iraq and Kuwait; the men
would remain as "guests". On September 14, with no end to the crisis in
sight, Canada increased its commitment. The prime minister announced
that a squadron of eighteen twin-jet CF-18 fighters, capable of speeds of
2,000kph and of filling either an attack or an interceptor role, would proceed to the Gulf from Canada's NATO bases at Baden and Lahr, Germany.
The aircraft, armed with 20mm guns and Sidewinder and Sparrow missiles, were to provide cover for the Canadian ships as they patrolled their
assigned areas in the middle of the Persian Gulf, some 500 kilometres
from Iraq. The deployment would put another 450 pilots and groundcrew,
men and women, into the Gulf. The squadron (increased to twenty-four
aircraft in January 1991 to allow for normal maintenance and any losses)
was to be located at Doha, Qatar, at hurriedly constructed bases dubbed
"Canada Dry One" and "Canada Dry Two"; Canadian headquarters was
located in Bahrain. Initially, ground protection came from a company of
infantrymen from the Royal Canadian Regiment. The CF-18 squadron—the
"Desert Cats"—became operational on October 8, and its capacities were
soon enhanced by a Boeing 707 air-to-air refueling tanker.

On October 1, just days after the Iraqi president promised "the mother
of all battles" if his conquest of Kuwait was challenged, HMCS *Athabaskan*
began its blockade enforcement duties by stopping an Indian liner north-
bound for the Iraqi port of Umm Qasr. "It was a friendly visit," one officer
said, "it's standard operating procedure." Six additional vessels were challenged that day by radio or inspected by the ship's Sea King helicopter,
called "Hormuz Harry" by its crew of four. At the same time the Canadians, and notably their force commander, Commodore Kenneth Summers,
were refining their command and control procedures with the dozen or
more navies (including Belgium, Britain, Denmark, France, Greece, Italy,
The Netherlands, Australia, Argentina, and the Soviet Union) operating a
giant hundred-ship fleet in the area—a task made easier by years of NATO
exercises that had standardized procedures among NATO fleets and other
Western powers. By Christmas the Canadian ships were patrolling an area
stretching from Bahrain to the Straits of Hormuz, and had boarded twenty

vessels and made almost one-quarter of the inspections undertaken by the allied fleet.

The sailors, like all other troops in the Gulf, lived with the fear of chemical attack, for the Iraqis had Scud missiles that could be armed with nerve gases or other chemical agents. This meant that anti-gas drills, always a part of the Canadian Forces' training, had to be treated seriously, and in the hot climate of the Gulf—38 to 45°c—that forced serious inconvenience on everyone. Nerve gas antidotes, consisting of atropine and a Canadian-developed substance called HI-6, were standard issue, but they might be dangerous for some users, and the Canadian Forces' antidote took at least seventeen seconds to mix and inject; too much time, said some. Moreover, the gas protection suits were cumbersome and claustrophobic at the best of times; in the terrible heat of the Middle East the difficulties of fighting in such equipment were severe indeed.

Meanwhile, as the huge U.S. buildup of troops and equipment went on frantically, the pressure on Iraq continued at the United Nations. On November 29, 1990 the Security Council accepted an American resolution to authorize the use of "all necessary means" to get Iraq out of Kuwait by a deadline of January 15. In Ottawa, members of Parliament hotly debated Canada's role in the Gulf, with the Liberal and NDP speakers offering support for the country's troops while simultaneously urging that economic sanctions be given more time to work, and objecting to giving the government a blank cheque. "Canadians deserve to know clearly what Canada is being committed to," said NDP leader Audrey McLaughlin. As a non-permanent (two-year) member of the Security Council, Canada had more voice than usual at the U.N. The Mulroney government backed the Security Council resolution in Parliament and carried its position by a vote of 111–82, and in New York Canada co-sponsored the U.S. resolution and voted for it.

Did this mean war? Not yet, or so Secretary of State for External Affairs Joe Clark maintained: "That is up to Iraq. It is not too late to solve this peacefully."

There was a glimmer of hope in mid-December when Iraq announced the release of the remaining hostages, a group that included forty-one Canadians. But though there were near-continuous discussions by intermediaries shuttling back and forth among the concerned capitals, there seemed little interest in Baghdad in considering any withdrawal from Kuwait; indeed the formerly independent state, much of its movable wealth looted by Iraqi officials and soldiers, was summarily incorporated into Iraq as its nineteenth province. A week before the deadline of January 15, Mulroney indicated that if war broke out Canada was prepared to consider changing its forces' role from a defensive to an offensive one. The Canadians in the Persian Gulf area, now numbering 1,700, watched and waited as the clock ticked down.

The suspense ended on the night of January 16 when American, Saudi, British, and Kuwaiti aircraft struck targets in Iraq and Kuwait with "smart" bombs and conventional "iron" weapons. At the same time sea-launched cruise missiles, capable of astonishing accuracy, devastated Iraqi command and control centres. "Desert Shield" had become "Desert Storm", and the Cabinet in Ottawa authorized its forces to take a limited offensive role. That meant that CF-18s could conduct sweep and escort missions over war zones, while the naval vessels could accompany ships bombarding coastal targets. "It is with no satisfaction that we take up arms," the prime minister said, "because war is always a tragedy. But the greater tragedy would have been for criminal aggression to go unchecked." In a vote that was not taken in the House of Commons until January 22, the Liberal opposition supported the government's position; the NDP did not. (The NDP stand was likely closer to the public's mood: a poll showed that 53 per cent wanted Canadian troops to play only a defensive role.) At the same time as it made public Canada's changed role, the government announced that it would send the hundred-bed 1st Canadian Field Hospital, based at Camp Petawawa, Ontario, to Saudi Arabia with some 130 medical personnel and 400 supporting troops. Two 16-member surgical crews duly flew to Saudi Arabia before the end of January.

The air war against Saddam proceeded without pause. Day after day, Iraqi military installations and civilian command and control centres were hammered from the air. The Iraqis retaliated by firing Scud missiles at targets in Saudi Arabia, the United Arab Emirates, and Israel—a nation that, though not directly involved in the war, remained the Number One enemy. There were fears in the Allied camp that the Israelis might retaliate and that this might drive the Arab states out of the alliance. But the Israelis, protected to a substantial extent by American-manned Patriot anti-missile defences, remained calm despite the provocation and the loss of life. The great coalition remained firm.

For the Canadian pilots flying over Kuwait and Iraq, the air war was at once exhilarating and terrifying. The Iraqi air force had been largely grounded in the opening hours of the war, so the threat was primarily from anti-aircraft defences. Even so, a constant watch had to be kept for enemy fighters. "I didn't see anything," one pilot said of his first sortie. "I was too busy looking for enemy planes to notice anything else." "Every time you fly," another pilot said, "you think maybe today will be the day the Iraqis come up to meet you." Weather permitting, the pilots flew up to twenty-five sorties a day— "about six times more than a normal squadron would fly" in peacetime, said Colonel Roméo Lalonde, the commander of the Canadian Air Task Group. But Lalonde insisted that his pilots would not be switched to a ground-attack role. "Absolutely not. We don't have the munitions here and we don't see any requirement for them."

But on February 1 Ottawa again expanded the squadron's role, declaring its mandate to be "to engage and eliminate enemy aircraft", a phraseology that included hot pursuit. That was not realistic, Lalonde argued. The Iraqi air force had "gone to ground. The bombers are not being opposed. If it is not yielding anything, why are we doing it?" The role was then changed once more, to stress air cover for the allied naval fleet, but on February 11 visiting Lieutenant-General Fred Sutherland, the head of the Canadian Forces' Air Command, declared that the CF-18 pilots were eminently capable of playing a ground-attack role after only a brief retraining period. (At the same time Lieutenant-General Kent Foster, the Canadian land forces commander, told the press that there was a contingency plan for the dispatch of a mechanized brigade of up to twelve thousand ground troops to the war zone.)

Finally, on February 20, the Department of National Defence announced that the Desert Cats would take up a ground-attack role within two weeks. The CF-18s were to be fitted with 225-kg bombs and cluster bombs to attack ground targets of all types, including armoured vehicles, supply lines, and troop concentrations. It was, Defence minister Bill McKnight said, "a logical evolution of our role in this conflict", and Canada would join eight other nations in playing this role in the air war. There were protests from Opposition parliamentarians, but by this point public support for Canada's role in the war had grown dramatically. When asked if they favoured their armed forces going to war against Iraq, 58 per cent of those polled said yes while only 38 per cent said no. The kneejerk anti-Americanism that had characterized much of the criticism of the war had begun to subside. Across the country, tens of thousands attached yellow ribbons to car aerials, trees, or front doors as a sign of support for the troops, and in Toronto billboards delivered a simple message: "To the Canadian troops in the Gulf we have two words to say: Thank You."

By the third week of February the air war seemed to have run out of targets, and the only question remaining was when the attack on the ground would commence. Peace efforts aimed at securing Iraqi withdrawal from Kuwait speeded up, and the U.N. was again the scene of feverish activity. But there was no success, and on February 24 the coalition's powerful ground forces launched themselves into Iraq and Kuwait. At the same time the CF-18s made their first ground-attack sorties, ahead of schedule. The Iraqi defences, supposedly well dug in and protected by oil-filled moats, wire, and mines, turned out to be virtually worthless, and the much-vaunted abilities of the Iraqi army melted in mass surrenders. "It's not Desert Storm," columnist Richard Gwyn of the *Toronto Star* wrote, "it's Desert Slaughter." The ground war lasted for just one hundred hours, with a ceasefire and *de facto* Iraqi surrender at midnight on February 27.

The result of the war was unquestionably decisive. Kuwait was liberated, though the retreating Iraqis set hundreds of that tiny state's oil wells afire, leaving a massive economic and environmental disaster in their wake. Allied troops occupied a large portion of southern Iraq, and civil war, destined to be crushed by the remnants of the Iraqi army, erupted almost at once in the rest of the country. Iraqi fatalities were believed to number at least a hundred thousand and almost as many troops had been captured. Coalition fatalities were under two hundred in all; fortunately not a single Canadian was included in that number.

The hard task of trying to bring peace to the whole Middle East remained, but for Ottawa the job now was to pull its troops out. Fifty left for Canada on March 2, and eight CF-18s headed out three days later for their German bases, where they were met with a hero's welcome. More would follow, including the field hospital's surgeons, who, happily, had had little work to do. While most of the Canadians headed for home, the destroyer HMCS *Huron* sailed for Gulf waters to continue to enforce U.N. sanctions and, as the Defence department said, to "contribute to the process of restoring peace and security in the region". At the same time, twenty-three combat engineers flew into Kuwait from their base at Lahr to help locate and dispose of land mines and the awesome amount of military munitions either abandoned in the precipitous Iraqi retreat from Kuwait or dropped by Allied aircraft. "This is going to be a nightmare," one soldier said.

That was true enough, but at least the nightmare of a terrible war had ended. In the process, the Canadian Forces had played their small yet important role creditably. The United Nations, despite charges that it had acted as little more than an American puppet, had perhaps found itself filling the collective-security role envisaged by its founders in 1945. The Soviet Union and the U.S. had overcome their longstanding mistrust to act with unprecedented co-operation, and the Israelis and much of the Moslem world had stifled their hatred in the interests of a solution to the threat posed by Iraq.

Moreover, those who argued that participation in the war would destroy Canada's reputation as a peacekeeper soon had their position confounded. On April 14, External Affairs minister Joe Clark announced that the U.N. had asked the country to provide 300 soldiers to serve as part of a 1,440-member United Nations Iraq Kuwait Observation Mission on the Iraqi–Kuwaiti border for one year. What New York needed, Clark said, were engineers to help clear mines, and they would be provided by the 1st Engineer Regiment, based at Chilliwack, B.C. By May 1, the Canadians were setting up their camp near Kuwait City, readying themselves for their dangerous work.

In late April, as well, the secretary-general of the U.N. hinted that Ottawa would be called on to provide an infantry battalion some eight hundred strong for a projected peacekeeping force in the western Sahara. A long war between Polisario guerrillas and Morocco came to a close when the Security Council adopted a report calling for repatriation of refugees and a referendum; the peacekeepers would organize the refugee movement and patrol the desert. Canadian peacekeeping was alive and well.

THE WORTH OF PEACEKEEPING

The war against Iraq was not a classic example of U.N. peacekeeping. Much like the Korean War forty years before, it was an American-directed and American-sponsored war, notwithstanding the sanction of the Security Council and the participation of many nations. It was also a war to resist unprovoked and undoubted aggression, and in that sense it fit clearly within the boundaries defined by the Charter of the United Nations. Whether the Gulf War is a harbinger of future U.N. military operations is unclear, though if the U.S.S.R. and the U.S. remain on good terms, concerted action against aggressors will be a live possibility.

Including the war against Iraq, almost 85,000 Canadians have served on U.N. and other peacekeeping missions around the world, including virtually every operation that could be so designated. This is a proud record, and there is no doubt that peacekeeping has become one of the centrepieces of Canadian foreign policy. The government, except on two or three occasions, has welcomed the opportunity to play its part in preserving peace; even when it was reluctant, Ottawa ultimately acceded to U.N. requests.

For a country such as Canada, peacekeeping provides the opportunity to carve out an area of independent military expertise. And certainly it has been useful. Peacekeeping may have accomplished little towards long-range peace in Cyprus, the Indian subcontinent, or the Middle East, but it has helped the world pick up the pieces after wars, and it has aided in the search for and maintenance of ceasefires. The Iran–Iraq war was brought to a close by the combatants' exhaustion, but peacekeeping provided a face-saving way towards peace; even the Control Commission in Vietnam, though scarcely a success, provided a cover to mask American withdrawal. So substantial has our role been that when the 1988 Nobel Peace Prize was awarded to U.N. peacekeepers, the Canadian armed services believed, with substantial justification, that the prize was really meant for them.

But why is it that the Canadian Forces are so good at peacekeeping? One answer is experience. National Defence Headquarters has studied the problems, run the staff and troop exercises, and learned how to react to U.N. requests with speed and efficiency. In some cases Canadians are wanted because we are a Western nation, to create balance on a peace-keeping force. In others it is because, as a NATO ally geared up for partici-pation in a European war, we have extensive logistical, signals, and air capacities. In other words, it is often less our impartiality (however valu-able that may be) than our alliance commitments that make us so useful.

In the early days, the military was less than enthusiastic about the demands of the U.N. The forces were training to fight the Russians in Europe, and peacekeeping was just a distraction that pulled scarce techni-cians and specialists away from that fundamental task. But by the end of the 1980s, as the threat posed by the Warsaw Pact waned and as the U.S.S.R. and Eastern Europe set out on the tortuous path to democracy, the military's view of peacekeeping began to alter. Without a believable Soviet threat, it becomes difficult to justify well-equipped armed forces—unless a new role can be found. Peacekeeping fills the bill neatly, and the Canadian Forces have now become peacekeeping's biggest supporters in Ottawa.

There is nothing wrong with this. The need for peacekeeping is sure to continue; in Cambodia or in Kashmir or in the Gulf, there will always be a war to be stopped and a peace to be restored. Canada needs armed forces, men and women who have the skills and courage to handle the nation's hard chores in an unknowable future—and if peacekeeping is one way to help keep them, then peacekeeping should be welcomed. But the cautious response—the demands for ceasefires, time limitations, mediation, and other preconditions—this too must be remembered. Peacekeeping, yes; but peacekeeping only when it has a chance to succeed and when it does not expose our service personnel to unacceptable risks.

Official war artist Ted Zuber lugged his sketch pads, videocam, and paints across the Gulf area, from base to ship to hospital—along with his gas mask and chem-suit. His instructions from the Canadian War Museum were to record history through an artist's eye—as he saw it, as it happened. Many of these on-the-spot sketches will be the basis for alkyd paintings.

Sentry Bunker CD 1 A private of the Van Doos guards "Canada Dry 1," one of the Canadian bases, his light machine-gun at the ready. Note his Tilley hat, official gear for Canadian troops in the Gulf. A Velcro side opening on the gas mask bag beneath his elbow lets him don the mask in the regulation nine seconds.

HQ *R22eR* Two Grizzly armoured cars sit ready outside the sandbagged headquarters of the Van Doos at Canada Dry 2, with jerrycans of gas (also sandbagged) in the foreground. Note the regimental flag on the right.

Heather On HMCS *Protecteur*, Canada's supply ship in the Gulf, a woman soldier tries out a Javelin anti-aircraft missile launcher. Though women are still banned from "combat positions," that category seems to be shrinking year by year.

Starboard Observer As a Hornet refuels in mid-air from this Air Transport Command 707 tanker, the operation is monitored by an observer at the rear of the 707; he keeps the engineer informed and warns of any problems.

HMCS *Protecteur* replenishes HMCS *Terra Nova* (left) and HMCS *Athabaskan* (right) in the Persian Gulf. *Protecteur* can simultaneously transfer ship fuel, aviation fuel, fresh water, heavy stores, mail, and troops to two ships, while under way.

An army gunner put aboard *Athabaskan* to operate the Blowpipe anti-aircraft missile system. The ships also carried hastily installed rapid-fire Phalanx CIWS (close-in weapons systems), visible above the gunner, and *Terra Nova* had eight Harpoon anti-ship missiles as well.

A boarding exercise on *Protecteur*. The Sea King helicopter was far from modern, but was updated for the Gulf with improved navigation and communications equipment, including infrared detection. It carries a "chaff" dispenser to foil radar-guided missiles, and can launch flares to throw off heat-seeking missiles.

Canada's warplane in the Gulf, the Hornet—the McDonnell-Douglas F-18, known as the CF-18 in Canada—carries Sidewinder and Sparrow air-to-air missiles and has a combat radius of 600 nautical miles, fully loaded.

Decontamination practice. Though Iraqi resistance evaporated in the face of opposition, fears of a chemical attack remained, and official handouts listed possible agents as "nerve, blister, blood, choking, vomiting, tear, stinging, and psychochemical." The cumbersome charcoal-lined chemsuits took as long as seven minutes to don; some soldiers carried plastic garbage bags to slide over their feet, to speed up the process.

An emergency drill simulating a shipboard explosion demanding helicopter evacuation of 12 "casualties" to *Protecteur,* which carried a full surgical team of 10. The men helping are stewards—food servers, mess managers, etc.—who double as stretcher-bearers in medical emergencies. Canada ultimately agreed to send a field hospital to Saudi Arabia, but the Iraqi surrender came before more than a portion of its personnel and equipment had been deployed.

ACKNOWLEDGEMENT OF PICTURE SOURCES

The government of Canada holds the copyright for most of the paintings reproduced in this book, and has given permission for their reproduction. Every reasonable effort has been made to trace ownership of other copyright materials. Information enabling the publisher to rectify any reference or credit in future printings will be welcomed.

Sources of colour illustrations are acknowledged following the legends on the colour plates in question. Unless otherwise indicated, all are from the Canadian War Museum, Canadian Museum of Civilization, National Museums of Canada. Photography at the museum was done by William Kent. Sources of black-and-white illustrations are as below. For reasons of space the following abbreviations have been used:

CWM:	Canadian War Museum
DND	Department of National Defence, Rockliffe Base
DNDO	Department of National Defence, Directorate of Exhibitions and Displays, Ottawa
OA:	Archives of Ontario
RCMI	Royal Canadian Military Institute
UN:	United Nations

Page i: DND (ISC90-479); ii: NAC (PA-131761); iii: NAC (C-3477); 5: Metropolitan Toronto Reference Library; 29: RCMI; 30 top: OA (AO 270); 30 bottom: NAC (C-31442); 31: NAC (C2775); 32 top: OA (S1480); 32 bottom: Saskatchewan Archives Board (R-A 3955); 33 top: NAC (C-21974); 33 bottom: NAC (C-5826); 34 top: Provincial Archives of Alberta, E. Brown Collection (B.5627); 34 bottom: NAC (C-17635B); 35 top: RCMI; 35 bottom: NAC (C-9129); 36 top: NAC (C-6078); 36 bottom: NAC (C-31500); 37 top: NAC (C-1277); 37 bottom: NAC (C-8401); 59: RCMI; 60 top: Collection of Prof. Desmond Morton; 60 bottom:NAC (C-8400); 61 top: NAC (C-24631); 61 bottom: NAC (C-128778); 62: NAC (C-14923); 63 top: NAC(C-6399); 63 bottom: NAC (C24627); 64: NAC (C-51799); 83:NAC (PA-128767); 84 top: RCMI; 84 bottom: RCMI; 85: OA (S 1243); 86 top: NAC (PA-16427); 86 bottom: NAC (PA-16431); 87 top: NAC (C-7987); 87 bottom: NAC (PA-113039); 88: NAC (C-10464); 89: NAC(PA-143954); 120 top: NAC (PA-128858); 120 bottom: NAC (PA-179972); 121: NAC (PA-133340); 122 top: Collection of Prof. David Marshall; 122 bottom: NAC (SF-838); 123 top: NAC (PA-128819); 123 bottom: NAC (PA-129109); 124 top: NAC (PA179973); 124 bottom: NAC (142233); 125: NAC (PA-178945); 126 top: NAC (PA-144973); 126 bottom: NAC (PA-128804); 145: NAC (PA-152036); 146 top: NAC (PA-138203); 146 bottom: NAC (PA-125625); 147: NAC (PA-138217); 148 top: NAC (PA-151994); 148 bottom: DND (PL-51684); 149: NAC (PA-169866); 150 top: DND (PL-50136); 150 bottom: DND (PL-50474); 151: DND (RE-21085); 152 top: DND (PL-55753); 152 bottom: DND (PL-52195); 179 top: NAC (PA-132638); 179 bottom: NAC (PA-129113); 180: NAC (PA-128806); 181: NAC (PA-140790); 182 top: NAC (PA-161642); 183: NAC (PA-132632); 184: NAC (PA-132637); 185 top: NAC (PA-132635); 185 bottom: NAC (PA-151509); 186 top: NAC (SF-8001); 186 bottom: NAC (PA-128831); 187: DND (IXC88-342); 209 top: DND (PMR74-829); 209 bottom: DND (PMR74-830); 210 top: NAC (PA-146519); 210 bottom: NAC (PA-151200); 211: DND; 212 top: DND (PL-107581); 212 bottom: DND (PL-107522); 213: DND (PL-107482); 214: UN (62265); 215 top: UN (124321), Y. Nagata; 215 bottom: UN (128414), Y. Nagata; 233 top: DND (CYP74-123-25); 233 bottom: DND (CYP74-36); 234 top: DND (ISC84-351); 234 bottom: DND (IXC88-369); 235 top: DND (UNC64-009-6); 235 bottom: UN (7881); 236 top: DND (UNC62-209-11); 236 bottom: National Aviation Museum (13154); 237 top: DND (VN73-276); 237 bottom: DND (VN73-273); 238: DND(VN73-282); 239: Sgt. Bob Fraser, RCMP; 240 top: DND (ISC90-515); 240 bottom: DND (ISC90-761); 241: DND(ISC90-741); 252: DNDO, courtesy Ted Zuber; 253 top: DNDO, courtesy Ted Zuber; 253 bottom: DNDO, courtesy Ted Zuber; 254: DNDO, courtesy Ted Zuber; 255 top: DND Base Halifax (HSC901069-541); 255 bottom: DND (ISC90-2069A); 256: DND (ISC90-2325); 257: DND (IWC90-530-8); 258: DND (IWC90-494-23); 259: DND (ISC90-2276A).

Index